SEE HOW MANY WAYS THIS BOOK CAN HELP YOU FIND A NAME THAT'S RIGHT!

★ There are over 3000 basic names, plus variations, to choose from.

★ Each name is defined and explained, and each has a phonetic spelling so that you can sound it out to be sure that it harmonizes with your surname.

★ Each name source is identified. You can select one from your ethnic heritage or one from a group you admire—perhaps an American Indian, Swahili or Israeli.

★ If you believe in numerology, the name-and-number relationships are explained for you.

★ If you want to create an individual name, here are suggestions: for example, inverting favorite names, varying parents' names, combining or respelling other names.

WHY SETTLE FOR ONE OF THE ESTABLISH-MENT NAMES? SELECT A NAME WITH MEANING FOR YOU AND YOUR BABY
from
THE NEW AGE BABY NAME BOOK

THE
NEW AGE
BABY NAME
BOOK

BY

SUE BROWDER

WARNER BOOKS

A Warner Communications Company

Special Thanks to the many religious leaders, professors, and Hindu, Arabic, American Indian, and African students without whose help this book could not have been written.

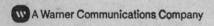

CONTENTS

Part I

CHAPTER 1

Introduction

The Yoruba-speaking people of Nigeria have a proverb: "Consider the state of your life before you name a child." And that is essentially what many parents are doing today as they seek distinctive ethnic or contemporary names for their children. In this book you will find meanings and pronunciations, when needed, for thousands of heritage names from cultures throughout the world—African, Oriental, East Indian, Russian, European, Latin and South American, Scandinavian, Eskimo, Hawaiian, as well as the most truly American culture, that of the American Indian. Ecological, flower, peace, and astrological names are listed as well. In addition, Americans are constantly creating new names which reflect changing cultural consciousness, and these, too, have been collected from recent newspaper birth columns. You may want to use the names exactly as they are listed, or you may decide to use them as a base for creating a totally personalized name for your baby, in which case Chapter II and parts of

Chapter III will give you pointers on making up a name of your own.

At any rate, when choosing a contemporary name, you will probably want to consider a few modern fashions. For instance, many people today use what were once considered only nicknames as formal given names. Newspaper records show Lexie becoming more popular than Alexandra, and Lisa more often used than Elizabeth, and a number of these shortened names have been listed. Several possible explanations have been offered for this trend toward shorter names, the most probable being (1) Americans' characteristic informality; (2) a searching for prettier, more efficient, or more unusual names; and (3) a loss of the superstition which created nicknames in the first place. Nicknames, it seems, were originally used and still are in some parts of the world to hide one's real name from evil spirits, the idea being that, as in the fairy tale "Rumpelstiltskin," someone has only to know a person's name to control him. Because of this belief, members of some African and American Indian tribes still consider it rude to ask someone his or her name, and when asked will often simply reply, "I forgot it" or "I have none."

Another modern trend is the tendency to use boys' names for girls. Many traditionally masculine names like Harper, Lindsey, and Darcy are as popular today for girls as for boys. This same practice can be found in many older cultures. Most American Indian and Hawaiian names, for example, can be used for both boys and girls, and perhaps the trend in this country has resulted from less emphasis on stereotyped masculine and feminine roles. In recognition of this fashion, boys' names that have been adopted in recent years by girls are listed in the girls' section.

A further trend is to seek names with deep, personal meaning for the parents, and ultimately, of course, for the child. Americans have become alienated, for any number of reasons, from their ethnic heritages, and as a result have long ago lost track of name meanings. Today a woman called Barbara may not know her name means

10

"stranger," and even if she does, the meaning is just another word; it has nothing to do with her personally. In many other cultures, however, names are considered a part of man's soul and as such have profound personal significance. A Hopi Indian called Quoiavma, or "Sunrise," once told me his name was a picture. "It means," he said, "the golden sun coming up over the misty mountains and glimmering on hazy smoky-blue waters while the morning birds chirp in the rustling green trees." Once, Sunrise recalled, he rose before dawn to take photos from the floor of the Grand Canyon, and when he showed the pictures to his clansmen, they said, "That is your name." The modern return to heritage and ethnic names is one attempt to regain lost meaning, and in this book we have tried wherever possible to get beyond a name's literal meaning to show you the picture, the connotations and traditions, that brought the name into being.

You should remember, too, that ethnic names are not limited to blacks and American Indians. Buddhists, Moslems, and Jews, as well as Spanish, Polish, and Irish Americans, to name just a few, all have ethnic identities. If your last name were Leibowitz, for example, you might want to give your little girl the pretty Polish name Melcia instead of the English equivalent Amelia. Or Henka rather than Harriet. And names that at first glance may seem rather awkward, like the Czech Anezka, often seem much more attractive when properly pronounced, in this case AH-nehzh-kah, the *zh* sounding like the *z* in *azure*.

Or perhaps you would like to name your baby after a favorite relative, but somehow his name, John for instance, seems too ordinary. Then you might consider one of the many variations of John—the Russian Ivan, the Irish Shane or Sean, or the Swedish Jens. Many names have also been listed to help you if you have mixed feelings about naming your baby "junior." Fewer babies are named junior today than fifty years ago, perhaps because many parents feel the child deserves a unique, individual name of his own. Researchers, incidentally, have supported this trend in finding that most boys dislike being called junior. If the father's name were Daniel, you might compromise between Daniel and a totally different name by calling the baby Dani, the modern Israeli form of Daniel, used for both boys and girls. If the baby were a girl, you could, of course, name her Daniela, but you might prefer one of the modern or ethnic forms of Daniela: Dana, Danice, Danit, Danett, Dania, or Danya.

About twenty common-sense rules have been established telling how to pick a name, but they all basically reduce to this: The name should sound pleasant and not have strong possibilities for embarrassing, derogatory nicknames, like Piggy or Fatso. The old rules that a name should clearly designate sex and not be too unusual, as we have pointed out, are disappearing. Generally for euphony it is suggested that children with two- or three-syllable family names should receive two given names, one with one syllable and the other with two syllables. One-syllable family names, on the other hand, should probably have given names of two or three syllables each.

Because of society's rising complexity, a middle name is practically essential today, and if you have a common surname, you may even want to select three given names for your child to avoid identity mix-ups. It is not at all uncommon in other parts of the world (among the Chinese and American Indians, for instance) for a child to have as many as ten names, which he collects for each important event in his lifetime—entering school, graduating, getting married, and so forth. Some Americans, of course, have been given long strings of names for other reasons. A Mr. Jackson Ezekiel David James Nathaniel Sylvester Willis Edward Demosthenes Henderson of Charlotte, North Carolina, was so named because his mother hoped one of these rich uncle namesakes would remember the boy in their will. Unfortunately for J.E.D.J.N.S.W.E.D., the wealthy old men all died without giving him a cent. Which brings us to a last rule: In case of family disputes, pick the name you and your mate like best.

One final word. The entries in this book have been carefully selected to screen out names which sound highly unusual or awkward to Americans, but for those seeking an ethnic name which is a bit more unusual we have included subentries under many names to give you a wider selection to pick from. The Yoruban name Apara, for instance, has listed beneath it the names Molomo, Kosoko, Banjoko, Durosimi, and Akisatan. A few names in this book may seem comical or even weird to our Americanized tastes, but for this reaction the Yoruba have still another proverb: "He who does not understand the cry of the palm bird complains of the noise it makes."

CHAPTER 2

How to Create a Name

Creating a totally unique name for a child is traditional in many cultures. The Chinese have few "common" first names because each child is believed too special to be given a name many others have used before him. The same is true of some American Indians who believe a person's name is his soul and so must be totally personal. In fact, it is said of many an Indian paradise that you have only to tell the gods your name to be admitted. Among these Indians, then, if two people accidentally end up with the same name, one of them will choose a new one. The Purim Kukis, a tiny Tibeto-Burmese tribe in Manipur State in China, actually have clan monopolies on names, and if anyone takes a name from another clan, he is fined a pig and a pot of rice brew, but allowed to keep the name.

In many cultures original names are created from an event in the father's life, such as the Miwok name Lipetu, meaning "bear going over a man hiding between rocks," referring to a close call the father had with a grizzly. Or the child might be named for an event at birth; for instance, the Miwok girl called Huyana ("rain falling") was probably born during a rainstorm. Another favorite custom, that of naming children for the first object one of the parents sees after birth, accounts for unusual names like the Zuni Indian Taci ("washtub") and Tiwa ("onions").

The ways to create your own name are, of course, limited only by your imagination, but the most common methods today include the following.

Anagrams

Creating a name anagram, of course, involves taking a word which has special meaning to you and switching the letters until you have a pleasant-sounding name. "Peace" might become Capee or Ceepa, "earth" can be switched to Retha, and so forth.

Telescoping from Contemporary Newsmakers

Basically telescoping simply involves dropping letters from a word until you arrive at a suitable name. If you wish to telescope from the name of a person you admire, Martin Luther King for example, you might shorten the name to Marin or Marnin. Or Kahlil Gibran can be changed to Kabran. You might also telescope and then juggle the letters to create a name. Hence, Golda Meir might be shortened to (Go)lda Me(ir), which can then become Melda.

Telescoping from Trends

This process simply involves using the first letters of words to create a name. You might create a "brotherhood telescope" from the words peace, independence, equality, and truth, producing the name Piet. Or you might create the "ecological telescope" Tesa from the words trees, earth, streams, and air. Another possibility is to use first letters from a favorite saying, book or song title, and so forth.

16

Inversions

To create a name by inversion, you merely switch the syllables in a familiar name. Examples are Mary to Ryma, Morena to Remona, the flower name Dahlia to Liadah, Marco to Comar, the Spanish Blanco to Coblan, and Donald to Alddon.

Names from the Father's Name

A boy, of course, can be named after his father by simply adding "junior" or by shortening the father's name. Donald might name his son Donal or Doni. Similarly, a girl can be named after her father by adding one of dozens of feminine suffixes. The combinations are virtually endless. For example, from the name John a girl might be called Joni, Jonie, Jony, Jonine, Jonisa, Jonitta, Jonitte, Jonit, Jonica, Jonitka, Jonitsa, Joniki, Jonanne, Jonilla, Jonsy, Jonette, Jonia, Jonya, or Jonalee, to name only a few. These, in turn, could be spelled with an initial *John* in place of *Jon,* two *n's* instead of one, and so forth.

Names from the Mother's Name

The most popular way to name a boy after his mother is to use her maiden name. Thus, a boy is often named Ward, Grey, Parker, Harris, Clark, Davis, Ross, Cole, Sanders, or whatever. Again, as with the father's name, the mother's name can be shortened and used with male suffixes. Hence, the name Mary could become Marston, Marton, Marten, Marnett, Marsin, Marson, Marald, Mardy, Marle, Marley, Marrand, Marick, Marwin, Marris, Marren, Marnand, and so forth. In the same way, Maria could become a feminine Mari, Marine, Marisa, Marica, or Maritsa, to name but a few. See examples from the above section for other common feminine suffixes.

Inventing Names by Combining Those of the Parents

This method of making up names is practically self-explanatory. The parents' first or first and middle names are written down and letters are simply dropped, added, or juggled until a pleasant name is formed. Joseph and

Ellen might name their little girl Joselle, or Daniel and Susan might call their boy Dansan. The first letters of the parents' names could also be used to form a new name. For instance, Gerald and Ida Adams might call their daughter Gia.

Apheresis

Apheresis involves dropping unaccented syllables from the beginning of a name. Since this has already been done with many more familiar names (Tilda from Matilda, Beth from Elizabeth), you probably will want to start with a more unusual name if you choose to try this method of naming. Examples of apheresis are the Hebrew Arella to Rella, the Russian Amaliya to Maliya, and the American Indian Aponi to Poni.

Apocopation

Apocopation is apheresis reversed. In other words, you drop unaccented last syllables to create a new name. Again we have common examples such as Elisa from Elisabeth or Nicol from Nicholas. You might shorten the Ibo name Atuanya to Atuan, the Swahili Azizi to Azi, or Delano to Delan.

Diminutives

After using apocopation, you might choose to create what is known as a diminutive by adding a pet ending. For example, you might drop the final syllable of Arna and add the suffix -ette to produce Arnette. The Arabic Fatma plus -ina becomes Fatina, and the more common Sharon becomes Sharita, Sharette, Sharma, and so forth. The examples under "Names from the Father's Name" give you typical masculine endings to get you started, while a few common feminine endings are listed under "Names from the Mother's Name."

Combinations

Combinations are made almost exactly like names invented by combining those of the parents, except that you go a step further and create a new name with a specific, personal meaning. For instance, Aubi could be created by combining the two Hebrew names Avirice, meaning "air" or "atmosphere," and Burura, meaning "clean" or "pure." The name Aubi, then, might express your hope for the future—a clean atmosphere with pure, fresh air.

Sex Switches and Respellings

Sex switches and respellings are obvious. Examples of boys' names already being used for girls include Harper and Jonny, Gari from Gary, and Darsey from Darcy. Respelling usually involves changing i to ie or y or vice versa, k to c or the reverse, or e to i or y, producing examples like Caryn, Ellyn, Robyn, Kari, Kary, Karyn, and the like. Another possibility is to capitalize a letter in the middle of a name, creating names like MariAnne and ArLene.

Naturally many of these methods can be applied to heritage names. But if you are most interested in ethnic names, you will find other ideas in Chapter III, which gives examples of the most typical names in various cultures. There is also a section on how to create a numerological name for your baby.

CHAPTER 3

Choosing an Ethnic Name

You will probably find many ethnic names you like, perhaps from heritages widely different from your own. For this reason, to give you a general background on a particular name, we have included the following summaries of traditions, customs, and naming practices of the major cultures included in this book.

African

Naming customs vary greatly among African peoples, but the types most commonly found denote the time of birth ("born on Sunday"), the order of birth ("first-born daughter"), a physical characteristic, or a recent family incident. Because of the high infant-mortality rate in Africa, Ghanaians and many other African peoples do not name a child until the seventh day to see if he will live, and many names reveal a concern the child will die. Some children, in fact, are believed to be reincarnated spirits who quickly enter and leave this world, and such infants are given "born-to-die" names in an attempt to prevent them from returning to the spirit world. Kaya, a common Ghanian name, means "stay and don't go back (don't die)," while the Yoruban name Kosoko says "there is no hoe (to dig a grave with)."

Some of the most fascinating African names come from Yoruban and Ovimbundu proverbs. Examples are Cilehe, from "Just let it stink, let it be," meaning if you bother it, you will make it worse; Kanene, from "a little thing in the eye is big"; and Ayondela, "a little tree bends and bends, as we all bend toward death." Among the Ibo of Nigeria, short-sentence names are popular, and include names such as Dumaka, "help me with your hands," and Nnamdi, "my father is alive."

Another common African source of names is the spirits. The Ibo god Chi, for instance, gives rise to Cinese ("Chi is protecting"), Cis (which simply means "Chi"), and Chinelo ("thought of Chi"). Chi is a personal god thought to stay with a person from the moment of conception to death, and is believed to be the cause of all sorts of misfortunes as well as successes.

Included in this book are Hausa, Ibo, Ovimbundu, Bari, Yoruban, Swahili, and other African names, as well as several early Afro-American names. Some African heritage names can also be found among Arabic entries.

American Indian

Most common among the North American Indians are imaginative ecological names taken from plants, animals, the stars and moon, and natural phenomena. While many other cultures name children after nature, the Indian, with his detailed observations and close association with nature, always goes further, creating names such as Taipa, "valley quail spreading its wings as it alights," and Tiponya, "great horned owl sticking her head under her body and poking an egg that is hatching."

As these examples indicate, most Indian names imply much more than their literal meanings suggest. To a stranger Luyunu merely means "to shake the head sideways," but to Luyunu's friends his name is really "bear taking off a leg or arm of a person while eating him."

Because of these hidden meanings, Indian names have often been misunderstood. "Sweaty Blanket" does not indicate the brave has B.O. or a dirty bed but that he is a tireless rider.

Because of a strong belief in each person's individuality and unique soul, an Indian seldom takes one of his parents' names. Instead his name may mirror a proud event in his father's life. Wakiza ("desperate fighter"), for example, may refer to a battle won without weapons, and Kijika ("walks quietly") to a time the older man noiselessly sneaked up on a deer in the forest. Similarly, a child born during a storm may be given a name as imposing as Shappa ("red thunder") or as whimsical as Lokni ("rain coming through a small hole in the roof").

In contrast, some Eskimos *must* give a newborn child a relative's name if the relative recently died, the idea being that only through their names do the dead return to this world. In the same Eskimo tribes, however, it is taboo to name a child after a living relative because the name would then be saddled with two bodies, one of which it is believed would have to die.

Because of the tendency to create new names, there are no "most common" Indian names. The most typical types, however, in addition to ecological names are magical names taken from gods, war and peace names, and names which simply have pretty meanings, such as Halona ("happy fortune") and Onida ("the looked-for one").

Arabic and Muslim

Arabic and Muslim names have remained virtually unchanged for over two thousand years, possibly the reason Arabic has so strongly affected names in many cultures. Nearly every country has a version of the Arabic Leila ("born at night"), and a high percentage of Swahili names are simply slight variants of the Arabic.

Many popular Arabic names come from the ninety-nine qualities of God listed in the Koran: Karim ("generous"), Kamil ("perfect"), Hakeem ("wise"), Kadar ("powerful"), and Nasser ("victorious"). These, in turn, are often prefixed with Abdul, Abdel, or Abd, meaning "servant of."

23

Abdel Nasser, as an example, means "servant of the victorious One." Muslim names, on the other hand, are usually derived from those of the Prophet Muhammad's descendants or immediate family: Ali, Hashim, and Hussein for boys, and Fatma, Ayasha, and Hinda for girls. The Prophet's name, with its estimated five hundred variants, is often considered the most popular name in the world, and a pious Muslim saying goes, "If you have a hundred sons, name them all Muhammad."

Next in popularity to religious names are those describing an abstract quality or virtue. Girls are named Amineh ("faithful"), Marid ("rebellious"), and Zarifa ("graceful"), while boys are called Sharif ("honest"), Nabil ("noble"), and Zaki ("intelligent"). Similar are Rafi ("exalting") and Yasar ("wealth"), names which, according to Orthodox Muslims, Muhammad disdained because they were too proud.

Although less common than a century ago, animal names are also used today. Typical are Hamal ("lamb") and Numair ("panther"). Nature names like Rabi ("fragrant breeze") and occupation names like Harith ("ploughman") also appear frequently.

To avoid using one's name too casually, considered the peak of rudeness, Arabs often attach prefixes to names. In this way, Sharif's father might be called Abu Sharif ("father of Sharif") and his mother Um Sharif ("mother of Sharif") instead of by their own given names. Similarly, Bin, Binte, or Ibn ("daughter of" or "son of") followed by the father's name is often used in place of a child's actual given name.

Astrological, Occult, and Other Magic Names

Astrological names are bestowed according to time of birth in the hopes that such names will be propitious with the stars. A child born under Leo might be given a name meaning "lion," the symbol of that sign of the zodiac, or one meaning "sun," which governs Leo. In China if the astrologer who casts the baby's horoscope on the third day of life finds too many wood influences, he may correct this evil by giving the child a metal name, because metal

24

conquers wood, or a name meaning "earth," since earth produces metal. Names meaning "iron," "rock," or "hammer" are also thought to improve the baby's health or fate.

Japanese color names like Akako ("red") and material names like Tetsu ("iron") also stem from ancient Oriental beliefs about magic. The color red, believed to cure diseases and ensure good health, was once considered a potent amulet, while the material names probably date back to an ancient idea that demons and evil spirits were born of the Stone Age and hence feared metals, especially iron. It was thus thought if a tiny baby girl were named Tetsu, the evil spirits would shun her for a child with a less frightful name.

If you are looking for a magical or astrological name, you will find all of the above types, as well as some delightful magic names used in incantations to summon or exorcise spirits, plus diety names from the Egyptian *Book of the Dead*, often considered the original record of magic. A fascinating group of names are those of the English Gypsies, which have been listed because of their close kinship with fortune-telling and the supernatural. Hindu names also offer dozens of possibilities, since the Hindus often name their children after gods to bring them luck and salvation.

Chinese

Chinese parents create an individual name for each child, usually making certain all the names in the family "go together." Thus, Precious Jade's sisters might be named Precious Jewel and Precious Peace. Also, unlike in most other cultures, Chinese first and middle names are selected to have a good combined meaning, the idea being a good name gives social status.

In the past some parents selected the most repulsive names they could think of, examples being "swine urine" and "cat vomit," hoping that evil spirits would be fooled into thinking the child was unloved and would leave him alone. Occasionally even today boys are given girls' names to deceive the demons, who supposedly prefer to harm males.

Because Chinese names are so individual, few common names exist, and to have a true Chinese name, you should create one of your own. A few names have been included in the list to give you possible ideas and words to work with such as Mu Lan ("magnolia blossom") and Mu Tan ("tree peony blossom"), examples of the many Chinese flower names. However, you will probably want to use a good Chinese-English dictionary, too. One additional reminder: When studying Chinese names, don't forget that Chinese surnames are written first and the given names last.

Hawaiian

Many Hawaiian names today are adaptations of English or Biblical names. Some are similar to the English names, such as Dorisa for Doris, while others have been changed more significantly, Akoni for Anthony, for example. Although Hawaiians have many short names, they also have some of the longest in the world, and the custom of giving a child an English first name with a Hawaiian middle name sometimes produces fascinating combinations. One example is David Kekoalauliionapalihauliuliokekoolau Kaapuawaokamehameha, nicknamed Kekoa Kaapu. While such names often seem odd to outsiders, they usually have melodic, picturesque meanings, the above being "the fine-leafed koa tree on the beautiful green ridges of the Koolau (mountains)." The same boy's sister was named Kapualehuaonapalilahilahiokaala, or "the lehua flower blooming on the steep ridges of Mount Kaala."

In this book you will find shorter names with similarly pretty meanings. Alaula ("light of early dawn" or "sunset glow") and Aolani ("heavenly cloud") are typical, and can be given to both boys and girls.

Many pretty Hawaiian names are created by the parents from an incident at birth. For instance, if a father looked up and saw a seagull shortly after his daughter was born, she might be named Iwalani ("heavenly seabird") or perhaps Iulani ("the highest point of heaven"). The names listed, therefore, are only samples of the many names you can create yourself. Some of the most often

26

used elements in names include Lani ("sky" or "heavenly"), Pua ("flower"), Olu ("gentle"), Mele ("a song" or "poem"), Lei ("wreath" or "child"), Ipo ("darling"), Iao (name of a star), Kapu ("sacred"). Malu ("peace"), Nani ("beautiful"), and Ola ("life" or "health"). Two common names, in fact, are combinations from this list: Pualani, which means "heavenly flower," and Puanani, "beautiful flower." Another example would be Melei from Mele plus Lei, meaning "song child."

Hindustani

Most Hindu names come from the many Hindu gods, who are actually manifestations of the One God. Common boys' names include Kistna, Hanuman, Siva, Rama, Narain, and Valli, while Davaki, Devi, Sakti, and Ratri are popular for girls.

Although high castes were once legally forbidden to marry anyone with a "plebeian" nature name, girls today are often named after rivers, flowers, trees, animals, and stars. The Hindus, like some Chinese and African people, also believe an ugly name will trick demons into thinking the child is not worth notice. So some children bear names like Klesa ("pain") or Kirwa ("worm").

The many suffixes added to Hindu names make the combinations and variants of one name almost endless. In the Punjab, where children are named after common words, Nath ("lord") becomes Natha, Nathi, Natho, Nathan, Nathu Rai, Nathu, and Nathi Mall, to name only a few variations. Most of the entries in the name list are simple forms of Hindu names, and to create your own name you might add any of about sixty suffixes used today, some of which can be considered names themselves. The more common ones are Rai ("prince"), Lal ("cherished"), Ram ("god"), Mall or Scna ("warrior"), Singh or Simha ("lion"), Autar ("incarnation"), Das or Dasa ("slave"), Gupta ("protector"), Guha ("secret"), Varma ("shield"), Putra ("son"), Datta ("gift"), Vala ("mine" or "from"), Tirtha ("ford"), Sagara ("ocean"), Pandita ("scholar"), Ananda ("bliss"), and Ji ("soul" or "life"). As an example, you might take Kali, which

27

is another name for the goddess Sakti, and add the suffix -*das* to create Kalidas, meaning "slave of Kali" or "devoted to Kali." Or since the Hindus often split long names in two, you might pick one of the above elements as a middle name.

Japanese

The most typical Japanese girls' names denote virtue, with examples being Setsu ("fidelity"), Shizu ("quiet" or "clear"), and Sumi ("the refined"). Similarly, many other names have an implied virtue meaning. For instance, Umeko, meaning "plum blossom child," also connotes wifely devotion, while a name from the lotus blossom implies all the Buddhist concepts of a heaven where immortal souls sleep enveloped in lotus buds until they are admitted to paradise.

The Japanese also use order-of-birth and number names for children. Hence, we find Ichi, meaning "one," all the way up to Man, or "ten thousand." The smaller numbers often indicate order of birth, the higher ones, such as eighty, a hope for longevity; and very large round numbers, such as ten thousand, were once considered good omens. Numeral names, of course, leave opportunities for whimsy, as in the family of children named "ten dollars," "one hundred dollars," and "one thousand dollars," or the boy called "1-2-3-4-5-6-7-8-9-10."

The most common girls' names include Chika or Chikako ("near"), Kiku ("chrysanthemum"), Suzu ("little bell"), and Taka or Takako ("lofty"). Common for boys are Taro ("first male"), Jiro ("second male"), Saburo ("third male"), and Akio ("bright boy").

You can create your own boy's name by using any of a number of prefixes, the most common of which are Toku ("virtue"), Masa ("good"), Zen ("just"), Michi ("righteous way"), Yu ("courage"), and Shin ("faithful"). Masataro, for example, means "good first-born male," and so forth. You will find other major elements to use with these prefixes in the regular name lists. Similarly, you can create your own girl's name by adding the suffixes -*ko*, -*yo*, or -*e* to regular name elements.

28

Thus, Kiku and Suzu might become Kikuko and Suzuko.

Hebrew

Jewish people have traditionally given their children two names, one purely Hebrew and another secular, both of which are supposed to be similar in sound or meaning. In some cases, both names are the same.

In Israel, where the most common name today is Moshe, it has become popular to choose a name which sounds unmistakably Israeli, yet is easy for Gentiles to pronounce and remember. Names of this type often end in *n* and have no more than four consonants: Doron, Rimon, Givon, and the like. In Israel, as in the United States, the trend is toward shortened names. Zlatopolsky becomes Paz, and Taranto, Tal. Other formerly long names include Dan, Gal, Kol, Nir, Niv, and Ziv. At one time animal names, like Lieb, or "lion," were widely used, but the modern trend is toward plant and flower names, such as the feminine Nurit, meaning "little yellow flower."

Hebraizing names by rearranging the letters is popular in Israel, and was recommended by the late Moshe Sharett as well as other leaders. Thus, Kleinman becomes Kenan, Neurath, Nur, and so forth. You will find many of these shortened forms in the name list, as well as longer names you may want to abbreviate yourself.

Numerology and Number Names

Many cultures believe numbers have magical powers or in some way influence fate. In Japan, where round numbers were once thought to be good omens, children are still occasionally named Sen ("thousand"), Michi ("three thousand"), or Yachiyo ("eight thousand generations"). Lest these examples seem merely an inscrutable Oriental custom, a man in Stanford, California, was named 4E Chittenden, and another American's birth-certificate name read Willie 5/8 Smith.

Many other beliefs are embodied in numerology, begun by the Greek philosopher Pythagoras, whose fascination for ciphers led him to number the letters of the alphabet.

The result was numerology. One success story involves commentator and columnist Hedda Hopper, who supposedly was a loser as Elda Furry, a bit more successful as the married Elda Hopper, but never really began to achieve fame until a numerologist selected the name Hedda.

There are no "numerologically good" first names as such because the complete name must be counted. To do so, add the numbers of the letters in a name, including the middle and last names, according to this chart.

1	2	3	4	5	6	7	8	9
A	B	C	D	E	F	G	H	I
J	K	L	M	N	O	P	Q	R
S	T	U	V	W	X	Y	Z	

You will probably come up with two digits—81 for example. Add the digits to get the name's destiny number, in this case 9 (8 plus 1). If you have two digits, which add up to another two digits, 98 for example, which gives you 17, simply keep adding until you get a number under 10, in this case 8 (1 plus 7.) Eleven is seldom reduced to 2 because 7 and 11 are considered master numbers, bestowing great intelligence and leadership abilities.

Generally the qualities associated with each number are as follows: 1, creative; 2, friendly, a follower; 3, artistic; 4, home-loving, peaceful; 5, a traveler, seeker of truth; 6, scholarly, with a social conscience; 7, intelligent, a leader; 8, ambitious, organized; and 9, just, righteous, a conscientious objector.

Russian

To point up Russian nationality, parents in the Soviet Union have been urged to give their children Russian-sounding names, like Ivan, Vladlen, Vladislav, Anna, Vera, and Sofia. In fact, more foreign-sounding names have been ridiculed, the Russian *Gazette* commenting that names like Azalia, Ella, Alfred, and Henry are not only unpatriotic but sound almost ludicrous.

Unlike many other people, the Russians seldom name their children after political leaders because the name may suddenly fall into disgrace. When Khrushchev replaced

Stalin, for example, the names of the late leader and his top advisers were wiped from the slates, and boys called Josef or Stalin and girls named Stalina hastened to choose names more favorable to the Khrushchev regime. Now, of course, Nikita is frowned upon.

Probably no other people in the world uses pet forms and diminutives more extensively than do the Russians. A girl named Agneshka, the Russian development or equivalent of the English Agnes, can be called Nessa, Nessia, Agnita, Agnya, Gusya, Nyusha, Ahniya, Nyushka, and Agnesa, all of which are in a sense her names. In addition, each pet name has an implied meaning. Names ending in -ka for instance, are used in anger, while those ending in -usha or -ya are special terms of endearment.

Scandinavian

Most Scandinavian names refer to leadership in battle, bravery, or Norse mythology. The Swedish Lars means "crowned with laurel," a victory symbol; Akin is "descent of the eternal king"; and Bodil means "commanding." You will find few peace names among these hardy peoples, with a few exceptions which begin with *Fred*.

The Scandinavians have a number of good, individualistic names, such as Hamar ("a symbol of man's ingenuity") and Einer ("individualist" or "nonconformist"). These northern countries are also an excellent source for short masculine names—Alf, Alrik, Arens, Garth, Arni, and Jens, as examples. You can find many beautiful girls' names, too, including Arla, Disa, Gressa, and Meri.

While many Scandinavians, particularly Norwegians, have common Biblical names, such as John, Peter, Ester, and Evelyn, it is fashionable today to give children names with a more Nordic flavor. Common names include Bjorn, Sven, Knut, Jens, Lars, Josef, Harald, Johan, and Ulrik. Popular for girls are Katrina, Ingrid, Helga, Dorotea, Jonina, Else, Astrid, and Rakel.

Slavic

Under Slavic names we include Polish, Slovak, and Czech or Bohemian names. At first glance some names listed may seem awkward, but the Slavic practice of pronouncing words with the stress on the first syllable and with the soft *sh* instead of *s*, *zh* in place of *z*, makes these names almost melodious. Anezka becomes AH-nehzh-kah, and Anicka is pronounced AH-neesh-kah.

Many typical boys' names end in *-slav* or the Polish *-slaw*, which means "glory." Some of the more popular Czech names are Radomil ("love of peace"), Jarslav ("glory of spring"), Bohdan ("God-given"), Bohumir ("peace of God"), Filip, Jan, Jakub, Josef, Karel, Jiri, Pavel, Tomas, and Vilem. Common for girls are Bela, Ludmila, Maria, Rusalka, the above-mentioned Anezka, Svetla, and Zofie. Also, many girls' names are created by simply adding *-a* to a boy's name, making Pavela from Pavel for instance.

Although Polish names typically end in *-slaw* (masculine) or *-slawa* (feminine), these are usually replaced by shorter nicknames. The pretty Tesia (TE-shuh) from Hortensja and Truda from Giertruda are examples.

Spanish

Spanish names, used in Spain, most of South America, Central America, Mexico, various islands, and a few other countries scattered around the world, are usually taken from the calendar of saints, and a "typical" name will have religious connotations. For girls Maria is so popular that additional names relating some quality of the Virgin have been added to differentiate among the thousands of Maria Garcias and Maria Chavezes. For this reason, you will find Maria de los Dolores ("Mary of Sorrows"), which is often shortened to Lolita, Lola, of simply Dolores; Maria de la Cruz ("Mary of the Cross"); and many similar names. Widely popular forms of such Virgin names include Luz and Lucita, from Maria de la Luz ("Mary of the Light"); Carmen ("Mary of Scarlet"); Jesusa ("Mary of Jesus"); and Suela, from Maria del Consuela ("Mary of Consolation"). The popular name, Pilar, meaning "pillar," used for both boys and girls, also refers to the Virgin, who stands as the base or pillar of the Christian religion.

Occasionally you will see combinations of other names

with Maria, a technique you may want to use to create your own Spanish name. Thus, Maria plus Ines produces Marines, and Maria plus Flora gives you Mariflor. Other examples are Maria and Romona for Marona, and Maria and Linda for Marinda.

The most popular Spanish boys' names have as many pet forms as English names. Francisco, for instance, has at least sixteen forms, some of the more common being Chico, Paco, Pancho, Curro, and Paquito. The favorite names for boys throughout the Spanish-speaking world are Juan, Jose, Pablo, Pauel, Pedro, Rafael, Mario, Manuel, Jaime, Luis, and Miguel.

Turkish

Because of intense national pride, the Turks have been encouraged to exchange names with foreign derivations for names derived exclusively from Turkish. Cemal ("beauty"), Halim ("gentle" or "patient"), and Kabil ("Cain") are being replaced with the Turkish Cahil ("young"), Deniz ("sea" or "storm"), and Halil ("intimate friend"). As a result, the old source of names—the Koran—is less popular today than a few years ago. Still quite common, however, are the Koran names Hasan, Mehmet, Ali, Ibrahim, Osman, and Suleyman.

Turkish given names are traditionally more important than in some other cultures because until the 1930's surnames were not used. Hence, like the Chinese and many American Indians, Turkish people often change or add to a boy's name, at each important event in his life. A boy, therefore, could receive names upon birth (the umbilical names), circumcision, his first day of school, graduation, and marriage, as well as several nicknames. Girls' names, on the other hand, tend to be fewer and more stable.

Astrological Guide

THE TWELVE SIGNS OF THE ZODIAC

Aries..............................March 21st through April 20th
Taurus.............................April 21st through May 20th
Gemini.............................May 21st through June 20th
Cancer.............................June 21st through July 22nd
Leo................................July 23rd through August 22nd
Virgo....................August 23rd through September 23rd
Libra...................September 24th through October 23rd
Scorpio...............October 24th through November 22nd
Sagittarius.......November 23rd through December 22nd
Capricorn...............December 23rd through January 20th
Aquarius................January 21st through February 19th
Pisces........................February 20th through March 20th

Pronunciation Guide

The symbols used in this book represent the following sounds.

A..*a* as in *at*
AH..*a* as in *father*
AW..*aw* as in *hawk*
AY..*ay* as in *say*
E..*e* as in *met*
EH...............................almost *a* in *mate*, only shorter
I..*i* as in *bit*
IGH...*i* as in *rise*
OH ....*o* as in *note*
OW..*ow* as in *how*
OO..*oo* as in *foot*
OO:..*oo* as in *moon*
UH...*u* as in *under*
ZH...*z* as in *azure*

It should be understood that in some instances pronun-
ciations can only be approximate because there are no
English equivalents for many sounds in other languages.
Also, the exact American Indian tribes using some names

have been lost, in which cases pronunciations have been Anglicized. Occasionally a name will contain a single consonant as a separate syllable. Such syllabic consonants are designated by a dot (e.g., K.) after the letter. Stress is indicated by capital letters, except in a few Hindu and Oriental names which have no accented syllables.

Part II

Girls' Names

Aba (ah-BAH) Ghanaian name for a girl born on Thursday.

Abebi (ah-beh-BEE) Popular among the Yoruba of Nigeria, this name means "we asked for her and she came to us." A variation is Abeni.

Abina (ah-bee-NAH) Akan name from Southern Ghana for a girl born on *Benada,* or Tuesday. Other variations are Abena and Abana.

Abiona (ah-BEE-oh-nah) Yoruban name for any child born during a journey. Also a boy's name.

Abira (ah-BIR-ah) This Hebrew name means "strong." Also spelled Adira.

Abital (ah-BEE-tahl) Popular in Israel for both girls and boys, Abital means "my father is dew." Avital is a variant spelling.

Ada (ah-DAH) Hebrew for "an ornament." The name

may also be derived from the Teutonic word for "happy" or the Latin for "of noble birth."

Adamina Originally derived from Hebrew, Adamina means "daughter of the red earth." Astrological name for girls born under the earth signs of the zodiac: Capricorn, Taurus, and Virgo.

Adamma (ah-DAHM-mah) "Child of beauty." Used by the Ibo of Nigeria.

Adara (uh-DAH-ruh) Derived from Greek and Arabic, this name means "virgin," the symbol of the zodiacal sign Virgo.

Adela (ah-DEH-lah) Spanish name meaning "noble." Another variation in Spanish-speaking countries is Adelina. Adela is also popular in Germany, where other variants include Adelia, Adele, and Adelle.

Aderes (ah-de-RAYS) Hebrew for "an outer garment" or "a cape." A common variation is Aderet.

Adesina (ah-DAY-see-nah) Often used by the Yoruba of Nigeria when the parents have waited a long time for a child. The meaning is "the coming of this baby has opened the way (for more children)."

Adia (ah-DEE-ah) Swahili name meaning "gift" or "present," implying the child is a gift from God.

Adie (ah-dee-AY) Hebrew for "ornament." A variant is Adiella, "the Lord's ornament."

Aditi (ah-dee-tee) Hindustani for "free and unbounded." In Hindu lore Aditi is the mother of the gods and is often asked to bestow blessings on children and cattle or to grant protection and forgiveness.

Adoette (ah-doh-AY-tuh) North American Indian name which means "big tree" and was probably given to a child born beneath a tree or believed to be akin to a tree spirit.

Adrienne French name meaning "dark one."

Adya (ah-dyah) East Indian name given to a child born

40

on Sunday. Adya is derived from the words *Teluga Adivaram,* meaning Sunday.

Afina (ah-FEE-nah) Rumanian nature name meaning "blueberry."

Afra (AH-frah) Hebrew name for a young female deer.

Agata (AH-gah-tah) "Good" or "kind." This name is used in Bulgaria, Czechoslovakia, Italy, Latvia, Poland, Sweden, and Spanish-speaking countries. Other Polish variants are Aga and Atka. The English development of the same name is Agatha.

Agate A magic name. The agate stone is said to cure the bites of scorpions and snakes, soothe the mind, drive away polluted air, and stop thunder and lightning. The stone is also believed to make one independent, an eloquent writer and speaker, and a favorite of princes. Wearing the agate around one's neck allegedly gives one victory over enemies.

Agda (uhg-DUH)Turkish name for a kind of candy. It implies the child is sweet as honey.

Agla A famous magic name which is said to be taken from the first letters of the Hebrew phrase *Ataw Gebor Leolan Adonai,* which means "Thou art mighty forever, Lord." The words were used as a charm by rabbis and some Christians until the sixteenth century to exorcise demons. The same magic name was also used in Germany, where it was thought to be derived from *Allmachtiger Gott, losch-'aus,* meaning "Redeem, Almighty God."

Agnella This pretty Italian name means "pure one." Another form used today in Italy is Agnola. The English equivalent is Agnes.

Ahava (ah-HAH-vah) Hebrew for "beloved." Variants are Ahuva and Ahuda.

Ahimsa (ah-heem-sah) This Hindu name comes from the spiritual virtue of nonviolence, which is interpreted as not injuring any living thing, even in thought.

41

Ahira (ah-HEE-ruh) "Related to the sun." Occult name for a girl born under Leo, which is ruled by the sun.

Ah Kum (ah koo:m) Chinese name meaning "good as gold."

Ah Lam (ah lahm) Chinese for "like an orchid."

Aida (igh-EE-duh) Popularized in Italy by the Verdi opera of the same name, Aida means "happy."

Aila (IGH-luh) Finnish name which comes from the Anglo-Irish for "light bearer." Another Finnish variation is Aili. The English equivalent is Ailene.

Aimee French for "loved one." The name originally comes from the Latin Amy.

Aiyana (igh-YAH-nah) North American Indian flower name meaning "eternal bloom."

Aja (ah-jah) Hindustani for "a goat," the symbol of the zodiacal sign Capricorn. Aja is also the name of a tribe in India.

Ajuji (ah-JOO:-jee) The Hausa of Africa always give this name to the surviving child of a woman whose children have always died. According to the tradition, when the baby is born, the grandparents take the child out to the refuse heap, or the juji, and pretend to throw it away. After this gesture to the demons, the mother rushes out and reclaims her child.

Akako (AH-kah-koh) Japanese for "red." This was once a magical name, red being considered a charm to cure diseases, particularly blood ailments. In one ancient Japanese tale, a powerful tree spirit is conquered because men attacking it painted their faces red, wore red shirts, and tied a red cord about the tree's trunk. Although the superstition is no longer believed, the name remains.

Akanke (ah-kahn-KEH) "To know her is to pet her." A Yoruban nickname.

Akasma (UH-kuhs-muh) Turkish flower name meaning "white climbing rose," referring to the clematis.

Akela (ah-KAY-lah) Hawaiian form of Adelle, "noble."

Aki (ah-KEE) Japanese name for a girl born in autumn. Other Japanese seasonal names are Haru, "spring," Natsu, "summer," and Fuyu, "winter."

Akilah (AH-kee-lah) Arabic for "intelligent" or "logical."

Akosua (ah-KOH-soo:-ah) Used in Ghana for a child "born on Sunday."

Alake (ah-lah-KEH) Yoruban nickname meaning "one to be petted if she survives." Given to an unhealthy child.

Alala (uh-LAH-luh) From the Greek for "Mars's sister" or "war goddess." Astrological name for girls born under Aries and Scorpio, which are ruled by the fiery planet Mars.

Alamea (ah-luh-MAY-uh) Hawaiian for "ripe" or "precious."

Alameda (ah-la-MAY-dah) This North American Indian name means "cottonwood grove." In Spanish the same name means a "promenade."

Alana (uh-LAH-nuh) Hawaiian for "an offering" or "light and buoyant."

Alani (ah-LAH-nee) Hawaiian nature name referring to any kind of orange or orange tree, particularly the oahu tree, with its oblong, fragrant leaves used for scenting cloth. Also a boy's name.

Alaqua (ah-LAH-quah) North American Indian name for the sweet gum tree.

Alauda Gallic nature name meaning "lark."

Alaula Hawaiian nature name meaning "light of early dawn" or "sunset glow." This name, like most Hawaiian names, is given to either sex.

Albertine (AHL-bair-ti-nuh) Latvian for "noble and brilliant." The English development of the name is Alberta.

43

Albinka (al-BEEN-kah) From the Latin Albinia, meaning "blond" or "white," this Polish name is the equivalent of the English Albina.

Aleeza (ah-LEE-zah) Hebrew for "joy" or "joyful." Variant spellings are Aliza, Alizah, Alitza, and Alitzah.

Aleka (ah-LAY-kah) Pet form of Alexandra used today in Greece. It means "helper and defender of mankind."

Alena (ah-LAY-nah) A favorite Russian diminutive. See Olena.

Aleta (ah-LEH-tah) Spanish name meaning "little winged one." Derived from Latin. The English development is Alida.

Aletea (ah-leh-TEH-uh) Contemporary Spanish name meaning "the truth."

Alexandra Common Russian name meaning "helper and defender of mankind." Russian variations and pet forms are Alya, Shura, Shurochka, Sacha, Sashenka, Lesya, and Olesya.

Algoma (ahl-GOH-mah) "Valley of flowers." North American Indian name.

Alhena (ahl-HEE-nuh) Originally from the Arabic for "a ring." The name refers to a third-magnitude star in Pollux, part of the constellation Gemini, the Twins. A child born under the sign Gemini is said to be versatile and brilliant, fickle yet unselfish.

Ali Contemporary American form of Alice or Alison, meaning "truthful."

Alicia (ah-LEE-see-uh) Spanish, Italian, and Swedish name from the Greek for "truthful." The Hawaiian form of the same name is Alika.

Alike (ah-LEE-keh) The Ibo of Nigeria use this as an abbreviation of the name Alikeocopeleabola, which means "girl who drives out beautiful women." The name is given because the child herself is lovely.

Alile (ah-LEE-leh) "She weeps." Used by the Yao-speaking people of Malawi for a child born into unfortunate circumstances.

Alima (ah-LEE-muh) "Sea maiden." Astrological name for girls born under the water signs of the zodiac: Cancer, Scorpio, and Pisces.

Alina (a-LEE-nah) Used in Poland and Russia, this name means "bright" or "beautiful." Russian pet forms are Alya and Lina.

Alita (ah-LEE-tah) Spanish name meaning "noble." Variant forms are Adelina, Adelita, Dela, and Lela. See also Adela.

Aliza (ah-LEE-zah) Hebrew for "joyous." See Aleeza.

Alka (AL-kah) Polish for "noble" or "brilliant."

Alkas (AHL-kahs) North American Indian name meaning "she is afraid."

Alleen Dutch name meaning "alone."

Alma (AHL-mah) Spanish and Italian name which literally means "soul" or "spirit," with a connotation of nourishment. In other words, the child feeds one's soul or lifts the spirit.

Almira (ahl-MEE-ruh) Hindustani name which means "clothes basket." The Hindus believe God is manifested in everything, and thus children in India are often named after common household objects. Each time the name is pronounced, God's name is pronounced, an act considered a step toward salvation. In Arabic Almira means "fulfillment of the Word" or "truth without question."

Alnaba (ahl-NAH-bah) The Navaho Indians often name their girls after events of war. This name means "wars passed each other," indicating two battles raged in opposite directions.

Aloha (ah-LOH-hah) This familiar Hawaiian name has connotations of love, affection, mercy, kindness, charity, greetings, and farewell.

45

Alohi (ah-LOH-hee) Hawaiian for "shining" or "brilliant." Also a boy's name.

Alona (ah-LOH-nah) A shortened form of the Hebrew nature name Alonaw, or "oak tree." The masculine form is Alon.

Altsoba (ahl-TSOH-bah) Navaho name meaning "all are at war." See Alnaba.

Aludra (uh-LOO:-druh) From the Greek and Arabic for "virgin." Astrological name for a girl born under Virgo, the Virgin.

Alumit (ah-loo:-MEET) Currently used in Israel, Alumit means "girl" or "secret." Variants are Aluma, Alumice, and Alma.

Alverta Contemporary Greek name meaning "noble and brilliant."

Alzubra (ahl-ZOO:-bruh) Derived from Arabic, this name refers to a tiny star of the fifth magnitude in the constellation Leo, the Lion. Hence, given to a child born under that sign.

Am (uhm) Vietnamese for "lunar" or "female principle." The latter refers to the Oriental concept of the universe, which states that in the beginning two sources of energy existed—male and female—and from these the world was born.

Ama (AH-mah) Southern Ghanaian name for a girl born on Saturday, from the Akan word *Memenda*. Also used among Fanti-speaking people. Other Ghanaian day-of-the-week names are Akosua, "born on Sunday"; Ajua, "born on Monday"; Abmaba, "born on Tuesday"; Ekua, "born on Wednesday"; Aba, "born on Thursday"; and Efua, "born on Friday."

Amadika (ah-mah-DEE-kah) "To be beloved." From the Wataware tribe of Southern Rhodesia. This is a name a mother gives herself if her life has been filled with tragedy; the connotation is "once my husband loved me, but he doesn't anymore."

Amalia (ah-mah-lee-ah, with the stress falling on one of the first three syllables, depending upon the language) Currently used in Hungary, Poland, Rumania, and Slovakia, this name is derived from the Gothic word *amala,* meaning "industrious." The English equivalent is Amelia.

Amaliya (ah-mah-LEE-yah) Russian development of the French Aimee, meaning "beloved."

Amara (ah-MAH-rah) Esperanto development of the Biblical Mary, meaning "bitter." In Portugal and Brazil, Amara becomes Amargo.

Amaris "Child of the moon." In astrology the moon is the ruler of the sign Cancer, the Crab. Early astrologers believed Cancer was the constellation through which souls passed from heaven into human bodies.

Amata (ah-MAH-tah) Spanish name meaning "beloved." The English equivalent is Amy.

Amaui (uh-MOW-ee) A gentle Hawaiian thrush which is a dusky olive brown.

Amayeta (ah-mah-YEH-tah) Miwok Indian name meaning "big manzanita berries."

Amber (AHM-ber) Arabic name taken from the semi-jewel, used in ancient magical healing rites. The clear reddish-yellow stone contains bits of plants, insects, and feathers.

Ambika (ahm-BEE-kah) One of the more than one thousand Hindu names for Sakti, goddess of power and destruction. This one means "the mother."

Ami Contemporary American spelling of Amy, beloved.

Amina (ah-MEE-nah) Popular Muslim name meaning "peace" or "security." Amina was the Prophet's mother.

47

Amineh (a-MEE-na) Common Arabic admirable-quality name meaning "faithful."

Amira (ah-MEE-ruh) Hebrew for "speech" or "utterance."

Amissa (ah-MEE-suh) This Hebrew name means "friend," or when used as a variant of Amita, "truth." Another spelling is Amisa.

Amma (ah-mah) A mother goddess worshipped in India. Other Hindu mother goddesses are Mata; Amba; Mahamba or Momba, Mumba, or Bimba; and Ellama or Elamma.

Amoke (ah-moh-KEH) "To know her is to pet her." Nickname among the Yoruba of Nigeria.

An (an or ang) Vietnamese for "peace," "safety," or "security."

Ana Hawaiian development of Anna, "graceful."

Anaba (ah-NAH-bah) Navaho Indian name meaning "she returns from war." See Alnaba.

Anabela (ah-nuh-BEL-ah) "Graceful" or "beautiful." Hawaiian form of Annabelle.

Anala (ah-NAH-luh) Often used for boys, this Hindu name means "fire" and is another name for Agni, the god of fire.

Ananda (ah-nuhn-dah) Hindustani for "bliss." Often used in India as a name component to create new names.

Anastassia (ah-nah-stah-SEE-ah) Very popular in Russia, this name comes from the Greek "of the Resurrection" and was introduced into Russia through the church. Pet forms are Nessa, Nastia, Asia (ah-SEE-ah), Tasya, Tasenka, and Stasya. In Czechoslovakia a common pet form is Stasa.

Anda Used in most Spanish-speaking countries, this name means "going." A variation is Andeana, "a walker" or "a goer."

Andulka (AHN-doo:l-kah) As common in Czechoslovakia as Susie or Jane is in the United States, this name means "little graceful one." The English equivalent is Anne.

Ane (AH-neh) Hawaiian development of Anne, from the Hebrew for "graceful."

Anela (AH-nel-ah) "Angel." This name was used by early Hawaiian Christians to designate the few pagan gods they still believed in.

Anevay (ah-neh-VIGH) North American Indian name meaning "superior."

Anezka (AH-nehzh-kah) A very popular girl's name in Czechoslovakia, Anezka means "pure." Other Slovak forms are Agnesa (AHG-nehsh-ah) and Agneska (AHG-nesh-kah). The English equivalent is Agnes.

Angela Currently used in both Greece and the United States, this name means "angel" or "one who brings good news." See Evangelia for other Greek variations.

Angeliki Contemporary Greek name meaning "angelic." A variation is Angelica.

Angeni (ahn-GAY-nee) North American Indian name meaning "spirit angel."

Angie Common contemporary American form of Angela, meaning "angel" or "one who brings good news." Often used today as an independent name.

Anica (ah-NEE-kah) Popular Spanish name which means "graceful." Other Spanish forms are Anita, Nita, and Ana. The English equivalent is Anne.

Anicka (AH-neesh-kah) Common Czech name meaning "graceful." Other popular forms in Czechoslovakia are Anna, Andula, and Anuska.

Anila (uh-nee-lah) Hindu name for the wind god, with whom the forty-nine godlings of the wind are associated. Also a boy's name.

Aniweta (ah-NEE-weh-tah) Common among the Ibo of Nigeria, Aniweta means "Ani (a spirit) brought it." This is typical of the many Ibo short-sentence names, which usually mention the child's birth, future, or a hope of the parents. Also a boy's name.

Anna (AH-nuh) One of the most common Russian names, Anna means "graceful." Pet forms are Anuta, Asya, Anya, Anka, and Nyura, the peasant form.

Anona Earth name from the Latin for "yearly crops." Used for girls born under the earth signs of the zodiac: Capricorn, Taurus, and Virgo.

Anthea (ahn-THAY-ah) Flower name from the Greek for "lady of flowers."

Antonetta (AHN-toh-neht-tah) Slovak name meaning "priceless." The same name is occasionally used in Sweden. The English equivalent is Antonia.

Anya (AHN-yah) Popular in Latvia, Estonia, Russia, and the Ukraine. See Anna.

Anzu (AH-N.dsuh) Japanese for "apricot," the emblem of the fair sex. In Western lore the apricot symbolizes timid love.

Aolani (ow-LAH-nee) Delicate Hawaiian name meaning "heavenly cloud."

Apangela (ah-pahn-GAY-lah) The African Ovimbundus of Angola take many names from proverbs. This one comes from the saying *(W)a pangela ka mali ungende,* or "One who intends not to finish her journey." A possible connotation is the child may not live.

Apara (ah-PAH-rah) Yoruban name meaning "one who comes and goes." This is one of the many Abiku, or born-to-die, names in various African languages. An old superstition says that certain children are the incarnation of evil spirits which enter and leave the world, and Abiku names are bestowed to keep the child from dying.
Other Yoruban born-to-die names are Molomo, "don't go back (to the spirit world)"; Kosoko, "there

50

is no hoe (to dig a grave with)"; Banjoko, "sit down (or stay) with me, meaning "don't desert me"; Durosimi, "wait and bury me, meaning "don't die before me"; and Akisatan, "rags are not finished (with which to bury you)."

Aponi (ah-POH-nee) North American Indian name meaning "butterfly." The Pima Indians believe their Creator took the form of a butterfly and fluttered all over the world until He found the best place for man.

Aprilette From the Latin for "open." Astrological name for a girl born in April, under either Aries, the Ram, or Taurus, the Bull.

Aprili (ah-PREE-lee) Swahili name for a girl born in April.

Aquene (ah-Kay-nay) North American Indian name meaning "peace."

Arabela (ah-rah-BEH-lah) Spanish for "beautiful altar." The English equivalent is Arabella.

Arah (AH-rah) "Lion cub." The name refers to the constellation and zodiacal sign Leo, the Lion.

Ararita (ah-rah-REE-tah) Occult name used in hexagram rituals to banish and invoke spirits. Ararita is taken from the first letters of the words in the incantation meaning "One is His Beginning; One is His Individuality; His Permutation is One."

Araxie In Armenia the Araxie River, from which this name is derived, is known as an inspiration to poets.

Arcite From the Latin for "archer." Astrological name for a baby born under Sagittarius, the Archer.

Ardilla (ahr-DEE-yah) Spanish for "squirrel."

Arella (ah-RAY-luh) Hebrew name meaning "angel" or "messenger." An alternate spelling is Arela.

Arete (ah-RAY-teh) Contemporary Greek name meaning "graceful" or "lovely." The English equivalent is Grace.

Aretha From the Greek for "best." The name is gaining popularity in the United States because of singer Aretha Franklin. A modern Greek variation is Arethi, pronounced AIR-re-thee.

Argemone (ahr-geh-MOH-neh) Flower name from the Greek for "poppy," the source of opium.

Aria (AIR-ee-uh) Occult name for a girl born in the Age of Aquarius, an astrological era of two thousand years of peace and brotherhood which began in March, 1948, when the sun left the Piscean constellation of turmoil and entered Aquarius.

Ariel (ah-ree-AYL) Hebrew for "lioness of God." Other common variations are Ariela and Ariella.

Arista (ah-REE-stuh) Latin for "harvest." A designation for the zodiacal sign Virgo, the Virgin, maiden of the harvest. Virgos are the intellectuals of the zodiac, practical, analytical, and skeptical.

Ariza (ah-REE-zuh) Hebrew name with the unusual meaning "cedar panels." Other forms used today in Israel include Arza, Arzice, and Arzit.

Arlet (ahr-let) Hindustani name for an East Indian spice.

Arna (AHR-nah) Hebrew nature name meaning "cedar tree." Other variants are Arnice and Arnit.

Arnina (ahr-NEE-nuh) A form of Arona, the feminine of Aaron, which is currently used in Israel. Other modern variations are Arni, Arnice, and Arnit. Many meanings have been given for this name, including "mountain," "singer," "to shine," and "messenger."

Artha (ahr-tah) Hindustani for "wealth" or "worldly prosperity," a goal which the practical as well as spiritual Hindus regard as one of the four ends of man.

Arziki (ahr-ZEE-kee) "Prosperity." A conventional African Hausa name used as late as the 1930's for a man's first female slave.

Asa (AH-sah) Japanese name for a child "born in the

52

morning." Other time-of-day names are Cho, "born at dawn," Yoi, "born in the evening," and Sayo, "born at night."

Asabi (ah-sah-BEE) Yoruban nickname meaning "one of select birth."

Asela (ah-SEH-lah) Contemporary Spanish nature name from the Latin for "slim ash tree."

Aselli (ah-SEHL-lee) Two stars in the constellation Cancer, the Crab. Those born under that sign are said to be sensitive, protective, and lovers of history.

Asenka (AH-sen-kuh) Used in Latvia, Estonia, and Russia, this name comes from the Hebrew for "graceful." Hundreds of variations come from the same source, including the English Anne. Estonian and Latvian variants include Aneta, Anichka, Anita, Annushka, Anya, Anyuta, Asya, and Nyura.

Asisa (ah-SEE-sah) Hebrew for "juicy" or "ripe."

Asiza (ah-SEE-zah) The African Dahomey believe the asiza are spirits who dwell in the forests and grant magical powers to man.

Asoka (ah-shoh-kah) Hindu name taken from the so-called non-sorrow flower, which allegedly blooms orange or scarlet when touched by the foot of a gentle maiden.

Asta (AH-stah) Very popular today in Norway as a modern form of Astrid, from the Old Norse for "divine strength." Asta is also an English name, derived from the Greek *aster,* meaning "like a star" and referring to the aster flower.

Astera Israeli flower name derived from the aster, which, because of its star-shaped leaves, has been called the starflower. Another form used today in Israel is Asteria.

Astrid One of the most common Danish names today, from the Old Norse for "divine strength."

Asvina (ahs-vee-nah) Hindu name for a child born during the lunar month which corresponds to the zodiacal sign Libra. The symbol of Libra is the Balance and the ruling planet is Venus.

Asya (AHS-yah) Popular Russian diminutive. See Anna.

Atara (ah-TAH-ruh) Hebrew for "a crown." A common variant is Ateret.

Atida (ah-TEE-duh) Israeli name from the Hebrew for "the future."

Atira (ah-TEE-rah) Hebrew name meaning "a prayer."

Aud (aoo:d) "Deserted" or "empty." Because of the current Norwegian preference for names with a distinctly Scandinavian sound, this is one of the most popular in Norway.

Audey Modern American name shortened from Audrey, "noble strength," and gaining popularity as an independent name.

Aulii (OW-lee) Hawaiian name meaning "dainty."

Auta (OW-tah) Given by the Hausa of Africa to a child of either sex born when the mother is well past child-bearing age. Variations are Yar Tsofuwa (female) and Dan Tsufuwa (male), which mean "baby of an old woman."

Avasa (ah-vah-sah) Hindu name from the Sanskrit for "independent."

Avena (ah-VAY-nuh) "Oats" or "oat field." Earth name for girls born under the earth signs of the zodiac: Capricorn, Taurus, and Virgo. Some astrologers advise such an earth name if a child's horoscope contains too many metal influences. An earth name restores the balance of the elements because earth produces metal and therefore controls it.

Averill From the Old English for "born in April." An especially good astrological name for an Aries child. Variant spellings are Avril, Avrill, and Averyl.

54

Avi (ah-VEE) Israeli name meaning "my father" or "my God."

Aviva (ah-vee-VAH) Hebrew for "springtime," with a connotation of youthfulness and freshness. Also spelled Avivah.

Avivi (ah-vee-VEE) Related to Aviva, this modern Israeli name means "springlike." Avivice and Avirit are also used.

Awanata (ah-wah-NAH-tah) Miwok Indian name for the turtle, prominent in some Indian myths. The Korusa, for instance, believe that in the beginning there was only the Old Turtle swimming in a limitless ocean. He dived down, brought up a mouthful of dirt, and created the world.

Awenita (ah-way-NEE-tah) "A fawn." North American Indian name.

Awendela (ah-wayn-DAY-lah) "Early day." North American Indian name for a child born just before sunrise.

Ayame (ah-ya-ME) Japanese for "iris," the Oriental emblem of the warrior and the Japanese flower of May. In astrology the iris is the "herb" of the moon, which governs the sign Cancer.

Ayasha (IGH-ish-ah) Common Muslim name which varies slightly throughout the Muslim countries of India, Turkey, Jordan, Persia, Egypt, and Arabia. Also spelled Asya. Ayasha was one of the Prophet Muhammad's wives.

Ayelet (ah-yeh-LAYT) Hebrew name for a deer or gazelle.

Aylette "The sea swallow." Pretty English nature name derived from Latin.

Ayita (ah-YEE-tah) "The worker." North American Indian name.

Ayla (ah-EE-luh) Hebrew name for the oak or terebinth tree.

Ayoka (ah-yoh-KAH) Yoruban name meaning "one who causes joy all around." This is usually a nickname rather than a given name, in the same category as Amoke.

Ayondela (ah-yohn-DAY-lah) Many African names derive from proverbs revealing some philosophy of life. Ayondela comes from the Umbundu saying "A little tree bends and bends, as we all bend toward death," indicating the high infant-mortality rate among the Ovimbundus.

Azami (ah-zah-MEE) Japanese for "thistle flower," an Occidental symbol of defiance and surliness.

Aziza (ah-ZEE-zah) Swahili for "precious."

Azize (uh-ZEEZ) Turkish for "dear," "precious," or "rare."

Azura (ah-ZHOO:-ruh) Ecological name meaning "clear blue sky."

Babara (buh-BAH-rah) Hawaiian form of Barbara, "stranger."

Baka (bah-kah) Hindu name meaning "crane," a symbol of longevity.

Bakula (bah-koo:-lah) A plant which according to Hindu myth bursts into bloom when sprinkled with wine from the mouth of a beautiful girl.

Balala (BAH-lah-lah) "You must eat much to grow." Used by the Mashona of Southern Rhodesia for a frail child.

Balaniki (bah-lah-NEE-kee) Hawaiian name from the Old French for "white one" or "fair one." The English equivalent is Blanche.

Barakah (BER-a-kah) Arabic name meaning "blessing." According to orthodox Muslims, the Prophet objected to this name as being too proud. He also disliked the names Rabah, "profit," and Aflah, "most successful."

Barbro A form of Barbara, "stranger," very popular today in Sweden.

Barika (bah-REE-kah) Swahili name derived from the Arabic for "bloom" or "be successful."

Batini (bah-TEE-nee) Swahili for "innermost thoughts."

Batya (bah-TEE-uh) Israeli name meaning "daughter of God." A variation is Basya.

Beatrisa (beh-ah-TREE-sah) Spanish name from the Latin for "she makes others happy." A pet form is Trisa.

Behira (beh-HEE-rah) Hebrew for "light," "clear," or "brilliant."

Bel (bayl) Hindu name for the sacred wood apple tree, the branches of which cannot be broken or used for firewood except by Brahmins.

Bela (BYEL-ah) "White child." Widely used in Czecho-slovakia for a fair-complexioned girl.

Belatha "Thou Essence, Air Swift-streaming, Elasticity!" An occult name used in incantations to invoke spirits.

Belia (beh-LEE-ah) Spanish variation of Isabel. See Belicia.

Belicia (beh-LEE-see-ah) Spanish variation of Isabel, "dedicated to God." Other forms are Belia and Belita.

Belinda (beh-LEEN-dah) Spanish for "pretty," this name originally comes from the Old Spanish *bella-linda.*

Bella "Nobly bright" or "beautiful." Used today in Hungary, where other spellings are Bela and Belle.

Belloma (bel-LOH-muh) From the Latin for "warlike" or "war goddess." Astrological name for girls born under Aries and Scorpio, which are ruled by the war planet Mars.

Bena (BAY-nah) This North American Indian name means "pheasant." The exact tribe from which the name comes is unknown.

Bene (BEH-neh) "Born on Fenibene," one of the eight

57

days in the African Kalabari-Ijaw market week. Other market-day names for girls are Kaladoku, "born on Ejibradokuene"; Kalaobuta, "born on Ejibrafeniobu"; Doku, "born on Opufedokuene"; and Obuta, "born on Feniobu."

Benita (beh-NEE-tah) Spanish name meaning "blessed." A common diminutive of Benedicta.

Berura (beh-ROO:-ruh) Modern Israeli name from the Old Hebraic Burura or Bururia, meaning "clean" or "pure." In the Talmud, Beruria is the only woman permitted to take part in legal discussions.

Beta (BE-tah) Used today in Czechoslovakia, in both Bohemia and Slovakia, this name means "dedicated to God." Other forms are Alzbeta, Betica, Liza, and Elizabeta.

Beti (BAY-tee) English Gypsy name meaning "little" or "small."

Betula (beh-TOO:-luh) Hebrew for "girl" or "maiden."

Bian (BEE-uhn) Vietnamese name meaning "to be hidden" or "secretive."

Bianca Popular Italian name meaning "white." Occasionally used in the United States.

Bibi (Bee-bee) Swahili term of politeness derived from the Arabic for "lady."

Bina (BEE-nuh) Used by two widely separated cultures. To the Israelis, Bina means "understanding" or "intelligence," and to the Arapaho Indians, it means "fruits." Another Hebrew variation is Buna.

Binti (BEEN-tee) Swahili for "daughter."

Birdella Teutonic nature name meaning "little elfin bird." Another variant is Birdena, "birdlike."

Birgit (BEER-git) Common in Norway, this name means "protecting." The variant Bergitte is one of the most common names in Denmark, as is Birgitta in Sweden.

Bitki (bit-KI) Turkish for "plant."

Blom (blahm) Afrikaans for "flower." The youngest Indo-Germanic language, Afrikaans is officially spoken in the Republic of South Africa.

Blum (bloo:-m) Yiddish for "flower." Often Anglicized to Bluma.

Bly This North American Indian name means "high" and was often bestowed in the hope that the child would grow tall. Also a boy's name. In Afrikaans the same name means "happy."

Bo (boh) Chinese for "precious."

Bobina (BOH-beh-nah) "Brilliantly famous." Czech nickname for Roberta, which is also used in Czechoslovakia. Other Czech forms are Roba and Berta.

Bohdana (boh-DAH-nah) "Given by God." Popular in the Ukraine as the feminine form of Bohdan. A pet form is Danya. Bohdan Chmelnyckyj was a famed seventeenth-century Cossack leader.

Bona Hebrew for "a builder."

Bonita Spanish name meaning "pretty."

Brett Traditionally a boy's name, Brett is gaining popularity in the United States as a girl's name. It means a "Briton." Also spelled Bret.

Brigida (bree-K(H)EE-dah) Spanish and Italian name meaning "strength" or "protecting." In Spanish the *g* is pronounced with a strongly aspirated sound like the *ch* in *loch*. The shorter form Brigid is one of the most popular names in Ireland today.

Brita "From Britain." Used in Norway. Also spelled Brit.

Brona Originally from the Greek *Berenike*, meaning "coming before victory," Brona is currently used in Czechoslovakia. The English equivalent is Berenice.

Brooke "Dweller by the brook." Masculine American name now often used for girls.

Bua (BOO:-uh) Vietnamese for "hammer." Bua also means "written charm" or "amulet," appropriate because such metal names are often thought to bring luck or good health.

Cai (kay) Vietnamese for "female."

Caimile (chigh-MEE-lee) Proverb name used by the African Ovimbundus. Caimile comes from the sorrowful saying *Ca imile li loluka; epota li citiwe li kunduka*, "A tree bears fruit, the fruit falls to the ground; a family has children, and they all die."

Calida (kah-LEE-dah) Spanish for "warm" or "loving."

Caltha (KAHL-thuh) This flower name comes from Latin and means "marigold" or simply "yellow flower."

Cam (kam) Vietnamese for "orange fruit" or "to be sweet."

Camila (kah-MEE-lah) Derived from a Latin word for a beautiful ceremonial girl who helped in ancient pagan rites, Camila is still used as a Spanish name. The English equivalent is Camille.

Camilla American name meaning "born free."

Candi (KAHN-dee) Colloquial Spanish form of Candida, "bright" or "white."

Candra Astrological name meaning "moon," ruler of the sign Cancer. In the tarot pack Pisces corresponds to the card of the moon.

Capri Astrological name for a child born under Capricorn, the Goat. Capricorn literally means "the goat-horned," and Capri is simply "the goat."

Cara (ka-ra) Vietnamese for "diamond" or "precious gem."

Cari (kah-RI) Turkish for "flowing like water." Also a contemporary American name which began as a variant spelling of Carrie, a nickname for Carol, "womanly." The English pronunciation is, of course, KAIR-ee.

Carine (kah-ri-NAY) Armenian name, the meaning of

which is uncertain. In English the same name is used as a variation of Cara, "beloved" or "friend."

Carita Italian name meaning "charity," derived from the Latin *caritas*.

Carlota (kahr-LOH-tah) Spanish and Portuguese development of the French Charlotte, meaning "petite" or "feminine." Carlota is one of the most popular Portuguese names today. A Spanish pet form is Lola.

Carly Gaining popularity in the United States as an independent name, this was once a nickname for Caroline, "little womanly one."

Carmen Spanish name from the cult of the Virgin Mary. Shortened form of Maria del Carmen.

Carna Israeli name meaning "horn." The exact Hebrew word is Karnis. Other forms used today are Carnis, Carnit, Carniela, and Carniella. All variations are also spelled with an initial *k*.

Caron (kah-ROHN) French name meaning "pure."

Catava (chah-TAH-vah) Ovimbundu proverb name from the saying *Ca tava otulo; ca patala olongembia,* "It consented sleep; it protested pain." Loosely translated, this means she wanted to sleep, but was in too much pain to do so. Other Ovimbundu proverb names include Ciyeva, "You hear it, but you don't do it," and Cakusola, "If you loved, you followed the messenger," The latter is a name for a child born shortly after the parents have been honored in some way.

Celia (SE-lee-uh) Swedish name meaning "dim-sighted." The Spanish and Italian form is Cecilia.

Celina (tsel-LEE-nah) Contemporary Polish name which comes from the Latin for "heavenly." Other Polish forms are Celestyn, Celestyna, Cela, Celek, Celinka, Celka, Cesia, Inka, and Inok.

Cella Italian nickname for Francesca, "free one" or "from France."

61

Cerella (se-REH-luh) "Of the spring." Astrological name for girls born under the spring signs of the zodiac: Aries, Taurus, and Gemini. A variant is Cerelia.

Cerise French for "cherry."

Chaitra (CHAY-truh) Hindustani name for the lunar month corresponding to the zodiacal sign Aries. Given to a child born under that sign.

Chandi (chahn-dee) "Angry" or "fierce." One of the more than one thousand names for the Hindu goddess Sakti. Another variation used in India is Chanda, sometimes loosely translated as "the great goddess." See Sakti for further information.

Channa (chah-nuh) Nature name from India for a variety of chickpea. According to traditional Hindu mythology, all herbs, plants, and trees were "fathered by heaven, mothered by earth, and rooted in the primeval ocean."

Chandra (CHAHN-druh) Hindu name for the moon or the moon god. See Candra for its astrological implications.

Chavi (CHAH-vee) English Gypsy name meaning "child" or "daughter." A variation is Chavali, "girl."

Chaya (ki-YAH) Hebrew for "life" or "living."

Chenoa (chay-NOH-ah) North American Indian name meaning "white dove," with the connotation of peace in nature.

Cher "Dear" or "beloved." Modern French name also used in the United States.

Chika (chee-KAH) Japanese name meaning "near," possibly in the sense of near and dear. A popular variation is Chikako.

Chilali (chee-LAH-lee) "Snowbird." North American Indian name.

Chimalis (chee-MAH-lees) "Bluebird." North American Indian name.

Chimene (shee-MEHN) Modern French name from the Greek for "hospitable."

Chiriga (chee-REE-gah) African Wahungwe name meaning "she is the girl of poor parents." Derived from the words *ka riga,* "to rob of everything."

Chitsa (CHEET-sah) North American Indian name meaning "fair one."

Chizu (CHEE-zoo) Japanese name meaning "a thousand storks." In Japan the stork was once a symbol of longevity, and the name is a holdover from this belief. A popular variation is Chizuko.

Cho (choh) Japanese for "butterfly."

Choomia (CHOO:-mee-uh) English Gypsy word for "a kiss."

Christel German name meaning "Christian." Other pet forms used in Germany today are Christa, Stine, and Tina. The English equivalent is Christine.

Chu Hua (chuh hwah) Chinese for "chrysanthemum." In China the chrysanthemum is the flower of autumn and the month of October. In Occidental astrology it is the flower of Scorpio.

Chuma (CHOO:-mah) Used by the Mashona of Southern Rhodesia, this name means "beads."

Chun (CHWUN) Chinese for "spring."

Cilehe (chee-LAY-heh) Ovimbundu proverb name from *Ci lehe no; oi kaile,* "Just let it stink, let it be." Loosely translated, the saying means if something is bad, just leave it alone or you will make it worse. Another version of the same saying is "Let it stink, it is his own," meaning we all must handle our own problems.

Cilka (CHEL-kuh) Slavic pet form of Cecilia, from the Latin for "dim-sighted." The name was probably once given to babies with small or squinted eyes.

Cinofila (chee-noh-FEE-lah) Ovimbundu name from the

proverb *Ocina o fila te nda o ci lia,* "A thing you die for only if you eat it." The saying is used to describe the hunter who overcomes all obstacles to find meat.

Cocheta (shoh-CHAY-tah) "The unknown." North American Indian name.

Cholena (choh-LAY-nah) "Bird." North American Indian name.

Cipriana (see-pree-AH-nah) Spanish development of the Greek *Kupris,* meaning "from the island of Cyprus." The Zuni Indians borrowed this name from the Spanish, changing it to Sipiana.

Clareta (klah-REH-tah) Popular in Spanish-speaking countries, Clareta comes from the Latin for "brilliant" or "bright." Also spelled Clarita.

Cohila (cho-HEE-luh) African Ovimbundu name from the proverb *Ca uhila onene, kutima ku vala,* "It is silent on the part of the young, at heart it hurts." In other words, the young are quiet about the things that hurt them.

Corah (KOH-rah) From the Hindustani word for "unchanging."

Crystal "Clear as crystal." In the occult world crystal banishes nightmares, dissolves enchantments, and allows one to have magical visions. It is so delicate, say the occultists, it can be bruised by honey.

Cytheria (sigh-THEH-ree-uh) Another name for Venus, ruler of the zodiacal sign Libra. Libras are the romantics of the zodiac. They are said to be peaceloving, easygoing, and lovers of beauty.

Dacey "Southerner." Modern American name once used only for boys. Also spelled Dacy and Dasi.

Dagania Hebrew for "corn" or "ceremonial grain." A variant is Daganya.

Daggi Estonian development of an Old German word

meaning "glorious day," "famous thinker," or "glory of the Danes." Another spelling in Estonia is Dagi.

Dagmar "Glory of the Danes." Danish name which is also used in the United States. Not as popular in Denmark as it once was.

Dagny Very popular in Norway, this name is the feminine form of Dag, meaning "day."

Dalila (dah-LEE-lah) Swahili for "gentle."

Dalit (dah-LEET) Hebrew name meaning "to draw water" or "a tree branch." Another form is Dalice.

Damita Spanish for "little noble lady."

Dana In Celtic mythology Dana was the mother of the gods. Originally a masculine name, however, it is used today as a girl's name in the United States and parts of Scandinavia. The Hebrew Dana, is a form of Daniel.

Danett Contemporary American name created from Daniela, "God is my judge." A modern feminine form of Daniel.

Danica (DAH-nets-uh) Current Slavic name meaning "morning star."

Danice This modern American name is either a form of Daniela, "God is my judge," or an alternate spelling of Denice, "follower of Dionysus," the Greek god of wine. The shorter Dani is also gaining popularity in the United States as an independent name.

Danit (dah-NEET) A feminine Hebrew form of Daniel, Danit means "to judge." Other forms are Danya and Dania, "judgment of God."

Danya (DAHN-yah) Popular nickname in the Ukraine. See Bohdana. Also an Israeli name. See Danit.

Darda (DAWR-dah) Modern Hungarian name meaning "a dart," or from the Hebrew meaning "pearl of wisdom."

Darsey Modern American development of the boy's name

Darcy, meaning "from a fortress" or "black man." Also spelled Darsy and Darcie.

Daru (DAH-roo:) Hindu name which comes from a species of pine or cedar called the *devadaru* "divine daru." An ancient Hindu sacrificial post was allegedly carved from this wood.

Dasha (DAH-shah) Popular Russian pet form of Doroteya, from the Greek for "gift of God."

Dede (DEH-de) In Ghana the Ochi- and Ga-speaking people use this for a first-born daughter.

Deedee Hebrew for "beloved." The abbreviated form Didi is often used in Israel as a pet form of Jedidiah. Also a boy's name.

Degula (deh-GOO:-lah) Hebrew for "excellent" or "famous."

Dela Spanish diminutive meaning "hope." See Alita.

Delle (DEH-luh or dehl) From the Hebrew for "jar." This is another name for the constellation Aquarius, the Water Bearer. Given to a child born under that sign. A variation is Deli.

Delora "From the sea coast." Used for girls born under the water signs of the zodiac: Cancer, Scorpio, and Pisces.

Delu (day-LOO:) Conventional Hausa name for the first girl born after three boys. Iggi is often given in place of Delu. See Kapuki for other examples of African serial names.

Dena (DAY-nah) North American Indian name meaning "a dale" or "a valley."

Denebola (de-NE-boh-luh) A bright star in the tail of the constellation Leo, the Lion. Hence, a name for a child born under that sign. A shortened form is Denie.

Derora (deh-ROH-rah) Modern Hebrew nature name meaning "flowing brook," "bird," particularly the swallow, or "freedom." Variants are Derorice and Derorit.

Deva "Divine." Hindu name for the moon goddess.

Devaki (dah-vah-KEE) "Black." Hindu name for the goddess who was the mother of the powerful god Krishna. Krishna was such an energetic baby that when only twenty-seven days old, he kicked a demon to death. His energy continued into later life: he allegedly had 16,108 wives and 180,008 children.

Devi (DAY-vee) "Goddess." One of the many names for the Hindu goddess of power and destruction, Sakti.

Devora (day-VOH-rah) Russian development of Deborah, "a bee." Also spelled Debora.

Dezba (DEHZ-bah) Common Navaho name meaning "going to war." See Doba.

Dickla (dee-KLAH) Used as a girl's name in Israel, Dickla means "a palm tree" or "a date tree." Other common forms are Dikla, Diklice, and Diklit.

Dina Popular as a nickname for many names, including the Greek Kostantina and the Russian Dinah. The African Wahungwe give the nickname to a boy who is always seeking a comfortable place to sit, the meaning being "he sat down wherever he went."

Dinka The Dinka are a tribe of about a million people who have lived since remote times on the plains around the Southern Nile. Concerned about equality among men, the Dinka believe if a man hoards more possessions than he needs, he upsets the balance of nature.

Diota (dee-OH-tuh) "Jar with a neck and two handles." This is another name for the constellation Aquarius, the Water Bearer. Given to a child born under that sign.

Disa Contemporary American name originally derived from the Old Norse for "active sprite" or the Greek for "double." It seems to be gaining popularity today, possibly because of the number-one American favorite, Lisa.

Dita (DEE-tah) Czech name meaning "rich gift." Other Czech variations include Ditka and Edita. The English equivalent is Edith.

Diza Hebrew for "joy." Other forms are Ditza and Ditzah.

Doba (DOH-bah) Navaho Indian name meaning "there was no war." With few exceptions, Navaho girls' names commemorate war.

Dodie Hebrew name meaning "beloved." David and Davida come from the same source. Other forms are Doda and Dodi.

Dolore (doh-LOH-re) Hawaiian form of Dolores, "sorrows."

Dolores Popular in Spanish-speaking countries as a shortened form of the Virgin name Maria de los Dolores, "Mary of the Sorrows," which refers to the seven tragic events in the life of Mary. Other Spanish forms are Doloritas, Dolorcitas, Lolita, and Lola.

Domini (DAH-mi-nee) Used today as an independent name in the United States, Domini was once a pet form of Dominica, "belonging to God," or a variation of Domina, "lady."

Doni American creation from Donna, "lady," or Donalda, "ruler of the world." Also used recently are Donni and Dawni, the latter from the older name Dawn, "daybreak."

Dooriya (DOO:-ree-yuh) Romantic English Gypsy name meaning "the sea," from the Irish Deire, "the deep." A pet form is Dooya.

Dorit (doh-REET) Hebrew for "a generation." Currently used in Israel, where a variation is Dorice.

Dorisa Hawaiian development of the Greek Doris, meaning "from the ocean." The original Doris in Greek mythology was the daughter of the god of the sea.

Dorlisa German development of the Greek Dorothea, "God's gift." Other common German variations are Dora, Dorle, and Thea. The English equivalent is Dorothy. Forms used in other parts of the world include Dorolice, French; Dorte (DOHR-teh), Norwegian; and Doroteya (doh-roh-TAY-yah), Russian, with pet forms Dosya and Dasha.

Dory Originally a boy's name, Dory is being used today for both sexes. The name means "golden-haired."

Dosya (DOHS-yah) Popular Russian pet form of Doroteya. See Dorlisa.

Drina (DREE-nah) Popular diminutive of the Spanish Alejandrina (ah-leh-hahn-DREE-nah), meaning "helper and defender of mankind."

Drisana (dree-SAH-nah) Sanskrit for "daughter of the sun." Occult name for a girl born under Leo, the Lion, which is ruled by the sun. The name is often shortened to Drisa.

Dua (DOO:-ah) Astrological name which means "of two natures," referring to the dual, often contradictory temperament of those born under Gemini, the Twins.

Duci (DOO-tsee) Contemporary Hungarian name meaning "rich gift." Other forms used in Hungary are Edith and Edit.

Dudee (DOO:-dee) English Gypsy name for "a light" or "a star."

Durva (DOO:R-vah) This Hindu name comes from the durva grass, used in ceremonial worship.

Duscha (DOO:SH-hah) Russian for "soul." Used as an endearing term like the American "honey" or "sweetheart."

Dyani (d.YAH-nee) North American Indian name for "a deer." The deer was generally not considered as admirable as more ferocious animals like the bear, but a Tsimshiau Indian proverb states, "A deer, although

69

toothless, may accomplish something," meaning don't judge a man by outward appearances.

Eartha Nature name meaning "child of the earth." See Ertha.

Ebony This flower name also means "blackness."

Edda Popular Icelandic name meaning "poetry" or "composer (or singer) of songs."

Ede (AY-de) Russian form of the Old Norse Edda, "poetry." Because the name lacks a true Russian flavor, it is seldom used today.

Edena (e-DEN-ah) Hawaiian development of the Hebrew *'ednah,* meaning "rejuvenation." The English equivalent is Edna.

Edi Hawaiian form of the English Edith, "valuable gift." The Russian development of the same name is Edita.

Ega (AY-guh) "Palm bird." Yoruban name from the proverb "He who does not understand the cry of the palm bird complains of the noise it makes."

Eirene (ee-REH-nee) From the Old Norse Eir, this Greek name means "peace." While Eir was once popular in Scandinavia, the name is uncommon today.

Ela Polish nickame for Elwira, the English Elvira, meaning "white" or "blond." Polish variations include Wira, Wiera, and Wirke. Ela is also a shortened form of the Polish Melania, "dark in appearance" or simply "black" or "dark."

Eleni (eh-LEH-nee) Popular modern Greek name meaning "light" or "torch." Variations used in Greece are Elenitsa and Nitsa. Eleni was originally derived from the Greek Helene.

Elese (e-LES-e) Hawaiian form of Elsie, from the Old German Elsa, "noble."

Eli (AY-le) A form of Ellen, "light," used in Norway.

Elianora (e-lee-uh-NOH-ruh) Hawaiian form of Eleanor, which in turn is a form of Helen, "light."

Elidi (eh-LEE-dee) "Gift of the sun." Astrological name for a child born under Leo, which is ruled by the sun. The name is also appropriate for girls born under the other two fire signs, Aries and Sagittarius.

Eliora (eh-lee-OH-ruh) Hebrew for "the Lord is my light." Also spelled Eleora.

Elisa (eh-LEE-sah) Spanish name from the Hebrew Elisheba, "dedicated to God." Variations are Belita and Ysabel (ee-sah-BEL). The English equivalent is Elizabeth.

Eliska (EL-izh-kah) Czech development of either Alice, Greek for "truthful," or Elsie, Old German for "noble." The *s* in this name is pronounced like the *z* in *azure*.

Ellama (EL-lah-mah) Hindu name for a mother goddess worshipped as the guardian of South India. Also spelled Elamma.

Elli Estonian form of Helen, "light." See Leena.

Elma (el-MUH) Turkish name meaning "apple."

Elsa (AYL-sah) Popular in both Sweden and Spain, this name comes from the Greek Alethia, meaning "truthful."
Other variations used throughout the world are Alisa (Bulgarian); Alicia (Czech, Scandinavian, Spanish, and Italian); Alisz, Aliz, Alizka, and Lici (Hungarian); Alisa and Alya (Russian); and Alika (Hawaiian).

Else (AYL-se) Very popular today in Denmark, this name comes from the Old German Elsa, "noble."

Elverda (el-VAIR-duh) From the Latin for "virginal." Occult name given to a girl born under Virgo, the Virgin.

Elza Israeli name from the Hebrew for "God is my joy." In Russia the same name is occasionally used as a form of the Old German Elsa, "noble."

Ema Hawaiian development of Amy, "beloved," or

71

Emma, "universal." Similarly, the Hawaiian form of the English Emeline is Emalaina.

Emalia (em-uh-LEE-uh) In Hawaii this is used as a form of Emelia, from the Latin for "flatterer" or "flirt."

Emele (e-ME-le) Hawaiian name meaning "industrious" or "ambitious." In Brazil, Portugal, and Spanish-speaking countries the development of the same name is Emilia. The English equivalent is Emily.

Emuna (eh-MOO:-nuh) Hebrew for "faithful." An alternate spelling is Emunah.

Enola (ay-NOH-lah) The interpretation by some experts that this North American Indian name is simply "alone" spelled backward seems unsatisfactory because of the Indian tradition of bestowing names deeply and personally meaningful. No other explanation, however, could be found.

Erika Modern Swedish name meaning "always powerful" or "eternal ruler," derived from Old Norse. The English form is Erica.

Erin Irish for "peace."

Ertha "Child of the earth." Earth name for girls born under the earth signs of the zodiac: Capricorn, the Goat, Taurus, the Bull, and Virgo, the Virgin. Also spelled Eartha. Other variations include Erta Hertha, and Herta. Such earth names are often recommended by astrologers to correct a horoscope containing an imbalance of metal or water influences, since earth controls metal and destroys water. According to occultists, a good horoscope balances the basic elements—earth, fire, air, water, metal, and wood—to allow the universal order to work smoothly throughout the person's life.

Estrella Astrological name meaning "child of the stars."

Etenia (ay-TAY-nee-ah) North American Indian name meaning "the wealthy."

Etty Estonian development of Elizabeth, meaning "dedicated to God." Other Estonian forms are Betti, Elisabet, Elsbet, Elts, Etti, Liisa, and Liisi.

Eudice (ee-oo:-DEES) Modern Israeli form of Judith, which means "praise."

Eva (AY-vah) Originally from Hebrew, Eva means "life-giving." The name is used in Portugal, Germany, Italy, Spanish-speaking countries, Denmark, Greece, Bulgaria, Slovakia, Hungary, Rumania, Russia, Austria, Serbia, Sweden, Norway, and the United States.

Evangelia. (eh-vahn-GEH-lee-ah) Modern Greek name meaning "one who brings good news." Pet forms are Lia, Litsa, and Angela.

Evelina This name is used in Latvia, Russia, the Ukraine, Spain, Latin and South America, and the United States, and Evelina comes from the Hebrew for "life." See Eva. The Hawaiian form is Evalina, often shortened to Ewa, pronounced E-vah.

Eyota (eh-YOH-tah) North American Indian name meaning "the greatest." Often a boy's name.

Ezrela (ehz-RAY-luh) Israeli name meaning "God is my help" or "God is my strength." Variations used today are Ezraela and Ezraella.

Falda Icelandic name meaning "folded wings."

Fanya (FAHN-yah) Popular Russian nickname. See Fayina.

Fatma (FAHT-mah) Popular Arabic colloquial form of Fatimah. Also spelled Fatima, the name is used throughout the Muslim world, including Arabia, Jordan, Egypt, Iran, Turkey, and India. Fatimah was the favorite daughter of Muhammad and is believed to have lived from 606 to 632 A.D. She was married to Ali.

Fayina (figh-EE-nah) Russian and Ukrainian name meaning "free one." Other Russian forms are Faina, Fanechka (FAH-nesh-kah), and Fanya.

73

Fayola (fah-YOH-lah) Used by the Yoruba of Nigeria, this name means "good luck" or "walks with honor."

Felcia (FEL-shuh) Polish development of the Latin for "happy." Other common Polish variants are Felka, Fela, and Felicia. The English equivalent is Felice.

Felda From the Old German for "from the field." The name is given to girls born under the earth signs of the zodiac: Capricorn, the Goat, Taurus, the Bull, and Virgo, the Virgin.

Femi (FEH-mee) Pretty Yoruban name meaning "love me."

Fenelia (fay-NAY-luh) Common name among the English Gypsies. Its meaning is unknown.

Flo (floh) "Like an arrow." North American Indian name often used for boys.

Fonda (FOHN-dah) Spanish for "profound" or "well-based."

Fotina Contemporary Greek name meaning "free" or "from France." The English equivalent is Frances.

Franci (FRAWN-tsee) Hungarian development of Frances. Other variations are Fereng, Franciska, and Ferike.

Frida (FREE-duh) Used in Hungary, this name means "peaceful ruler." Other variants are Frederica and Frici. Frida is also currently used in Germany, where other forms are Frederike, Fritze, Fritzi, Fritzinn, and Riekchen. The Polish development of the name is Fryda, pronounced the same as Frida.

Gada (GAH-dah) This Israeli name is either a feminine form of Gad, "happy" or "lucky," or a Hebrew form of the Aramaic for "luck." Gada is also a plant name in Hebrew.

Gafna (GAHF-nah) Hebrew for "vine."

Gaho (GAH-hoh) North American Indian name meaning "mother."

74

Gaia (GIGH-uh) "The earth." Gaia was a Greek earth diety and the mother of Uranus. The name is used for girls born under the earth signs Capricorn, Taurus, and Virgo, and under Aquarius, which is ruled by Uranus. Another spelling is Gaea.

Gala (GAH-lah) Scandinavian name from the Old Norse for "singer."

Gali (gah-LEE) Hebrew for "a hill" or "a mound," or "a spring" or "a fountain." Other variants are Gal, Galice, and Galit.

Galina (gah-LEE-nah) Russian development of Helene, "light." The Greek name came into Russia through the Greek Orthodox Church. Popular diminutives include Jelena, Galinka, Galya, Yalena, and Lena.

Galya (GAHL-yah) Hebrew for "God has redeemed." Also used in Israel as a boy's name. In Russia it is a common pet form of Galina.

Ganit (gah-NEET) Hebrew for "garden." Gana and Ganice are also used today.

Ganesa (guh-NAY-shuh) East Indian name for the Hindu god of good luck and wisdom. Ganesa is depicted as a rotund, pink god, with an elephant's head and a snake tied about his potbelly. He has four hands, one holding either a shell or a water lily, the others a discus, an ax, and a modaka (a sweet riceball, which is his favorite food). Once while riding on his rat, Ganesa was allegedly frightened by a snake. He fell and his tummy burst. Dozens of modakas flew out, but he stuffed them all back inside him and re-tied the snake about his middle. The moon, who saw the whole episode, laughed and incurred Ganesa's wrath.

Gari Like many contemporary American girls' names, this one is a feminine form of a masculine name. Gari comes from Gary, meaning "spear" or "spear-man₂" and is also occasionally used as a boy's name.

Garuda (gah-ROO:-dah) East Indian name for the celestial Hindu sun-bird upon which the god Vishnu rides. See Salmalin, listed in the boys' section, for further information.

Gauri (GOH-ree) "Yellow" or "fair." One of the many designations of the Hindu goddess Sakti. This name refers to either the yellow harvest or the yellowish gauri buffalo, both associated with the goddess. See Sakti for further information.

Gavrilla (gahv-REE-luh) Hebrew for "a heroine" or "strong."

Gazit (gah-ZEET) Hebrew name meaning "hewn stone."

Geela (GEE-lah) Hebrew for "joy." Variations include Gilia, Gila, Gili, Gilal, Giliah, Gilana, Gilat, and Gilit.

Gelya (GAYL-yah) Russian pet form of Angeline, from the Old French for "angel" or "messenger."

Gemina (je-MEE-nuh) Astrological name for a girl born under Gemini, which is symbolized by the Twins and ruled by Mercury. Other variations include Geminine and Mini. Geminis are said to be versatile, restless, and high-strung and to have often contradictory needs and desires.

Gerda (GAIR-dah) Originally Scandinavian, from the Old Norse for "protection" or "enclosure," Gerda is used today as a Latvian nickname for Georgiana and an Estonian form of Gertrude.

Germaine French name from the Latin for "the German," which in turn comes from the Celtic for "the shouter." English forms are Germana and Germain.

Geva (GAY-vah) Hebrew for "hill." This modern Israeli name is also a place name in the Bible.

Gianina (jah-NEE-nah) Popular feminine form of the Italian Giovanni, meaning "God is gracious." Giovanna is also used in Italy. The English equivalent is Jane.

Gilada (gee-LAH-duh) Hebrew name meaning "my joy is eternal" or "my hill is a witness."

Gimra (GEEM-ruh) Hebrew for "ripened," "fulfilled," or "complete."

Gina (JEE-nah) Japanese for "silvery." According to an ancient superstition, the evil spirits and demons were born during the Age of Stone and hence feared the influence of metals. Although this belief is no longer common, metal names like Gina remain. In fact, in the Orient if a child has too many wood characters in his horoscope, he may be given a metal name to counteract this evil, since metal is believed to conquer wood.

Ginger From the Latin gingiber. Also the name of a spice.

Ginneh (GIN-neh) This name was borne by some of the first Afro-Americans taken from the Ginneh tribe of the Ivory Coast. When the names Ginny and Jinny were used by blacks, they were actually shortened from Ginneh rather than Virginia. In the course of several generations, however, the African origin and meaning were forgotten.

Giovanna (joh-VAHN-ah) Italian name. See Gianina.

Girisa (gee-REE-shah) "Mountain lord." One of the Hindu names for the god Siva. Also used in India as a boy's name.

Gisa (GEE-suh) Hebrew for "hewn stone." A variant is Giza, which is also a Teutonic name meaning "gift."

Gita (GEE-tah) A Slovak form of Margaret, "a pearl," and a Hebrew name from the Yiddish for "good." A Hebrew variation is Gitel.

Gitana (hee-TAH-nah) Spanish for "a gypsy."

Gizi (GEE-zee) Hungarian name from the Old German for "pledge" or "hostage." Also used in Hungary are Gizike and Gizus. The Latvian equivalent is Gizela, and the English, Giselle.

Gladi (GLAH-dee) Hawaiian development of the flower name Gladys, meaning "gladiolus."

Gleda (GLEH-dah) Icelandic name meaning "make happy" or "make glad."

Golda Israeli name meaning "golden-haired." Variants are Goldarina and Goldie.

Goldina "Golden one." In the occult world both the metal gold and the color gold are linked with the sun, ruler of the zodiacal sign Leo.

Greer Once a nickname for Gregoria, "watchful," Greer is now used in the United States as an independent name.

Gressa (GREH-sah) Nature name from the Norwegian for "grass."

Greta German and Austrian development of the Latin Margarita, "a pearl." Other variants used in these countries are Gretchen, Margarethe, Margarete, Grete, Gretal and Grethal.

Grete (GREH-te) Norwegian name meaning "grace." In Nordic mythology Gratie was one of the three Graces.

Gunda (GOO:N-dah) Very popular today in Norway, this name means "warrior" or "battle maiden."

Gurit (goo:-REET) Hebrew name for young animals, particularly lion cubs. Another form is Gurice. In astrology the Lion is the symbol of Leo.

Habibah (hah-BEE-bah) Arabic name which means "beloved." The popular masculine form is Habib. The Hebrew equivalent is Haviva.

Hadiya (hah-DEE-yah) Swahili for "gift."

Hagia (hah-GEE-uh) Hebrew name meaning "joyful" or "festive." In the Bible Hagia is masculine, but the name is used today in Israel for girls. Another form is Hagit.

Haley (HAY-lee) Originally used for boys, the name

Haley, meaning "ingenious" or "scientific," is now a common girl's name in the United States.

Hali (HAH-lee) Greek name meaning "sea." Astrologers use the name for girls born under the water signs of the zodiac: Cancer, the Crab, Scorpio, the Scorpion, and Pisces, the Fishes. A longer form is Halimeda, "thinking of the sea," often shortened to Hally or Hallie.

Halona (hah-LOH-nah) North American Indian name meaning "happy fortune."

Hama (hah-MAH) Popular Japanese name meaning "shore." A variant is Hamako.

Hamuda (hah-MOO:-dah) Hebrew for "precious" or "desirable."

Hana (hah-NAH) Japanese for "flower" or "blossom." Other forms are Hanako and Hanae. The Arapaho Indians use a similar name, pronounced HAH-nah and meaning "sky" or "black cloud."

Haniya (hah-NEE-yuh) Also spelled Hania, this Hebrew name means "resting place." Similar in form are the Israeli Hanice and Hanit, which mean "spear."

Hannele (hah-NEL-le) Modern German name from the Hebrew for "merciful" or "gracious." Other variations are Hanna, Hanne, and Hanni.

Hara (HAH-rah) "Seizer." Feminine form of the Hindu name Hari. Hari is one of the 1,008 names for the god Siva, the destroyer in the Hindu Triad.

Harper "Harp player." A boy's name now used in the United States as a girl's name.

Hasana (hah-SAH-nah) This name is always given by the African Hausa to a first-born female twin. The second-born, if a girl, is called Huseina, and if a boy, Husseini.

Hasina (hah-SEE-nah) Swahili for "good." In Hebrew the same name means "strong."

Hateya (hah-TEH-yah) Miwok Indian name from the word *hate,* "to press with the foot." The connotation is "bear making tracks in the dust." From the same source comes the name Hatawa, "bear breaking the bones of people or animals."

Heather Modern American flower name. The word actually dates back to the Middle English for "flowering heath." The purple heather is considered symbolic of admiration and beauty in solitude, and the white blossom supposedly protects one against danger.

Hedda German for "strife in battle." Czech variants are Heda, Hedvick, and Hedvika.

Hedia (heh-DEE-ah) Hebrew for "the voice (or echo) of God." Also spelled Hedya.

Hedy Slovak name from the German for "fight" or "strife." Also an American name which comes from the Greek for "sweet" or "pleasant."

Helene The source of hundreds of girls' names throughout the world, this Greek name means "light" or "torch." Other forms include Helena, Hawaiian; Onella, Hungarian; Eleni, Elenitsa, and Nitsa, Modern Greek; Eli, Norwegian; Elli, Estonian; and Helli, Finnish.

Helga (HEL-gah) Very popular today in Norway and Iceland, Helga means "pious" or "religious."

Helki (HEL-kee) Miwok Indian name from the word *hele,* "to touch." The connotation is "jacksnipe digging into the ground with its bill." The jacksnipe supposedly comes out of hiding only in winter. Also a boy's name.

Helli One of the most popular names in Finland. A form of the Greek Helene, "light."

Helmine Used today in Germany as a shortened form of Wilhelmina, meaning "unwavering protector." Other German forms are Minna, Mina, Mine, and Minchen.

Henka (HEN-kah) Polish development of the French word

for "ruler of the household." Other forms used today in Poland are Henia, Heniuta, and Henrieta. English equivalents are Harriet and Henrietta.

Hermina (HAIR-mi-nah) Czech name from the Greek for "child of the earth." Other Czech forms are Herma and Mina.

Hertha The Teutonic goddess of fertility and peace. The name also comes from the Old English for "earth." See Ertha for its astrological significance.

Heta (HEH-tah) Hopi Indian nickname which is a corruption of Yeta, the name for the traditional race to the village after the rabbit hunt. Used by the Rabbit Clan.

Hilary A masculine name, meaning "cheerful" or "happy," now used in the United States as a girl's name.

Hilda German for "battle maiden." This word is the source of many German names, including Hildegarde, "battle wind" or "battle fortress," Hildemar, "battle celebrated," and Hildreth, "battle counselor."

Hinda (HIN-dah) Common Muslim name. Hinda was one of Muhammad's wives. In Yiddish the same name means "a deer."

Hisa (hee-SAH) Japanese name meaning "long-lasting," with the connotation of longevity. Other popular forms are Hisako, Hisae, and Hisayo.

Hiti (HI-ti) Banti Eskimo name meaning "hyena." Such totemic names, symbolizing a person's close identification with an animal, are common in many cultures.

Hoa Vietnamese for "flower" or "peace."

Hoku (HOH-koo:) Hawaiian for "star." Like most Hawaiian names, this is used for both girls and boys.

Hola (HOH-lah) Hopi Indian name which comes from the *mahola,* a seed-filled club used by dancers in religious ceremonies.

Holly Nature name meaning "holy" or "holly tree." Traditionally the holly is symbolic of foresight and defense, and is the Occidental flower of December.

Hoshi (hoh-SHEE) Japanese for "star." A common varient is Hoshie.

Huata (hoo:-AH-tah) Miwok Indian name which means "carrying seeds in burden basket."
A principle source of food and material for making jewelry, seeds are frequently mentioned in Miwok names. Other examples include Helkimu "hitting bushes with seed beater," from *hele,* "to touch"; Howotmila "running hand down the branch of a shrub to find seeds for beads," from *howotu,* "beads"; Huatama ("mashing seeds in mortar"); and Kanatu ("making mashed seeds into a hard lump").

Hulda From Austria, this name means "gracious" or "beloved." The same name used today in Israel comes from the Hebrew for "weasel."

Humita (HOO:-mee-tah) Hopi Indian name for "shelled corn."

Huso (HOO:-soh) African Ovimbundu name from the words *ohuso yakai,* meaning the feigned sadness of a bride. The name is probably bestowed because the newborn baby is thought to resemble the bride in expression.

Huyana (hoo:-YAH-nah) Miwok Indian name which means "rain falling."

Iantha (ee-AHN-thah) A violet colored flower.

Idette (ee-DET-te) "Industrious." Used in Germany. The English equivalent is Ida.

Ilana (ee-LAH-nah) Hebrew for "a tree." A variation used in Israel is Ilanit. Also spelled Elana and Elanit.

Ilia (IGH-lee-uh) North American Indian name whose meaning is uncertain. The same name can be found in Roman mythology, in which Ilia is the mother of Romulus and Remus.

Ilka Used in most Slavic countries, this name comes from the word *milka,* meaning "flattering" or "ambitious."

Ilona Hungarian for "beauty." Ilona can also be considered a Hungarian form of Helen, "light" or "torch," in which case other forms include Ila, Ilka, Ilonka, Ilu, Iluska, Ica, and Lenci.

Ima (EE-mah) Japanese for "now." A variation is Imako. Other names relating in a general sense to time are Toki, "time (of opportunity)," and Toshi, "year (of plenty)."

Imala (EE-mah-lah) North American Indian name meaning "disciplinarian."

Imma (EEM-mah) "A pourer of water from a jug." Akkadian name for the constellation Aquarius, the Water Bearer. Given to a child born under that sign.

Indra An ancient Hindu god of power, once the most prominent god in the heavens and guardian of the eastern quarter of the compass. His power was usurped by Vishnu and Siva.

Ines (ee-NEHS) Spanish development of the Greek for "pure" or "virtuous." Also spelled Inez. The English equivalent is Agnes.

Inesita (ee-neh-SEE-tah) Pet form of Ines used in Spain and Latin and South America. The same name also appears among the Zuni Indians, who often received baptismal names from Franciscan friars.

Inessa (ee-NEH-sah) Russian development of Ines.

Ingrid "Ing's ride." In Norse mythology Ing was the god of the harvest, fertility, peace, and prosperity, who took an annual mythical ride on his golden boar whose tusks tore up the earth so men could plant seeds. Ingrid is one of the most common names in Norway, and is used throughout Scandinavia.

Inoa (i-NOH-ah) Hawaiian for "name" or "name chant."

Irina (ee-REE-nah) Russian name from the Greek for "peace." A popular pet form is Ira (EE-rah).

Irisa (ee-REE-sah) Russian for the name Iris. In Western astrology the iris is the "herb" of the moon, which governs the sign Cancer. In Japan the iris is the emblem of the warrior and the flower of May. A similar name is also found in Greek mythology, where Iris is the goddess of the rainbow and a messenger of the gods.

Isabel (ee-sah-BEL) Spanish development of the Hebrew Elisheba, "dedicated to God." Variations include Elisa, Belita, Ysabel, Isabelita, and Belicia.

Ishi (ee-SHEE) Japanese for "stone." One of the few material names in Japan. A variation is Ishie.

Istas (EE-stahs) "Snow." North American Indian name.

Ituha (ee-TOO:-hah) North American Indian nature name which means "the strong, sturdy oak."

Iuana (ew-AH-nah) North American Indian name which means "blowing backward as the wind blows over the waters of a bubbling stream."

Ivria (eev-REE-uh) From the Hebrew word *Ivri,* meaning "from the other side (of the Euphrates River)" or "from Abraham's land," the term originally used for the Hebrew people in the Bible. Other variants of the name are Ivriah and Ivrit, the latter being the Hebrew word for the Hebrew language.

Ivy From the Ivy vine, which was considered sacred in classical Greek and Roman mythology.

Iwalani (ee-wuh-LAH-nee) Popular Hawaiian name which means "heavenly sea bird."

Iwilla This name was used by Afro-Americans in the 1800's and is a creation from the sentence "I will arise again."

Iza (EE-sah) Polish. See Lilka.

Izabel (ee-zah-BEHL) Current Portuguese favorite. See Isabel.

Izusa (eh-ZOO:-sah) North American Indian name meaning "white stone."

Jael (yah-AYL) Used in Israel for both girls and boys, Jael is Hebrew for "wild she-goat" or "mountain goat." Also an astrological name for a child born under Capricorn, the symbol of which is the Goat.

Jacinta (hah-SEEN-tah) Spanish name for the hyacinth.

Jade From the jade stone, considered a supernatural charm in the Burmo-Tibetan region. When worn, jade allegedly strengthens weak hearts and diverts lightning. When tossed into water, it causes mist, rain, and snow. And if poison is poured into a cup made of the stone, the cup will supposedly crack.

Jaen (yah-AYN) Hebrew for "ostrich."

Jafit (yah-FEET) Hebrew for "beautiful" or "lovely." A common variation is Jaffa.

Jambu (JAHM-boo:) The mythical Hindu rose apple tree, so immense it supposedly overshadows the world.

Jamila (jah-MEE-lah) A favorite among Muslims, Jamila means "beautiful." The Prophet taught that ugly names should be changed, and he renamed a girl called Asiyah, or "rebel," Jamila.

Jana (YAH-nah) Common Polish and Latvian nickname. See Janina. Also occasionally used in Czechoslovakia.

Jani (JAH-nee) From the Swahili word for "leaf."

Janina (yah-NEE-nah in Poland, YAH-nee-nah in Latvia and Lithuania) Popular in Poland, Latvia, and Lithuania, this name comes from the Hebrew for "God is gracious" or simply "gracious" or "merciful." The English equivalent is Jane. Other variations include Jana and Zanna, Latvian; Janyte, Lithuanian; and Janeczka, Jasia, Nina, Jana, Joanna, Joasia, Joanka, Janka, and Zanna, Polish.

Jardena (yahr-DAY-nah) Hebrew for "to flow downward." The masculine form is Jordan.

Jarita (jah-REE-tah) Hindustani name. In East Indian legend Jarita was a bird mother who risked her own life to save her four sons in a burning forest, and as a result became human.

Jasmine Flower name, commonly used in India as Yasmine or Yasiman. The jasmine is considered symbolic of amiability and sweetness.

Jayne (JIGN) Hindustani for "victorious."

Jelena (yeh-LAY-nah) Common Russian nickname. See Galina.

Jemina (yay-MEE-nuh) Hebrew for "right-handed."

Jenica (zhye-NEE-kah) Contemporary Rumanian name from the Hebrew for "God is gracious." The English equivalent is Jane.

Jensine (YEN-seen) A favorite in Denmark, Jensine is a development of the Hebrew for "God is gracious."

Jesusa (heh-SOO:-sah) One of the most popular Spanish Virgin names, this is shortened from Mary (de) Jesus, or "Mary of Jesus." The common pet form Jesusita is also used by the Zuni Indians. Other Zuni variations are Chucha and Chuchita.

Jin (jin) Unusual Japanese name meaning "superexcellent." It is uncommon possibly because of an Oriental superstition that if a child receives too demanding a name, she will never live up to it.

Jina (JEE-nah) Swahili for "name."

Joana (ee-oh-AH-nah) One of the most common names in Brazil, Joana is a development of the Hebrew for "God is gracious."

Joby Originally a nickname for Jobina, "afflicted" or "persecuted," Joby is gaining use in the United States as an independent name. Also spelled Jobie and Jobi.

Joella (yoh-AYL-luh) Feminine form of the Hebrew Joel, meaning "the Lord is willing." Other forms used today in Israel are Joela and Joelle.

Jolan (YOH-lawn) Hungarian flower name from the Greek for "violet blossom." Variants are Joli and Jolanka. Latvian and Polish forms are Jolanta and Jola. The English equivalent is Yolanda.

Joletta Flower name meaning "violet."

Joline Contemporary feminine form of Joseph, "he will increase," used in the United States. Joline is much more common today than the older Josephine.

Jonina (yoh-NEE-nuh) Hebrew peace name meaning "dove." Variants include Jonit, Jonati, Yonit, and Yonita. See Yonina for other forms.

Jora Originally from Hebrew, Jora means "autumn rain." Astrological name for a child born under the autumnal water sign Scorpio. Also spelled Jorah.

Joyita (hoh-YEE-tah) Spanish pet form of Joyuela, which refers to an inexpensive but beautiful jewel. The shorter Joya simply means "jewel" or "gift."

Juanita (hwah-NEE-tah) Spanish development of the Hebrew for "God is gracious." Nita and Juana are pet forms.

Julieta (hoo-lee-EH-tah) Used with this pronunciation in Spain and Latin and South America. The name means "youthful one." Another form is Julia. The same names, of course, are also common in the United States.

Jun (JOO:N) Chinese for "truth" and Japanese for "obedient." Also a boy's name.

Junella "Born in June." Astrological name for a girl born under Gemini, the Twins, or Cancer, the Crab.

Jyotis (JYOH-tis) East Indian name which means the sun's light." For the Leos of the zodiac, whose sign is ruled by the sun.

Kachina (kah-CHEE-nah) North American Indian name meaning "sacred dancer."

Kagami (kah-GAH-mee) Japanese name meaning "mirror," in the sense of clear and pure reflections. A more common name with a similar meaning is Kyoko.

Kai (KIGH) Hawaiian for "sea" or "sea water." Also a boy's name.

Kaili (KIGH-lee) A Hawaiian diety. The name is used for both girls and boys.

Kaimi (KIGH-mee) "The seeker." A common Hawaiian name.

Kakalina (kah-kuh-LEE-nuh) Hawaiian development of the Greek *katharos,* meaning "pure." The English equivalent is Katherine. See Katina for variations used in other countries.

Kala (KAH-lah) "Black" or "time." One of the 1,008 names for the Hindu god Siva. Also a boy's name.

Kalama (kuh-LAH-muh) Hawaiian name meaning "the flaming torch." The name was borne by the wife of Kamehameha III, who ruled Hawaii from 1837 to 1847.

Kalanit (kah-lah-NEET) Israeli flower name. The kala-nit is a plant with cup-shaped, brilliantly colored flowers, common in Irsael's countryside.

Kalere (kah-LEH-reh) Used in the Niger Delta, this name means "small woman," a prediction the baby will be short in height when she grows up.

Kali (kah-LEE) "The black goddess" or "time, the destroyer." One of the many names for the Hindu mother goddess Sakti. See Sakti.

Kalila (kah-LEE-lah) "Girl friend" or "sweetheart." A pet name used in Arabic countries.

Kalinda (kah-LEEN-dah) Hindu nature name borrowed from the mythical Kalinda Mountains, from which the sacred river Jumna, or Jamna, flows. Kalinda literally means "the sun."

Kalindi (kah-leen-dee) The original name of the Jumna River, one of the seven sacred rivers in India. While in ancient times, nature names were considered lowly and even disgusting, today many Hindustani girls are named after rivers and flowers.

88

Kaliska (kah-LEES-kah) Miwok Indian name which means "coyote chasing deer." According to one Miwok legend, the coyote created the world and all the animals, and then held a conference on how he should build man. Each animal wanted man to be like him. The lion wanted him to have a loud roar, the bear wanted him to be silent and strong, and the beaver insisted he have a flat tail to carry mud on. But the coyote said he could think of something better than any one of these qualities, and that night while everyone slept, he stole the best ideas he had heard that day and created man.

Kalle (KAH-lee) "Strong." Used today in Finland. The English equivalent is Carol.

Kallie Once a nickname for Calandra, "lark," this is now an independent Christian name in the United States. Another possible source for Kallie is Calantha, "beautiful blossom." Also spelled Kalli, Kally, Calli, and Callie, and shortened to Kal or Cal.

Kaluwa (kah-LOO:-wah) The African Usengas believe that spirits who can never be reincarnated because their names have been forgotten are wandering the earth, working evil. To appease these demons, children are sometimes named Kaluwa, or "the Forgotten One."

Kalyca (kah-LEE-kah) Greek for "rosebud." Variants of this flower name are Kalica and Kalika. The shortened forms Kaly and Kali are also used.

Kama (KAH-mah) Hawaiian form of Thelma, "the nursling." The same name also comes from the Hindu god Kama, meaning "love." The god, according to mythology, rides a parrot and shoots flower-tipped love arrows from a sugarcane bow with a bowstring of bees.

Kamali (KAH-mah-lee) Mashona name from Southern Rhodesia. Also used for boys. Kamali is a spirit believed to protect newborn babies when there is illness in the village.

89

Kamaria (kah-mah-REE-ah) Swahili name meaning "like the moon." In astrology the moon governs the sign Cancer.

Kamata (kah-MAH-tah) Miwok Indian name which reveals an unusual pastime among Miwok women. The meaning is "throwing gambling bones on the ground in a hand game."

Kameke (kah-MEH-ke) Derived from the African Umbundu word *omeke*, meaning "a blind person," and given to a child with small or squinty eyes.

Kameko (KAH-may-koh) Japanese name meaning "tortoise child," indicating a hope for longevity. Another common form is Kameyo, "generations of the tortoise."

Kamika (kuh-MEE-kuh) Hawaiian equivalent of the English Smith.

Kamila (KAH-mee-lah) Serbo-Croatian for "camel."

Kamilla (kah-MEEL-luh in Poland, KAH-mil-luh in Latvia) Contemporary name used in Hungary, Latvia, and Poland. From a Latin word for "helper at a ceremonial sacrifice." Polish variants are Mila and Kamilka. See Camila.

Kanani (kuh-NAHN-ee) Hawaiian for "the beauty."

Kane (KAH-ne) Japanese for "the doubly accomplished," from the verb *kaneru*, to do two things at once. In Japanese the same sound is also used for a character which means "bronze." Kaneko is a variant form.

Kanene (kah-NAY-ne) African Ovimbundu name from the proverb "A little thing in the eye is big."

Kanika (kah-NEE-kah) Used by the Mwera-speaking people of Kenya, this name means "black cloth."

Kanoa (kuh-NOH-uh) Hawaiian for "the free one." Also a boy's name.

Kanya (KAHN-yah) "Virgin." Hindu name for a child born under the zodiacal sign Virgo, the Virgin. Kanya is also another name for the goddess Sakti.

Kapera (kah-PEH-rah) Given by the African Baduma to a child born after many infants in the village have died. The name is derived from the words *ku pera*, "to end" or "to be finished," and the pathetic meaning is "this child, too, will die."

Kapila (kah-PEE-lah) Hindu name also used for boys. Kapila was an ancient Hindu prophet who taught that only through philosophical study can man attain unity with God. He is believed to be the god Vishnu in the fifth of his twenty-four incarnations.

Kapua (kuh-POO:-uh) Hawaiian for "blossom."

Kapuki (kah-POO:-kee) "First-born daughter." Used by the Bari, who live in Southern Sudan on the banks of the Upper Nile.
Order-of-birth names are common in Africa and sometimes become quite specific, as some of the following indicate: Poni ("second-born daughter"); Jwan ("third-born daughter"); Pita ("fourth-born daughter"); Sukoji ("first-born daughter following a son"); Kako ("girl born after one daughter has died"); Sumiti ("fish," for a child born after more than one baby has died); Bojo ("despiser of her twin," for a first-born female twin); and Jore ("full," for a second-born female twin).

Kapule (kuh-POO:-le) Hawaiian for "a prayer." Also the Hawaiian version of Deborah, "a bee."

Karayan (kah-rah-YAHN) "The dark one" or "the black one." Used as a surname in Armenia.

Kari Contemporary American form of Carol, "strong" or "feminine." Kari is also used today in Hungary. See Karoly.

Karida (KAH-ree-dah) Arabic for "untouched" or "virginal."

Karka (KAHR-kah) "Crab." Hindu name for a child born in the solar month Karka, under the zodiacal sign Cancer, the Crab.

Karla Czech and German development of the French word for "petite" or "feminine." Other German forms include Charlotte, Karoline, Lottchen, Lotte, and Lotti. Interestingly enough, the same name was borne by an Australian aborigine man and meant "fire." This Australian culture has such a taboo against speaking a dead man's name that when Karla died, his name was extinguished from the language and a new word for fire was introduced.

Karli (kuhr-LI) Turkish for "covered with snow" or "snowy."

Karma (KAHR-mah) Karma literally means "action." It embodies the Hindu principle which says that all of one's actions morally affect this or a future life. Karma can also be interpreted as fate or destiny.

Karmel "Vineyard," "garden," or "farm." Currently used in Israel, where other forms include Carmeli, Carmi, Carmia, and Carmiel. The Spanish form is Carmen, and the Italian, Carmine.

Karmiti (QAHR-mi-ti) Banti Eskimo nature name meaning "trees."

Karolina (kah-roh-LEE-nah) Russian and Hungarian development of the French for "petite" or "feminine." The English equivalent is Caroline.

Karoly (KAW-roh-lee) Modern Hungarian name which comes from the Teutonic word for "strong." Other Hungarian forms are Karosi and Kari.

Kasa (KAH-shah) Hopi Indian name from the *patsip-qasa*, "fur-robe dress," a type of lizard with a tough hide. The name comes from the Earth Cult.

Kasi (KAH-shee) One of the most common names among the Hindus of Madras, Kasi is the colloquial name for Banaras, one of the seven holy Hindu cities. During the epic period of India, the city was the capital for the Kasi tribe.

Kasinda (kah-SEEN-dah) Used by the African Ovimbundu for either a girl or boy born into a family which already has twins. Kasinda comes from the Umbundu word *osinda,* which literally means "the earth that blocks the passage behind a burrowing animal."

Kasota (kah-SOH-tah) "A clear sky." Ecological name from the North American Indians. It can be used, too, for girls born under the air signs of the zodiac: Gemini, Libra, and Aquarius.

Kassia (kahs-SEE-uh) Modern Polish name from the Greek for "pure." See Katina.

Kata (kah-TAH) Uncommon Japanese name meaning "worthy person." See Jin.

Kateke (kah-TAY-ke) Ovimbundu nickname from the proverb *Kateke tueya tua lia palonga; kaliye kalo peya oku lila povilindo,* "The days we came, we ate off dishes; now it comes to eating off wooden bowls." Loosely translated, the saying means "we have stayed too long and worn out our welcome." The name Kateke, then, is used for someone who seems nice at first, but becomes tiresome after you get to know her.

Katerina Used today in Bulgaria, Czechoslovakia, and Russia, Katerina comes from the Greek for "pure." Another form found in Russia is Yekaterina, with diminutives Katya, Katinka, Kiska, and Katuscha. For other forms used throughout the world, see Katina.

Katina Contemporary Greek name from the word katharos, which means "pure."
Hundreds of names throughout the world come from the same source, including the popular English Katherine. Other examples are Katerina, Kata, Katka, and Katuska (Czechoslovakian); Caron, Catant, Trinette, and Catherine (French); Kathe, Katrina, and Trine (German); Kati, Katalin, Katarina, Kata, Katinka, and Katus (Hungarian); Rina and Triine

93

(Estonian); Caterina (Italian); Kofryna (Lithuanian); Kassia, Kasia, Kasin, Kasienka, and Kaska (Polish); Catarina (Portuguese); Catalina (Spanish); Kolina and Kajsa (Swedish); Karena, Katla, and Karin (Norwegian); Katrin (Icelandic); and Katrya and Katerina (Ukrainian).

Katura (KAH-too:-rah) This Southern Rhodesian name comes from the Babudja words *ku tura,* which a mother may speak after giving birth. Loosely translated, the words mean "I feel better now." Literally translated, Katura means "to take a load from one's mind." Also a boy's name.

Katya (KAHT-yah) Popular Russian diminutive. See Katerina.

Kaula (KOW-luh) Hawaiian for "prophet."

Kaulana (kow-LAH-nuh) Hawaiian name meaning "fame."

Kaveri (kah-VAIR-ee) Hindu nature name taken from one of the seven sacred rivers of India. The sacred rivers play an important role in Hindu ceremonies, and it is believed that bathing in these rivers, particularly the Ganges, washes away man's most evil sins. In ancient times a man of high caste was forbidden to marry a girl with a nature name because her name indicated she was inferior. Today, however, many girls are given such names.

Kavindra (kah-VEEN-drah) Hindustani for "mighty poet." Often used as a name element only.

Kawa (kah-WAH) Japanese for "river."

Kaya (KAH-yah) Hopi Indian nickname, an abbreviation of the name Kaka-hoya, which means "my elder sister little." In Japan the same name means "a rush" or "a yew."

Kaya (kah-YAH) Ghanaian born-to-die name meaning "stay and don't go back." In the same category is the name Boba, "you have come again." See Apara for information on born-to-die names.

94

Kazu (KAH-zu) It is often difficult to determine the meaning of an Oriental name because the sound of the name may be associated with several different written characters, each representing a different meaning. This Japanese name, for instance, may mean "first" "a great number," or "obedient," depending on which character is used. A favorite variant is Kazuko.

Kealoha (ke-uh-LOH-huh) "The loved one" or "beloved." Popular Hawaiian name.

Kedma (KAYD-muh) Hebrew for "toward the east."

Kefira (keh-FEE-ruh) Hebrew for "young lioness." Good astrological name for a girl born under Leo, which is symbolized by the Lion.

Kei (KAY) A favorite in Japan, this name means "rapture" or "reverence." A common variant is Keiko.

Keiki (ke-EE-kee) Hawaiian for "child."

Kekona (ke-KOH-nuh) "Second." Hawaiian name for a second-born child.

Kelda Scandinavian name meaning "fountain" or "spring." The same name is also used in English, with the nickname Kelly.

Kelila (keh-LEE-lah) A favorite in Israel, this name means "crown" or "laurel," a symbol of victory and beauty. Another form is Kelula. Yiddish variants include Kaile, Kayle, Kyla, and Kyle.

Kelsi Once a nickname for Kelly, which in turn is short for Kelda, Kelsi is gaining popularity in the United States as an independent name. Also spelled Kelsy, Kelcy, Kelci, and Kelcie.

Kenda Ecological name meaning "child of clear, cool water." Also an astrological name for girls born under the water signs Cancer, Scorpio, and Pisces. A variant spelling is Kennda.

Kerani (ke-RAH-nee) Popular among the Todas of India, this name means "sacred bells."

Kesava (ke-SAH-vah) Hindu name which means "having much (or fine) hair." This is another name for the god Vishnu, or Krishna.

Kesi (KEH-see) Swahili name for a child born when her father is in trouble.

Kessie (KEH-see-e) Fanti or Ashanti name for a girl who is fat at birth. The masculine equivalent is Kesse.

Ketzia (ket-ZEE-ah) Hebrew name for a cinnamonlike bark. Hence, Ketzia has the connotation of fragrance. Another spelling is Kezia.

Kichi (KEE-chee) Japanese for "the fortunate." A more common Oriental name with a similar meaning is Yoshi.

Kiden (kee-DEHN) Bari name for the first daughter born after three or more sons. This birth-order feature is common among the Bari of Southern Sudan. See Kapuki for other examples.

Kiele (kee-EL-e) Hawaiian flower name meaning "gardenia" or "fragrant blossom."

Kikilia (ke-ke-LEE-uh) Hawaiian development of the Latin for "dim-sighted." The English equivalent is Cecilia. The African Kameke and the Slovak Cilka are similar in meaning.

Kiku (kee-KOO:) A favorite in Japan, this name means "chrysanthemum," an Oriental symbol of longevity and the Japanese flower of September. Common variations are Kikuyo and Kikuko. In Western astrology the chrysanthemum is the flower of Scorpio.

Kim Common American name with vague origins. The name may have been borrowed from the Koreans in the early 1950's, or it may be a nickname for Kimberly, from the Old English for "born at the royal-fortress meadow" or "ruler." A more imaginative reference says the name was telescoped from Kansas, Illinois, and Missouri, using the initial letters of those state names.

Kimama (ke-MAH-mah) Shoshone Indian name meaning

"butterfly." According to one American Indian legend, the Creator took the form of a butterfly and flew all over the world, looking for the best place to create man.

Kimi (KEE-mee) Japanese for "peerless" or "sovereign." Favorite variants are Kimiko, Kimiyo, and Kimie.

Kineks (KEE-nehks) North American Indian flower name meaning "rosebud."

Kini (KEE-nee) Like most Hawaiian names, this is used for both sexes. As a girl's name, Kini is a form of Jean or Jennie, "God is gracious." As a boy's name, it means "king."

Kirima (ki-ri-mah) Banti Eskimo name meaning "a hill."

Kirsi (KEER-see) The Todas of India derive this name from their word for the amaranth, one of various flowering plants. Also spelled Kiri.

Kisa (KEE-sah) A favorite Russian pet name meaning "kitty" or "pussycat."

Kishi (kee-SHEE) Japanese for "beach." This uncommon name probably connotes longevity rather than beauty.

Kiska (KEES-kah) Russian nickname meaning "pure." See Katerina.

Kismet (KIZ-met) Contemporary American name meaning "fate" or "destiny."

Kissa (kiss-SAH) Used in Uganda for a child born after twins.

Kita (kee-TAH) Unusual Japanese name meaning "north" and referring to old Chinese beliefs regarding direction and position.

Kiwa (KEE-wah) "Border." Japanese name for a child born on a border. A variation is Kiwako.

Klarika (KLAH-ri-kah) Hungarian and Slovakian name from the Latin for "brilliant" or "illustrious." A pet form used in both countries is Klara. The Ukrainian form is Klarissa or Klarysa.

Klementina (kle-men-TEE-nah) Bulgarian and Russian name which means "mild," "calm," or "merciful." Other Russian forms are Tina and Tinochka. English equivalents are Clementia and Clementine.

Klesa (KLEH-sah) Hindustani for "pain." The ugly meaning is given to a child possibly to ward off evil spirits. A Pali variant is Kilesa.

Koko (KOH-koh) Japanese for "stork," a symbol of longevity.

Kolenya (koh-LEHN-yah) Miwok Indian name which means "fish coughing," from the word *kole,* "to cough." According to a Karok Indian legend, the fish was the first living thing created. In the zodiac the Fishes are the symbol of Pisces.

Kolina (koh-LEE-nah) Swedish name from the Greek for "pure." See Katina.

Koma (koh-MAH) Japanese term of endearment, meaning "filly," "pony," or "like a pussycat." A common variant is Komako.

Kona (KOH-nah) Hindu occult name for a child born under Capricorn, which is ruled by the planet Saturn. Kona, "angular," is also another name for Saturn, the black god in Hindu mythology. At one time the name was given to a child in the hope of appeasing the god. See Sani, listed in the boys' section.

Konane (koh-NAH-ne) Hawaiian name meaning "bright as moonlight." Also given to boys.

Kori Contemporary American name derived from Cora, which in turn comes from the Greek for "maiden." Also spelled Kory and Korrie.

Kostya (KOHST-yah) Russian pet name for Konstantin, from the Greek for "firm" or "constant." Other popular variants of Konstantin are Kostenka, Kotik, and

Kostyusha. English equivalents are Constantia and Constance.

Kotha Occult name meaning "thou hollow one," used in incantations to invoke the spirits.

Koto (KOH-toh) Japanese for "harp."

Krishna (KREESH-nah) Usually used in India as a boy's name. Krishna is a Hindu incarnation of Vishnu, the god protecting all creation. It is believed that when some great evil has occurred, Vishnu, as protector, comes down to earth in human form as either Krishna or another incarnation, Rama. See Devaki.

Kristin (KREE-stin) "Christian." Widely used in Scandinavia, particularly Sweden and Norway. Other forms include Kirsten and Kirstin.

Krysta (KREE-stuh) Polish nickname for Krystyna, "Christian." Other Polish variations are Krystka, Krysia, and Krystynka. Since children in Poland are commonly known by nicknames, Krysta and Krysia are as popular as the formal given name Krystyna.

Kuai Hua (kwigh hwa) Chinese for "mallow blossom." In China the mallow blossom is the flower of September and symbolic of the power of magic against evil spirits. The English equivalent in meaning is Melba.

Kulya (KOO:L-yah) Miwok Indian name which means "sugar pine nuts burned black." The name may indicate that at birth there was so much excitement, the pine nuts on the coals were ignored and thus burned.
The pine was important to the Miwoks and frequently appears in their names. Other examples are Liptuye ("getting pine nuts from cones which have dropped to the ground"); Tukeye ("pine cones dropping and making dust," from *tukini*, "to throw end over end"); Istu ("sugar-pine sugar"); and Uskuye ("cracking sugar pine nuts").

Kumi (KOO:mee) Japanese name meaning "braid." A popular variation is Kumiko.

Kumuda (kuh-MOO:-dah) "Lotus." This flower is revered by both Hindus and Buddhists. The Hindus associate it with the birth of Brahma, and many Hindu dieties often sit enthroned upon its petals. The Buddhists, on the other hand, believe in a heaven where souls lie enveloped in lotus buds upon the Sacred Lake of Lotuses until they are admitted to paradise on judgment day.

Kuni (KOO:-nee) Japanese for "country-born." A variation is Kuniko, "country-born child."

Kuri (KOO:-ree) "Chestnut." A variant also used in Japan, often as a surname, is Kurita. "chestnut field." The chestnut tree occasionally appears in Oriental legends, including one story of a mythical tree so large its branches shaded several provinces, and so magical it could not be cut down.

Kurma (KOO:R-mah) Hindu name meaning "tortoise," the form the god Vishnu took when he churned the oceans. According to legend, from Vishnu's toe flows the sacred Ganges River, and from his naval sprouts a lotus which bears the diety Brahma on its petals.

Kusa (KOO:-shah) Hindu name from the sacred kusa grass, which is also called *darbha*. The grass has long leaves tapering to needle points and allegedly came from the hair of the god Vishnu in his incarnation as a turtle. A ring of kusa worn during sacred rites supposedly protects one against evil and purifies one of sin. An annual kusa festival is held on the eighth day of the moon during the month Bhadrapada (August–September), at which time an offering of the grass is believed to obtain immortality for ten of one's ancestors.

Kveta (CKVE-tuh) Czech name meaning "flower." Other variants are Kvtuse, Kvetka, and Kvetuska. The English equivalent is Flora.

Kwamina (kwah-MEE-nah) Used by some of the first Afro-Americans taken from the Gold Coast. In

America the name was quickly corrupted to Quo Miny, which probably accounts for its almost instant loss of popularity.

Kwanita (kwah-NEE-tah) Zuni Indian form of the Spanish Juanita, "God is gracious." The English equivalent is Jane.

Kyla (KIGH-lah) Yiddish name. See Kelila.

Kynthia Common Greek name meaning "moon." Astrological name for a child born under Cancer, which is governed by the moon. The English equivalent is Cynthia.

Kyoko (KYOH-koh) Japanese name meaning "mirror," possibly implying the child clearly reflects her parents' hopes.

Lahela (luh-HE-luh) Hawaiian development of the Hebrew for "ewe." Another variant is Rahela. The English equivalent is Rachel.

Lailie (LAY-lee) Hebrew name from the Arabic for a child "born at night." Variations are Laila, Laili, and Laylie.

Laka (LAH-kuh) Hawaiian name for the goddess of the hula. Laka also means "attract" or "tame."

Lakya (LAHK-yah) East Indian name for a child born on Thursday, from the word for Thursday, *Laksmanavaram*.

Lala (LAH-lah) Slovak name meaning "tulip."

Lalasa (lah-lah-shah) Hindustani for "love."

Lalita "Charming." One of the more than one thousand names for the Hindu goddess Sakti. See Sakti for further information.

Lana (LAH-nuh) Hawaiian name meaning "buoyant" or "to float."

Landa (LAHN-duh) "Child from the land." Astrological name for girls born under the earth signs Capricorn, Taurus, and Virgo. Occultists believe such names

101

overcome an imbalance of metal or water influences in a child's horoscope, since earth controls metal and destroys water (a principle known as solidity over insolidity).

Lani (LAH-nee) Pretty Hawaiian name meaning "sky" or "heavenly." Lani is found as an element in many other names, including Hokulani, "star in the sky"; Alohilani, "bright sky"; Ahulani, "heavenly shrine"; Kakaulani, "placed in the sky"; Pililani, "close to heaven"; Malulani, "under heaven's protection"; and Okalani, "of the heavens."

Laniuma (lah-nee-OO:-muh) Hawaiian for "geranium."

Lara (LAH-rah) Popular pet name in Russia. See Larissa.

Lari Once a nickname for Laura, "crowned with laurel," or Lara, "shining" or "famous," Lari is used today in the United States as an independent name. In astrology the laurel is the plant of the sun, which governs the sign Leo.

Larissa (lah-REE-sah) Russian name from the Greek for "cheerful one." Favorite nicknames are Lara and Larochka.

Laure French development of the Latin for "laurel" or "the air." Also used in France is the variant Laurette.

Lavinie (lah-VEEN-yuh) Modern French name meaning "purified" or "lady from Latium." The English form is Lavinia.

Layla (LAH-ee-lah) Swahili name from the Arabic Leila. See Leila.

Lea Hebrew name meaning "weary." A popular pet form is Lee. The Italian equivalent is Lia.

Leandra "Like a lioness." Astrological name for a girl born under Leo, the Lion. Other names for Leos include Leodora, "gift of the lion"; Leoine and Leoline, "of the lion family"; Leonanie, "lion's grace"; and Leona and Leonelle, "lionlike."

Ledah Hebrew name which simply means "birth."

Lee Chinese name meaning "plum."

Leeba "Heart." Used today in Israel.

Leena Estonian development of the Greek Helene, "light" or "torch." Other forms include Elli, Hele, and Lenni.

Lehua (le-HOO:-uh) Hawaiian name meaning "sacred to the gods." Also the name of a native flower.

Leila (LIGH-lah) Arabic name for a child "born at night." Other forms are Laila and Layla, the latter also used by the Swahili-speaking people of East Africa.

Leilani (lay-LAH-nee) Common in Hawaii, this name means "heavenly child."

Lela (LEH-lah) Popular Spanish nickname for Alita. See Alita for further information.

Lemi (LEH-mee) Zuni name. The exact meaning is unknown.

Lena Modern Israeli name which means "dwelling" or "lodging." Lena is also a nickname for the German Magdalene and the Russian Galina.

Lenka (LEHN-kah) Czechoslovakian development of the Greek Helene, "light" or "torch." Other forms include Helena, Hela, and Heluska.

Lenni Estonian name. See Leena.

Lenora Russian pet form of Eleonora, from the Old French for "light."

Lenusya (le-NOO:SH-yah) Used today in Russia as a pet form of Yelena, "lily flower." Another common pet form is Liolya.

Leor Israeli name from the Hebrew for "I have light." Also a boy's name.

Leotie (leh-oh-TEE-e) North American Indian name meaning "prairie flower."

Leska (LESH-kuh) Used in Czechoslovakia as a pet form of Alexandra, from the Greek for "helper and defender of mankind." Another variant is Lexa.

Lesya (LEHSH-yah) A favorite in Russia. See Alexandra.

Leta (LEH-tah) Swahili name meaning "bring," which may be combined with a second name to mean "bring happiness" or "bring luck." In English the same name is used as a shortened form of either Letitia, "gladness," or Latonia, a name identified with the Greek goddess Leto, mother of the moon and sun.

Leticia (leh-TEE-see-ah) Spanish name from the Latin for "gladness."

Levana Latin for "the rising sun." Used for Leos of the zodiac, whose sign is ruled by the sun.

Levia (leh-VEE-uh) Hebrew name meaning "to join." The masculine form is Levi.

Lewanna (leh-WAH-nuh) Hebrew for "the moon." Astrological name for those born under Cancer. Moon children tend to be the homebodies of the zodiac, conscious of ancestral ties, sensitive, and protective.

Lexa Czech nickname. See Leska.

Lexie Used today as an independent name, Lexie was once an American nickname for Alexandra, meaning "helper and defender of mankind."

Leya (LEH-yah) Spanish name meaning "loyalty to the law." Leya is also used by the Tamil of South India and Ceylon to designate the constellation and zodiacal sign Leo, the Lion.

Lia Modern Greek name meaning "one who brings good news." See Evangelia. Lia is also used in Italy. See Lea.

Lian Chinese name meaning "the graceful willow." The English Liana, used in the United States, comes from the liana vine, a brilliantly blossomed tropical climbing plant.

Lida (LEE-dah) Russian diminutive. See Lidiya.

Lidiya (lee-DEE-yah) Introduced into Russia by the Greek Orthodox Church, this name means either "happy" or "from Lydia," an ancient country in Asia Minor. Favorite variants are Lida and Lidochka.

Lien (lay-ehn) Chinese for "lotus." The buds, blossoms, and seeds of the eight-petal lotus are all visible simultaneously, and hence in China the flower is considered a symbol of the past, present, and future. The lotus also symbolizes purity, and a familiar proverb in China is "The lotus springs from the mud." See Kumuda for Buddhist beliefs regarding the flower.

Liene (LI-e-ne) Latvian name from the Latin for "she is alluring."

Lien Hua (lay-ehn-hwah) Chinese for "lotus flower. In China the lotus is the flower of summer and July, and a symbol of perfection and purity. See Lien.

Li Hua Chinese for "pear blossom." In China the pear blossom is the flower of August and a symbol of purity and longevity.

Lihwa (LEE-hwah) The given name of the Chinese princess Chang Lihwa, who lived during the last of the Ch'en dynasty (583 to 589 A.D.) and was renowned for her beauty, particularly her glossy black hair, which was said to be seven feet long. Notice that Chinese surnames are written first, given names last.

Lila (LEE-luh) Hindu name which refers to the concept of the free, playful will of God. Also a Polish nickname for Leopoldine, "bold defender of the people."

Lilia (lee-LEE-uh) Hawaiian name for the lily flower. A pretty variation is Liliana (lee-lee-AH-nuh). English equivalents are Lily and Lillian.

Liliha (lee-LEE-huh) "Disgust." The name of a woman governor of the Hawaiian isle of Oahu during the 1820's.

Lilika (lee-LEE-kah) Modern Greek development of the Latin *lilium,* meaning "lily flower."

Lilith From the Arabic word meaning "of the night." In Eastern mythology Lilith was Adam's first wife. She was created separately from Adam, and was the first feminist, challenging Adam's authority as head of the household. When Adam was too stubborn to compromise, Lilith left him, and God tried to make up for the fiasco by creating Eve from Adam's rib so there would never be any doubt of man's superiority over woman. Eventually Lilith supposedly became a demon.

Liljana (LEEL-yah-nah) Serbian name for the lily flower. See Lenusya.

Lilka (LEL-kuh) Polish name meaning "famous warrior-maiden." Common variants are Ludka, Iza, Lodoiska, Ludwika, and Luisa.

Lilli (LIL-ee) Estonian development of the Latin word for the lily flower.

Liluye (lee-LOO:-ye) Miwok Indian name which means "chicken hawk singing when soaring."
The chicken hawk appears in a number of Miwok names including Noksu ("smell of chicken hawk's nest"); Yutkiye ("chicken hawk lifting ground squirrel from the ground"); Yuttciso ("lice thick on a chicken hawk," from *yutuk,* "stick on"); Putepu ("chicken hawk walking back and forth on a limb"); Tiwolu ("chicken hawk turning its eggs with its bill while they are hatching"); and Toloisi ("chicken hawk tearing a gopher snake with its talons").

Lina (LEE-nah) Russian diminutive of Angelina, Adelina, and Carolina.

Linda (LEEN-dah) Spanish for "pretty one." This is the source of the common English name Linda.

Lindsey Traditionally a boy's name, Lindsey is gaining popularity in the United States as a girl's name. The various spellings found include Linsey, Lindsy, Lindsay, and even Linnzi. The name probably means "pool on an island" or "from the isle of the serpents."

Liolya (lee-OHL-yah) A favorite nickname in Russia. See Yelena.

Liona (lee-OH-nuh) Hawaiian for "lion." In astrology the Lion is the symbol of Leo.

Lirit (li-REET) Modern Israeli name which means "poetic," "lyrical," or "musical."

Lisa (LI-suh) A Scandinavian favorite from the Hebrew Elisheba, "dedicated to God." According to a recent name study, Lisa is the most popular girl's name in the United States.

Liseli (lee-SEH-lee) Common Zuni Indian name. The meaning is unknown.

Liseta (lee-SEH-tah) Contemporary Spanish name from the Hebrew for "dedicated to God." See Isabel and Belicia for other variations.

Lisette (lee-SET-te) German development of Elizabeth, "dedicated to God." Other German forms include Else, Elisabet, Elsbeth, Elschen, Elis, Ilse, Lise, Lisa, Liese, and Betty.

Lissa Used today as an independent name, Lissa was once an American nickname for Melissa, "honey" or "a bee," or Millicent, "honest" or "diligent." The melissa plant is considered symbolic of sympathy and love, and is an Arabic emblem of rejuvenation.

Lissilma (le-SEEL-mah) North American Indian name which means "be thou there." The exact tribe is unknown.

Litlit (LEET-leet) North American Indian name which means "butterfly."

Litonya (li-TOHN-yah) Miwok Indian name which comes from the word *litanu,* "to dart down," and means "hummingbird darting down after having flown straight up." In the occult world the hummingbird is considered a love charm to enchant members of the opposite sex. Another Miwok Indian hummingbird name is Lumai, "humming of hummingbird's wings as it flies fast," from *lumana,* "to go past with a noise."

Litsa (LEET-sah) Modern Greek name. See Evangelia.

Livana (lee-VAH-nuh) Hebrew for "white" or "the moon." Also spelled Levana. In astrology the moon governs the sign Cancer.

Livanga (lee-VAHN-gah) African Ovimbundu proverb name from the saying *Livanga oku soka ku livange oku lia,* "Be first to think, but don't be first to eat." The proverb warns of the danger of being poisoned by rotten meat if one does not think first and check for spoiling.

Liviya (li-VEE-yuh) Hebrew for "lioness." Another spelling is Leviya. In astrology the Lion is the symbol of Leo. The variants Livia and Levia also mean "crown."

Livona (li-VOH-nuh) Hebrew for "spice" or "incense." Also spelled Levona.

Liza (LEE-zah) Popular in both Russia and the United States, Liza is a diminutive of the Russian Yeliza-veta, "dedicated to God." In Russia other forms of Yelizaveta are Betti, Lizanka, and Lizaveta, the peasant form.

Lizina (LI-zi-nah) Latvian development of Elizabeth. Variants are Liza and Lizite.

Lokelani (loh-ke-LAH-nee) "Heavenly rose." Hawaiian flower name.

Lola Hawaiian development of Laura, "crowned with laurel." Also a Spanish name. See Lolita.

Lolita Popular Spanish pet form of the Virgin name Maria de los Dolores, "Mary of the Sorrows." It can be further shortened to Lola. See Dolores for other forms.

Lolotea (loh-loh-TEH-ah) Zuni Indian development of the Spanish Dorotea, "gift from God."

Lomasi (loh-MAH-see) North American Indian name which means "pretty flower."

Loretta (loh-REH-tah) Spanish for "pure." In English the same name is considered a form of Laura, "crowned with laurel."

Lota Hindustani name which refers to a portable drinking cup. Traditionally Hindus often name their children after inanimate objects. See Almira for an explanation of the custom.

Lotta (LOHT-tah) A Swedish favorite meaning "petite" or "feminine." Originally derived from the French Caroline. In Germany the equivalent is Lotti.

Lucerne From the Latin for "life."

Lucita (loo:-SEE-tah) Spanish Virgin name shortened from Maria de la Luz, "Mary of the·Light."

Ludmila (LOO:D-mee-lah) Popular Czech name meaning "love of the people" or "dear to the people." A shortened form is Mila.

Luke (LOO:-ke) Hawaiian development of the Latin *lucia,* meaning "light" or "she brings light." The English equivalent is Lucy.

Lukina (loo:-KEE-nah) Ukrainian name meaning "graceful and bright." Also spelled Lukyna. The English equivalent is Luciana, which is a combination of Lucy plus Anne.

Lulani (loo:-LAH-nee) "The highest point in heaven." A lofty Hawaiian name for both girls and boys.

Lulu North American Indian name which means "rabbit." Lulu has also been used in the United States as a form of the Anglo-Saxon Lulie, "soothing influence."

Luna Zuni Indian name from the Spanish *luna,* "moon"

or "satellite." In astrology the moon rules the sign Cancer, while the tarot card of the moon corresponds to Pisces.

Lunetta Italian for "little moon." See Luna for the astrological significance of the moon.

Lusa Finnish form of Elizabeth, "dedicated to God."

Lusati (loo:-SAH-tee) African Umbundu name given to a child born after her father has recently died. Lusati comes from the word *olusati,* which refers to a stalk of maize and perhaps indicates the way it stands alone in a harvested field.

Lusela (loo:-SAY-lah) Miwok Indian name which means "bear swinging its foot when licking it."
Of all the animals, the bear is probably the most popular in Miwok names. Other bear names are Etumu ("bear warming itself in the sunlight," from *etumu,* "to sun oneself"); Etumuye ("bear climbing a hill," from *etumü,* "to climb a hill"); Heltu ("bear barely touching people as it reaches for them"); Kutattoa ("bear scattering intestines of a person as it eats him," from *kutatcnani,* "to discard unwanted garbage"); and Moemu ("bears sitting down to look at each other," from *mo'ani,* "to meet," and *moeye,* "to join.").

Lusita (loo:SEE-tah) Zuni Indian name from the Spanish Lucia, "light" or "she brings light." It could also be a corruption of the Virgin name Maria de la Luz. See Lucita.

Luyu (LOO:-yoo:) This North American Indian name has been interpreted as meaning "the wild dove," but is more accurately a Miwok Indian name meaning "dove shaking its head sideways," from the word *luyani,* "to shake the head."

Luz (loo:s) Like Lucita, Luz is a shortened form of the Spanish name Maria de la Luz, "Mary of the Light."

Macha (MAH-chah) North American Indian nature name meaning "the aurora." Since the exact tribe is unknown, an alternate pronounciation may be MAH-shah.

Machi (mah-chee) Japanese for "ten thousand." In Japan round numbers were once considered good omens.

Magara (MAH-gah-rah) The Mashona of Southern Rhodesia often give this name to a baby who cries so much, her mother doesn't know what to do. The name comes from the words *ku gara*, meaning "to sit" or "to stay," referring to the hours the mother sits beside her child.

Magda (MAHG-duh) Israeli name from the Hebrew for "a high tower." Magda is also used in Russia, where it is derived from the Greek for "of Magdala," a Palestinian city on the Sea of Galilee where Mary Magdalene once lived. Other forms are Magdalene and Magdaline (Hebrew), Magdalena (Czech), and Madalena (Spanish).

Magena (mah-GEH-nah) North American Indian name which means "the coming moon." In astrology the sign Cancer is ruled by the moon.

Magha (MAHG-hah) Hindu name for a child born during the lunar month corresponding to the zodiacal sign Aquarius, the Water Bearer.

Mahala (mah-HAH-lah) "Woman." North American Indian name. A similar name, Mahila or Mahela, is used in India and comes from Sanskrit, considered by some scholars to be the world's primal language.

Mahesa (mah-HEH-shah) "Great lord." One of the 1,008 names for the Hindu god Siva. Mahesa is also a boy's name.

Mahina (muh-HEE-nuh) Hawaiian for "moon." See Luna for the moon's astrological significance.

Mahira (mah-HEE-ruh) Hebrew for "quick" or "energetic." An alternate spelling is Mehira.

Makadisa (mah-kah-DEE-sah) This is a second name, or

nickname, among the African Baduma people and means "she was always very selfish."

Makana (muh-KAH-nuh) Hawaiian for "gift" or "present." The idea of a child as a gift from God is prevalent throughout the world, as evidenced by the Nigerian Aniweta, the Ukrainian Bohdana, the Russian Dasha, the Czech Dita, the Hungarian Duci, and the German Dorlisa, to name only a few.

Makani (muh-KAH-nee) Hawaiian for "the wind." Also a boy's name.

Makara (mah-KAH-rah) Hindu name for a child born under the zodiacal sign Capricorn, symbolized in the Occident by the Goat and in India by the Sea Monster.

Malia (muh-LEE-uh) Hawaiian form of Mary, "bitter." Another Hawaiian variation is Mele. Malia is also a Zuni Indian name, derived from the Spanish Maria.

Malila (mah-LEE-lah) Miwok Indian name which means "salmon going fast up a rippling stream."
Since it is a principal food source, the salmon is frequently mentioned in Miwok names. Other examples include Hahiyo ("salmon keeping mouth open when in shallow water"); Pootci ("cutting salmon's belly," from *putu*, "to open the belly"); Puta ("cutting open a salmon"); and Sata ("throwing salmon out of water"). See also Mituna.

Malina (mah-LEE-nah) This name, from the Tabascan language, is a favorite among Mexican Indians. It is sometimes used in the United States as a shortened form of Magdalene derived from the name of the Biblical town in which Mary Magdalene was born.

Malka Hebrew for "a queen."

Malu (MAH-loo:) Hawaiian for "peace." Another common Hawaiian name is Malulani, "under heaven's protection" or "beneath peaceful skies."

Mana (MAH-nuh) Hawaiian for "supernatural power."

Manaba (mah-NAH-bah) Navaho Indian name meaning "war returned with her coming." See Doba.

Manda (MAHN-dah) Spanish nickname for Armanda, "harmony" or "battle maiden." Also one of the Hindu names for Saturn, god of the occult. See Kona.

Mandara (mahn-DAH-rah) A mythical tree in the Hindu paradise under whose shade all cares are forgotten. According to ancient tree-worship beliefs, plants are not only conscious but able to feel pain as well. Each tree is believed to contain a tree spirit who must be given flowers and sweetmeats. In return, the tree may be consulted as an oracle and has the power to grant children fame and wealth. Before a tree is cut, the cutter prays to the tree diety so that the god will find another tree and not be angry with him.

Mandisa (man-DEE-sah) "Sweet." Used by the Xhosa-speaking people of South Africa.

Mandy Originally a nickname for Amanda, "worthy of love," Mandy is now an independent name in the United States. An alternate spelling is Mandi.

Manga (MAHN-gah) Used by some of the first Afro-Americans taken from the British Cameroons. Unattractive nicknames and family separations possibly caused the name to quickly disappear among future generations.

Mangena (mahn-GAY-nuh) Hebrew for "song" or "melody." Also spelled Mangina.

Mani From the prayer *om mani padme hum,* the first and greatest of all charms among Tibetan Buddhists. The meaning of the sacred words is unknown, but repeating them is believed to thwart evil and embody all wisdom and knowledge.

Manidatta (mah-nee-DAHT-tah) East Indian name from the Sanskrit for "pearl given." Like many other gems, the pearl was once believed to ward off evil spirits. In Occidental astrology the pearl is the stone of Gemini.

113

Mankalita (mahn-kah-LEE-tah) Zuni Indian form of the Spanish Margarita. See Margita.

Mansi (MAHN-see) Hopi Indian name meaning "plucked flower." Possible English variants are Mansy and Mancy.

Manya (MAHN-yah) A favorite Russian diminutive. See Mara.

Mapela (muh-PE-luh) Hawaiian name from the Latin *amabilis,* meaning "lovable." The English equivalent is Mabel.

Mara (MAH-ruh) Used in Russia, Serbia, Hungary, and Slovakia as a form of the Hebrew for "bitter." The English equivalent is Mary.
Other variants used throughout the world include Marya, Mariya, Masha, Manya, Marusya, Manechka, Mashenka, and Mura (Russian); Maria, Mari, Marcsa, Marika, and Mariska (Hungarian); Marija, Marica, Mica, Micka, and Mimi (Slovakian); Marija, Marica, Maritsa, and Marishka (Serbian); Marja (Finnish); Maring (Filipino); Maria, Marita, Mariquita, Marica, and Mariquilla (Spanish); and Mamie, Mari, Mollie, Marie, Maretta, Marilyn, Marla, Manette, Marilla, May, Pollie, Miriam, and Muriel (English).

Maralah (mah-RAH-lah) North American Indian name for a child born near the time of an earthquake.

Marci This modern American name was once a nickname for Marcia, "martial one," but is used today as an independent Christian name. Also spelled Marcie, Marcy, and Marsi.

Marea (MAH-reh-uh) "Child of Mars." Astrological name for girls born under Aries and Scorpio, which are ruled by the planet Mars. Other names for Mars children include Marcelina, "beautiful warlike girl," and Marca, "warlike" or "like Mars."

Marganit (mahr-gah-NEET) Hebrew flower name. The

marganit, with its red, blue, and golden blossoms, is native to Israel.

Margita (MAHR-gee-tah in Czechoslovakia, mahr-GEE-tah in Poland) Common in Czechoslovakia, Hungary, and Poland, this name comes from the Latin for "a pearl." The English equivalent is Margaret. In astrology the pearl is the stone of Gemini.

Other variations of the name include Margarid (Armenian); Marketa and Marka (Czech); Madge, Maggi, Meg, Meta, Greta, Marga, Marge, Marget, and Margette (English); Grete, Gretal, and Grethal (German); Margit, Margo, Gitta, and Rita (Hungarian); Margalis, Margalit, and Margalith (Israeli); Margrete (Norwegian); Margarita, Margisia, Gita, and Rita (Polish); Margo, Margarete, Margosha, and Rita (Russian); and Gita, Gitka, and Gituska (Slovakian).

Mari Contemporary American name. See Mara.

Maria The popularity of the Virgin's name in Spanish-speaking countries makes this the most common Spanish name in the world. The many variations include Dolores, Lucita, Luz, Jesusa, and Carmen. See Mara for other forms closer in spelling.

Marice Flower name from the Teutonic for "the marsh flower."

Marijana (MAH-rih-yah-nuh) Slovak name which combines Mary, "bitter," and Anne, "graceful." The English equivalent is Marian. See Mara.

Marini (mah-REE-nee) Swahili for "fresh, healthy, and pretty."

Marinita "Little one of the sea." Used for girls born under the water signs of the zodiac: Pisces, Cancer, and Scorpio.

Marisha (mah-REE-shah) Popular pet name in Russia. See Mara.

Marita (mah-REE-tah) Spanish form of Mary. See Mara.

Marja (MAHR-jah) Finnish name. See Mara.

Marlene (mahr-LEH-ne) German name from the Greek Magdalene, a place name for the town in which Mary Magdalene was born.

Marni Hebrew pet form of Marnina, which means "to rejoice."

Marta From the Aramaic Martha, "lady" or "mistress." The name is used today in Sweden, Norway, Rumania, Lithuania, Italy, Hungary, Bulgaria, Czechoslovakia, Poland, Russia, the Ukraine, Serbia, the United States, and most Spanish-speaking countries.

Marva (MAHR-vuh) Israeli plant of the mint family.

Marya Slovak development of Mary. See Mara. In India Marya is a boy's name, derived from the Sanskrit for "mortal man."

Marzia (MAR-zee-uh) "Martial." The name refers to the warlike quality associated with the planet Mars, which rules the zodiacal signs Aries and Scorpio.

Masago (mah-SAH-goh) Japanese name meaning "sand," probably referring to sand's eternal quality and expressing a hope for a long life for the child.

Masalina (mah-sah-LEE-nah) Zuni Indian name. The exact meaning is unknown.

Masha (MAH-shah) Classic Russian form of Mara, "bitter."

Masika (mah-SEE-kah) Swahili name for a child born during the rainy season.

Matana (mah-TAH-nah) Modern Israeli name meaning "gift."

Matilda From the Old German for "battle maiden," this name is used today in Estonia, Italy, Lithuania, Latvia, Rumania, Russia, Serbia, Sweden, Norway, the Ukraine, the United States, and Spanish-speaking countries. Tilda and Tilli are favorite pet forms in most of these countries.

Matrika (mah-TREE-kah) "Mother." One of the many names for the Hindu goddess Sakti. See Sakti for further information.

Matsu (MAHT-soo:) Japanese for "pine," an Oriental symbol of stability and firm old age, and the so-called flower of January.

Mausi (MAW-see) North American Indian name which means "plucking flowers."

Maya (MIGH-yah) Hindu term for God's "creative power," which includes His ability to act through man as well as to create life. According to sacred Hindu writings, "God resides in the heart of all beings, and by His maya moves them from within as if they were turned by a machine."

Mazal (mah-ZAHL) Hebrew for "a star" or "luck."

Meda (MAY-duh) North American Indian name meaning "prophet" or "priestess" or "edible root."

Medlar Flower name. The medlar is a small tree or shrub, with pink or white blossoms and brown, applelike fruit.

Mega (MEH-gah) Spanish for "gentle," "mild," or "peaceful."

Mehira (meh-HEE-ruh) Hebrew name. See Mahira.

Mei (may) Hawaiian form of the Latin *maia,* "great one." The English equivalent is May.

Mei Hua (may hwah) Chinese for "plum blossom." In China the plum blossom is the flower of January and winter, and a symbol of beauty and longevity. The Japanese equivalent is Umeko.

Meira (meh-EE-rah) From the Hebrew name M'eeraw, meaning "light." Popularized by Israeli Prime Minister Golda Meir, who changed her name from Golda Meyerson, following the Israeli custom of choosing a Hebrew name.

Mel (mehl) Portuguese for "honey."

117

Mela (MAY-lah) Hindu name which refers to a religious gathering. In Poland the same name is used as a pet form of Melania, "black" or "dark," other variants of which are Melka and Ela.

Melanie "Black" or "dark." Melanie is probably derived from Melanesia, the name of a region northeast of Australia where the people are predominantly dark-skinned. Melanesia literally, means "black islands." The Polish equivalent is Melania.

Melantha "Black flower." The name probably comes from the deep purple lily which once grew along Mediterranean shores.

Melba A form of Malva, gaining popularity in the United States. The name is derived from either the Greek *malako*, "soft" or "slender," or the Latin *malva*, "mallow flower." In China the mallow is considered a magic charm against evil, it is also the flower of September and the zodiacal sign Virgo.

Melcia (MELT-shuh) Polish name meaning "ambitious" or "industrious." Another form used in Poland is Amalia.

Meli (MEH-lee) Zuni Indian name from the English Mary or the Spanish Mere, both of which mean "bitter." Meli is also a Greek name meaning "honey."

Melia (MEH-lee-ah) Spanish pet form of Cornelia, pronounced Kohr-NE-lee-ah in Spain, which means "yellowish" or "cornel tree." A less common variation is Nelia.

Melisenda (meh-lee-SEHN-dah) Spanish development of the German for "honest" or "diligent." The English equivalent is Millicent.

Melka (MEL-kah) Polish nickname. See Mela.

Melosa (meh-LOH-sah) Spanish for "honeylike," "sweet," or "gentle."

Memdi (MEHM-dee) A North Indian plant from which

comes a henna dye used to stain the palms of hands and the soles of feet for religious ceremonies.

Menora (me-NOH-ruh) Modern Israeli name derived from the Hebrew for "a candelabrum." A more truly Hebrew form is Menorah.

Menta (MAIN-tah) Spanish plant name for the mint or peppermint.

Mere (ME-re) Hawaiian form of Mary. See Malia.

Meri (MEH-ree) Popular Finnish name which means "sea." In Hebrew the same name means "rebellious," and since it implies bitterness, it may come from Mary or Miriam.

Merida (meh-REE-dah) Spanish place name sometimes used as a girl's name.

Meriwa (me-RI-wuh) Banti Eskimo name with the unusual meaning "thorn." It may have been used as a magic name to ward off evil spirits, to trick them into believing the child was unloved because she had an ugly name.

Meryem (MAI-re-em) Turkish development of Miriam, "rebellious" or "bitter," or Mary, "bitter." Another form is Meryemana, referring to the Virgin Mary.

Mesha (MAY-shah) Hindu astrological name for a child born under Aries, the Ram. Mesha literally, means "ram."

Meta German for "a pearl." See Greta.

Mia Modern Israeli name derived from Michaela, a feminine form of Michael, meaning "who is like God?" In other parts of the world, including the United States, Mia is occasionally used as a pet form of Maria.

Miakoda (mee-ah-KOH-dah) "Power of the moon." Occult name for a child born under Cancer, which is ruled by the moon. The name was originally used by various North American Indian tribes.

Michi (mee-chee) Japanese for "the righteous way." In Japanese a much less common character associated with this sound means "three thousand," which expresses a hope that the family will extend for many generations.

Micka (MITS-kuh) Slovakian form of Maria, "bitter." Another favorite is Mica. See Mara.

Midori (mee-doh-ree) Unusual Japanese name meaning "green." Color names are rarely used today. At one time they referred to human qualities, Midori possibly indicating a hope that the child would be illustrious. Other color names include Ai, "indigo"; Aka, "red"; Iro, "color"; Kon, "deep blue"; Kuro, "black"; Murasaki, "purple"; and Shiro, "white."

Mieze (MEE-tse) German form of Maria. See Mitzi.

Migdala (mig-dah-LAH) Hebrew for "fortress" or "tower."

Migina (mee-GEE-nah) Omaha Indian name which means "moon returning," indicating the child was born during the new moon. Other Omaha moon names include Mihuca, "loud voice moon," and Mitexi, "sacred moon." In astrology the moon governs the sign Cancer, while the tarot card of the moon corresponds to Pisces.

Mika (MEE-kah) Used by widely separated cultures. Among the North American Indians, Mika means "the knowing raccoon." In Japan it is an abbreviation of *Mikazuki* "the moon of the third night (of the old lunar month)," and literally means "new moon." In Russia the same name is a pet form of Dominika, "belonging to the Lord" or "born on Sunday."

Miki (MEE-kee) Japanese for "stem," possibly referring to the family tree. A similar name is Mikie, pronounced mee-KEE-e.

Mila (MEE-lah) Czech nickname meaning "loved by the people." See Ludmila.

120

Milada (MIL-ah-dah) Czech name which combines
   words *mi,* meaning "mine," and *lada,* referring ᴜ
   the goddess of youth, fertility, and love. Milada,
   then, literally means "my love."

Milena (MI-leh-nuh) Used today in Slovakia, Milena
   comes from the Greek for "black" or "dark." The
   English equivalent is Melanie.

Mili (MEE-lee) Modern Israeli name meaning "who is
   for me." It may also be a form of Millicent or Millie,
   "honest" or "diligent."

Miliama (mi-lee-AH-muh) Common Hawaiian development of the English Miriam, derived from the Hebrew
   for "rebellious" or "bitter."

Milica (MI-lits-uh) Slovak form of Amelia, which comes
   from the ancient word *amal,* "hard work," occurring
   in many languages.

Mimi French form of Wilhelmina, from the Old German
   for "unwavering protector." In the United States
   Mimi has been used as a diminutive of Miriam,
   "bitter" or "rebellious."

Mimosa Flower name. Shortened forms are Mim and
   Mimi. The mimosa is a tropical shrub or tree, with
   spikes of small white, yellow, or pink blossoms.

Mina (MEE-nah) Hindu astrological name for a child
   born under Pisces, which is symbolized by the Fishes.
   Also used as a Czech pet form of Hermina, and as
   a German, Polish, and English nickname for Wilhelmina.

Minal (mee-NAHL) North American Indian name meaning "fruit."

Minda (MEEN-dah) "Knowledge" or "wisdom." Occasionally used in India.

Mindy An independent name today, Mindy was once an
   American nickname for Minna, "love.

Mineko (mee-NE-koh) Japanese for "peak," loosely
   translated to mean "mountain child."

Minette (mee-NET) French form of the German Wilhelmina, which means "unwavering protector." Other French variants include Guillelmine, Guilette, Wilhelmine, Mimi, and Guillaumette.

Minima (mi-NEE-mah) Used by some of the early Afro-Americans taken from the Bonny tribe of Southern Nigeria. In America Minima became Monime and seems to have disappeared after several generations, possibly because of the rapid alienation from African heritage, or because of the difficulty English-speaking people had in pronouncing African names.

Minna German form of Helmine, from the Old German for "love."

Minowa (mi-NOH-wah) North American Indian name which means "moving voice."

Mio (MEE-oh) Unusual Japanese name meaning "triple cord." No further explanation could be found.

Miquela (mee-QUEH-lah) Zuni Indian adaptation of the Spanish Micaela, "who is like God?" Another Spanish variant is Miguela, and the masculine form is Miguel.

Mir (meer) Czech for "peace."

Mira (MEE-ruh) A favorite form of Miriam used today in Israel. Other popular variations are Miri and Mirit.

Mirabella (mee-rah-BEHL-lah) Spanish for "beautiful." In the United States the name is often changed to Mirabelle.

Miri (MEE-ree) English Gypsy name meaning "mine." Also an Israeli form of Miriam.

Mirjam (MEER-yuhm) Finnish form of Miriam, "bitter" or "rebellious."

Missie Modern American name for a young girl.

Mitena (mi-TAY-nah) Omaha Indian name for a child born under the coming or new moon. In astrology the moon rules the domestic sign Cancer, while the tarot card of the moon corresponds to Pisces, the most mystical sign of the zodiac.

Mithuna (mee-TOO:-nah) Hindu astrological name for a child born in the solar month Mithuna, under the sign Gemini, symbolized by the Twins.

Mitra (MI-trah) A Hindu god of daylight and the sun.

Mituna (mi-TOO:-nah) Miwok Indian name from the word *mituye,* "to roll up." The connotation is "wrapping a salmon with willow stems and leaves after catching it." Other salmon names used by the Miwoks include Hunui, "fat salmon"; Litcitu, "salmon swimming in river", and Matcinina, "salmon jumping falls and missing."

Mitzi German name meaning "little bitter one." Other German forms are Maria, Marie, Mieze, and Milly.

Miwa (mee-WAH) Japanese for "the far-seeing." Commonly used with the suffix *-ko* to mean "far-seeing child."

Miya (MEE-yah) Japanese for "temple" or "Shinto." A favorite variation is Miyoko, "Shinto child."

Miyoko (MEE-yoh-koh) Japanese name which means "beautiful generations child." It can be shortened to Miyo.

Miyuki (mee-YOO:-kee) A Japanese favorite which literally means "deep snow," connotating the peaceful silence following a heavy snowfall.

Mizella (mee-ZEH-luh) Used by the English Gypsies. The exact meaning of this name could not be determined.

Moana (MWAH-nah) Hawaiian for "ocean."

Mona Miwok Indian name which means "gathering jimson weed seed." In English the same name is derived from the Greek for "just one" or the Italian for "my lady."

Mora (MOH-rah) Spanish name meaning "little blueberry."

Morasha (moh-RAH-shuh) Hebrew for "inheritance."

Morela (moh-RE-luh) Polish for "apricot."

Morena (moh-REH-nah) Spanish name from the Irish *Mairin,* meaning "little Mary" or "little bitter one." The English equivalent is Maureen.

Moriah (moh-REE-uh) Hebrew name which means "God is my teacher." Other variations include Moriel, Morice, and Morit.

Mozelle (mo-ZEH-le or Anglicized to moh-ZEL) From the Hebrew for "taken from the water." This name is used for girls born under the water signs of the zodiac: Pisces, Cancer, and Scorpio. Also spelled Moselle.

Mu Lan (moo:-LAHN) Chinese for "magnolia blossom." In China the Magnolia is the flower of May and a symbol of feminine sweetness.

Muliya (moo:-LEE-yah) Miwok Indian name which means "hitting farewell-to-spring seed with a stick as the seed hangs on the bush," from the word *mule* "to beat" or "to hit."
Other farewell-to-spring Miwok names include Eskeye ("farewell-to-spring seed which has cracked open on the bush"); Loiyetu ("farewell-to-spring in bloom"); Malkuyu ("farewell-to-spring flowers drying"); and Memtba ("tasting farewell-to-spring seed after it has been mashed with the pestle but while still in the mortar," from *memttu,* "to taste").

Mulya (MOO:L-yah) Miwok Indian name which means "knocking acorns off a tree with a long stick," from the word *mule,* "to beat" or "to hit." Among North American Indian tribes which had no corn, acorns and fish were the chief foods. One Indian legend tells how the acorn was created. It seems everyone loved the first-born man except the she-frog, who envied his beautiful legs. So the frog spit in the man's water, and he died. He had promised he would give the Indians their most valued possession, and from his ashes sprang the first oak, covered with acorns as large as apples.

Muna (MOO:-nah) Hopi Indian name which means "freshet" and was given to a child born during the season the streams rise. From the Cloud Cult.

Muneva (MOO:-nay-vah) Popular name among the Mashona of Southern Rhodesia for a child so thin she resembles the muneva, a type of net bag.

Mura (moo:-RAH) Japanese for "village," possibly indicating the child or her parents came to the country from a village.

Murrah (MOO:-rah) "Bitter." Arabic form of the Biblical Mary.

Mu Tan (moo:-TAHN) Chinese for "tree peony blossom." In China the peony, called the king of flowers, is the flower of March and spring, and a symbol of love and affection.

Nadia (NAH-dee-uh) Russian name meaning "hope." Also spelled Nadiya. Other forms used throughout the world include Nadine, English; Nadzia and Natka, Polish; Nada, Slovakian; and Nadya, Nadenka, Nadyusha, and Dusya, Ukrainian and Russian.

Nagida (nah-GEE-duh) Hebrew for "wealthy" or "ruler."

Nani (NAH-nee) Hawaiian for "beautiful." Also a modern Greek form of Anne, "graceful."

Nara (NAH-rah) North American Indian place name. Also Japanese for "oak," a symbol of steadfastness and stability. According to one prehistoric myth, man sprang from the oak, thus making it the most sacred of all trees.

Nari (NAH-ree) Japanese for "thunderpeal." A variation is Nariko, "thunder child."

Narilla (nah-REE-luh) English Gypsy name. Also spelled Narrila. The exact meaning is obscure.

Narmada (nahr-mad-dah) Hindu nature name taken from one of the seven sacred rivers of India. The rivers are invoked as dieties capable of granting fertility and wealth; and bathing in them is one of the religious duties required of all Hindus.

Nashira (na-SHIGH-rah) One of the bright stars in the constellation Capricorn, the Goat. This sign of the zodiac was once called the Mansion of Kings because the Roman emperor Gaius Octavius Augustus was born under its influence. Capricorns are said to be the executives of the zodiac, who, like their symbol the mountain goat, climb sure-footedly over obstacles to reach the heights.

Nashota (nah-SHOH-tah) North American Indian name meaning "twin." Used for girls born under the zodiacal sign Gemini, the Twins.

Nasnan (nahs-NAHN) Carrier Indian name meaning "surrounded by a song."

Nasya (NAH-see-ah) Hebrew for "miracle of God." Also spelled Nasia.

Nata (NAH-tah) Found in widely separated cultures, Nata is a North American Indian name for a speaker or creator, and a Hindustani name for a rope dancer. It is also used in Poland, where it means "hope."

Natane (nah-TAH-ne) Arapaho Indian name meaning daughter."

Natasha (nah-TAH-shuh) Slavic name meaning "born on Christmas."

Natesa (nah-TAY-shah) "Dance lord." One of the 1,008 names for the Hindu god Siva. More often a boy's name. Siva is usually pictured with either one or five faces, four arms, and a third eye, which appeared in order to save the world from darkness when his

126

wife playfully covered his two eyes with her hands. The third eye can allegedly turn men to ashes.

Natka (NAHT-kah) "Hope." See Nadia.

Navit (nah-VEET) Hebrew for "beautiful" or "pleasant." Also spelled Naava and Nava.

Neci (NE-tsee) Hungarian name from the Latin for "intense and fiery," referring to one who lives intensely.

Neda (NEH-duh) Slovak name for a child born on Sunday. Also possibly a feminine form of Edward, derived from the Old English for "prosperous guardian."

Nediva (neh-DEE-vuh) Hebrew for "noble and generous."

Neely Contemporary feminine form of Neal, "champion," used in the United States.

Neema (neh-EH-mah) Swahili name for a child born during a time of prosperity.

Neka (NAY-kah) North American Indian name meaning "the wild goose." This may first have been used by a proud father who, after Indian tradition, named his daughter for a feat he had accomplished, in this case the shooting of many wild geese.

Nelia (NEH-lee-ah) Shortened form of the Spanish Cornelia, "yellowish" or "cornel tree." Another variant is Melia.

Nelka (NEL-kuh) Polish nickname for Petronela, "rock." Other favorites in Poland are Nela, Petra, and Ela.

Nenet Occult name from the Egyptian *Book of the Dead,* often called the original book of magic. The goddess Nenet personifies the inert, motionless character of the primeval waters in which the Creator lived.

Nepa (NEH-pah) "Walking backward." This is another name for the constellation Scorpio, the Scorpion. Alchemists believed that iron could be turned to gold only when the sun was in this sign of the zodiac.

Nerissa "Daughter of the sea." Astrological name for girls born under the water signs of the zodiac: Pisces,

127

Cancer, and Scorpio. Variations are Nerice and Nerine, the latter being a flower name as well.

Nessa Russian pet form of Anastassia, "of the Resurrection." See Anastassia.

Netia (NEH-tee-ah) Israeli name meaning "plant" or "shrub." Other forms are Neta and Netta, also used in Israel as boys' names.

Netis (NAY-tis) North American Indian name which means "trusted friend."

Neva (NEH-vah) From the Spanish *nieve*, meaning "snowy" or "extremely white." Nevada, "white as snow" comes from the same source.

Neza (NEH-zhuh) Slovakian form of the Greek for "pure." The English equivalent is Agnes. Other forms used throughout the world include Agnessa, Bulgarian; Anezka and Anka, Czech; Agnes, Hungarian; Inez, Portuguese and Spanish: Agnessa, Nessia, and Nessa, Russian; Agneta, Scandinavian; and Ines, Spanish.

Niabi (nee-AH-bee) North American Indian name meaning "a fawn."

Nicoli Modern American creation from Nicole, "victorious army" or "victorious people." Another current variation is Nikki.

Nida (NEE-dah) Omaha Indian name for a mythical being or animal which crept elflike in and out of the earth. This was also a word for the bones of extinct mammals, like the mastodon.

Nika A favorite nickname in Russia for Dominika, "born on Sunday" or "belonging to God." Other variants are Domka and Mika.

Niki (NEE-kee) Modern Greek pet form of Nikoleta, "victorious army" or "victorious people." Another Greek variation is Nikolia.

Nili (NEE-lee) Current Israeli name for both girls and boys. It is an abbreviation of the words "the glory (or eternity) of Israel will not lie," from I Samuel

15:29. During the first World War, Nili was a pro-British and anti-Turkish underground organization in Palestine.

Nina (NEE-nah) North American Indian name meaning "mighty." In Spanish-speaking countries Nina, pronounced NEEN-yah, means "girl" and is occasionally used as a name.

Ninita (nee-NEE-tah) This Zuni Indian name probably comes from the Spanish Ninita, pronounced nee-NYEE-tah, which means "little girl."

Nipa (NEE-pah) "Stream." Nature name used today by the Todas of India.

Nirel (ni-RAYL) Israeli name from the Hebrew for "God's light" or "planted field." Also a boy's name.

Nirveli (neer-VEH-li) "Water" or "water child." Used by the Todas of India.

Nishi (nee-SHEE) Japanese for "west." A Japanese proverb goes, "From the east the root, from the west the fruit."

Nisse (NIS-suh) Scandinavian name meaning "friendly elf" or "friendly brownie." It has been Anglicized to Nissa.

Nita (NEE-tah) A Choctaw Indian name meaning "bear," and a Spanish variant of Anita, meaning "graceful." Another Spanish form is Anica.

Nitara (ni-TAH-rah) Hindu name from the Sanskrit for "deeply rooted." Also occasionally used in the United States.

Nitsa Popular today in Greece, Nitsa means "light." See Eleni.

Nituna (nee-TOO:-nah) North American Indian name meaning "my daughter."

Nizana (nee-ZAH-nah) Hebrew flower name meaning "bud." Other variations are Nitza and Nitzana.

Noga (NOH-guh) Israeli name from the Hebrew for "shining" or "morning light." Also a boy's name.

Nolcha (NOHL-chah) Israeli name from the Hebrew for "shining" or "morning light." Also a boy's name.

Nolcha (NOHL-chah) North American Indian name which means "the sun."

Nona From the Latin for "nine." A possible numerological name.

Nori (NOH-ree) Japanese for "precept" or "doctrine." Noriko, "doctrine child," is also used.

Noura (NOH-rah) Arabic name which means "light," indicating a hope that the child will bring illumination with her presence.

Nova (NOH-vah) Hopi Indian name which means "chasing (a butterfly)." From the Badger Cult.

Numa (NOO:-mah) Arabic form of the Biblical Naomi, which means "beautiful" or "pleasant."

Nuna (NOO:-nah) North American Indian name meaning "land."

Nunki (NOO:N-kee) A star in the constellation Sagittarius, the Archer, which influences those born under that sign.

Nuria (noo:-REE-ah) Currently used in Israel, Nuria means "fire of the Lord." Other forms are Nuri and Nuriel. These are also boys' names.

Nurit (noo:-REET) Modern Israeli name meaning "little yellow flower." Popular variations are Nurice and Nurita. The plant from which this name comes blooms annually in Israel.

Nusi (NOO-shi) Hungarian version of the Hebrew Hannah, "graceful." Other forms used in Hungary are Aniko, Anci, Annuska, Nina and Ninacska.

Nyura (NYOO:-rah) A favorite among Russian peasants. See Anna.

Oba (oh-BAH) Yoruban name for an ancient river goddess. Still a common girl's name.

Odelia (oh-DAY-lee-ah) Hebrew for "I will praise God."

Odera (oh-DAY-ruh) From the Hebrew for "plough."

Ogin (oh-GEEN) North American Indian flower name meaning "the wild rose."

Okalani (oh-kuh-LAH-nee) Hawaiian for "of the heavens" or "from heaven."

Oki (oh-KEE) Unusual Japanese name meaning "in the middle of the ocean," possibly for a child born at sea.

Okrika (ohk-REE-kah) Common name among the early Afro-Americans taken from the Okrika tribe of Southern Nigeria. In America the name was corrupted to Ocreka and then gradually disappeared.

Olathe (oh-LAH-thah) North American Indian name which means "beautiful."

Olayinka (oh-la-YEEN-kah) Yoruban name from the word *ola* meaning "honor," "wealth," or "abundance," and the suffix *-yinka,* implying one is surrounded by something. Hence, Olayinka means "honors (or wealth) surround me."

Olena (oh-LAY-nah) Current Russian name from the Greek for "light." Other names from the same source are Lenusya, Lila, Lyalechka, Lyalya, Alena, Alenka, and Alenushka.

Olesia (oh-LE-shuh) Polish name which means "helper and defender of mankind." A pet form is Ola. The English equivalent is Alexandra.

Olga Ancient Russian name which means "holy." Still one of the most popular names in Russia today. Favorite pet forms are Olia, Olenka, and Olechka. Also used in Czechoslovakia, Estonia, Hungary, Latvia, Poland, Sweden, the Ukraine, the United States, and Spanish-speaking countries. The name may first have been popularized by Saint Olga, who spread the Christian religion in Russia during the tenth century.

Oliana (oh-le-AH-nuh) Hawaiian for "oleander," a poisonous evergreen with white or red blossoms.

Olisa (oh-LEE-sah) Common in Africa among the Western Ibos of Onitsha, this is another name for Chukwu, or "God." Many Ibo name use Olisa as an element, including Belu Olisa, which implies nothing is possible without God's help or approval.

Oma (OH-mah) Arabic for "commander," and the feminine form of the popular Omar.

Omena (AW-me-nuh) Finnish for "apple."

Omusa (oh-MOO:-sah) Miwok Indian name which means "missing things when shooting with arrows," *omusa,* "to miss with arrows." Another connotation is "missing deer when trying to shoot them with arrows." In astrology the Archer is the symbol of Sagittarius. Other Miwok archery names include Selumtci ("shooting an arrow up in the air"); Sitki ("putting an arrow in the quiver"); Situtu ("taking an arrow from the quiver"); and Tuwume ("an arrow sticking into a pota ceremony pole").

Ona Lithuanian development of the Hebrew Hannah, "graceful." Other popular forms in Lithuania are Anikke, Annze, Ane, Onute, and Onele.

Onatah (oh-nah-TAH) The Iroquois corn spirit and daughter of the earth. Once when looking for fresh dews, Onatah was captured by the spirit of evil, who imprisoned her underground until the sun guided her back to her lost fields. She never again looked for dew.

Onawa (oh-NAH-wah) "Wide-awake one." Used by some North American Indians for a child who never sleeps and keeps his parents awake. The name may also indicate bright alertness.

Onella (OH-ne-lah) Hungarian equivalent of the English Nellie, which comes from the Greek for "light."

Oni (AW-nee) The Yoruba of Nigeria use this name for a child born on holy ground. Among the Benin of Nigeria, the same name means "desired" and is pronounced oh-NEE.

Onida (oh-NEE-dah) North American Indian name meaning "the looked-for one."

Orah Hebrew for "light." Other variants are Ora, Orit, and Orlice. Oralee, Orlee, and Orly have the slightly different meaning "light is mine."

Oredola (oh-RAY-doh-lah) Yoruban name which means friendship has brought honor."

Orenda (oh-RAYN-dah) Iroquois Indian name meaning "magic power," which refers to the power inherent in all things, from rocks to man. It is believed that with this force one can affect and control others, and that to own something with great strength can increase one's inner potential. The Huron Indians call the force Oki, while the Sioux name it Wakanda.

Oriana (oh-ree-AH-nuh) "Golden" or "dawning." Astrological name which refers to the sun-ruled sign Leo, the Lion. Variants are Oralia, Orlene, Orlann, Orelle, and Orelda.

Orino (oh-REE-noh) Japanese for "weaver's field." The name can be shortened to Ori, "weaver."

Orlenda (ohr-LEHN-duh) English Gypsy name from the Russian *orlitza* meaning "female eagle."

Ornice Hebrew name for a fir or cedar tree. Variations are Ornit and Orna.

Osen (oh-SEN) "Thousand." This unusual Japanese name is probably bestowed because of an old belief in the magical power of round numbers.

Oshun (oh-SHOO:N) The Yoruban goddess of the Oshun River.

Oya (AW-yuh) Miwok Indian name which literally means "to name," but connotes "naming or speaking of the kuiatawila bird (jacksnipe)." Also a boy's name.

Padma (PAHD-mah) "Lotus," the national flower of Hindu India. The padma, like the day lotus, is said to open by day and close at night. Other Indian names derived from varieties of the lotus are Nalina and Aravinda. In Hindu belief the god Brahma sprang from a mystical lotus which grew from the god Vishnu's navel.

Paka (PAH-kah) Swahili for "pussycat."

Palila (pah-LEE-luh) Hawaiian name which means "bird."

Paloma (pah-LOH-mah) Spanish for "dove," a symbol of peace. The name is given to a baby who coos.

Pandasala (pahn-dah-SAH-lah) African Ovimbundu name from the proverb *O pandasala utima wove; kutima wukuene ombala yikuavo,* "You search your heart; at the heart of another village another." Loosely translated, the saying means you can know your own sorrows, but not those of another.

Pandita (pahn-DEE-tah) Hindustani name meaning "scholar." Often used as a name element only.

Panya (PAHN-yah) A favorite Russian diminutive of Stephania from the Greek for "crowned one."

Papina (pah-PEE-nuh) Miwok Indian name which means "a vine growing on an oak tree."

Pati (PA-tee) Miwok Indian name which literally means "to break by twisting," but connotes "twisting willows for carrying fish." Other Miwok fish names include Putbana, "catching small fish with a basket," and Pumsono, "sucker fish jumping out of the water." In astrology the Fishes are the symbol of Pisces

Patia (PAH-tee-uh) Spanish Gypsy name which means "leaf," connoting the freshness of spring.

Paulita (pow-LEE-tah) From the Latin for "little," this name is used in Spain and Latin and South America. English equivalents are Paula and Pauline.

Pausha (POH-shah) Hindu name for a child born during the lunar month Pausha, which corresponds to the zodiacal sign Capricorn.

Pavla (PAHV-lah) Czech development of the Latin for "little." Another Czech form is Pavlina. English equivalents are Paula and Pauline.

Pazia (pah-ZEE-uh) Hebrew for "golden." Other variants used today in Israel are Paz, Paza, Pazice, and Pazit. Paz is also a boy's name.

Pedzi (PAYD-zee) Southern Rhodesian name derived from the Babudja verb *ku pedza,* "to finish." Pedzi literally means "finisher," and the name is bestowed on the last child a mother plans to have.

Peke (PE-ke) Used in Hawaii, this name comes from the Old German for "shining" or "glorious," which originally referred to an ancient German fertility goddess. The English equivalent is Bertha.

Pelcia (PEL-shuh) A favorite Polish nickname for Penelopa, from the Greek for "weaver." Other Polish diminutives are Pela and Lopa. The English equivalent is Penelope.

Pelipa (peh-LEE-pah) Zuni Indian name from the Spanish Felipa, which means "lover of horses." The name originally comes from the Greek. The English equivalent is Philippa.

Pemba (PEHM-bah) African Bambara word for the force of present existence. Working with Faro, the force of the future, Pemba makes the world go around, moves the stars, and directs the affairs of men.

Penda (PAIN-dah) Derived from the Swahili for "love" or "be fond of," Penda, means "beloved one."

Peni (PAY-nee) Carrier Indian name for both girls and boys. Peni literally means "his mind," and the name was once used by a Carrier pseudoprophet who claimed he communicated with the spirit world during cataleptic fits, and who maintained he could listen to people's minds. The Zunis used the same name, but an exact translation could not be found.

Penina (pay-NEE-nah) Hebrew for "coral" or "pearl." A variation is Peninit, and a common pet form, Penny.

Pepita (peh-PEE-tah) A favorite Spanish pet name for Josephine, the feminine form of Jose, which comes from the Hebrew for "addition" or "increase." The name became quite popular in Spanish-speaking countries after 1621, when the Pope named March 19th a festival day for Saint Joseph.

Perla (PER-luh) Slovakian name from the Latin for "a pearl." The English equivalent is Margaret.

Pilar (pee-LAHR) A favorite in Spanish-speaking countries, Pilar means "pillar" or "fountain base." The name actually refers to the Virgin Mary, pillar of the Christian religion.

Pilisi (pi-LEE-see) Hawaiian development of Phyllis, from the Greek for "a green branch."

Pinga (PEEN-gah) Hindustani for "dark" or "tawny." One of the more than one thousand names for the goddess Sakti. See Sakti for further information.

Pipal (PEE-pahl) A mythical Hindu tree which allegedly has its branches on earth and its roots in heaven.

Pita (PEE-tah) "Fourth-born daughter." A favorite name among the Bari of Southern Sudan. See Kapuki for other serial names.

Pokii (POH-kee) Hawaiian for "younger brother" or "younger sister."

Pollyam (poh-lee-YAHM) Among the Hindus of Madras, this is one of the most common names for girls and boys. Probably a shortened form of the name Poleramma for the goddess of the plague, and bestowed to appease the spirit and keep her from striking.

Poni (POH-nee) "Second-born daughter." A common name among the Bari of Southern Sudan. See Kapuki for other serial names.

Poppy The Occidental flower of August and the Chinese flower of December. In Occidental astrology the poppy is the "herb" of the moon, which governs the sign Cancer.

Posala (poh-SAH-lah) One of the many Miwok Indian names taken from the farewell-to-spring flower. Posala literally means "to burst," but the connotation is "pounding farewell-to-spring seed." Other Miwok farewell-to-spring names are listed under Muliya.

Prane (PRAH-ne) Lithuanian name from the Latin for "free one." Other forms used in Lithuania today include Pranute and Pranele. The English equivalent is Francis.

Pualani (pwah-LAH-nee) Popular in Hawaii, this name means "heavenly flower," probably referring to either the wild ginger blossom or the bird-of-paradise in bloom. Also common are Pua, "flower," and Puanani, "beautiful flower." A nickname is Puni.

Pakuna (poo:-KOO:-nah) Miwok Indian name which means "deer jumping when running downhill."
The graceful deer has inspired many Miwok names. Others include Ewentcu ("deer eating brush"); Muku ("deer making trail when walking back and forth"); Toloise ("deer lying down and looking up at someone coming"); Tolsowe ("deer's ears erect as it stands looking around"); and Yatcalu ("deer's antlers spreading wide").

Querida (keh-REE-dah) Spanish for "beloved."

Rabi (rah-BEE) Common Arabic nature name meaning "breeze," connoting a fragrant scent. Also a boy's name.

Rabiah (rah-BEE-ah) Arabic for "spring" or "breeze." See Rabi.

Radha (RAHD-hah) A woman in Hindu mythology who was a cowherd and a favorite of the god Krishna.

137

Radinka (RAH-den-kuh) Slovak for "energetic" or "active."

Radmilla (RAHD-mel-luh) From the Slovak word meaning "worker for the people."

Rahela (ruh-HE-luh) Hawaiian name. See Lahela.

Raizel (RAY-zel) Yiddish flower name which means "rose." Variants are Rayzel and Razil.

Rakel (RAH-kehl) A favorite in Sweden Rakel comes from the Hebrew for "a ewe." English equivalents are Raquel and Rachel.

Ramla (RAHM-lah) Swahili for "fortune teller."

Ramona (rah-MOH-nuh) Spanish for "mighty protector" or "wise protector." The masculine form is Ramon.

Randi Popular today in the United States, Randi was probably created as a feminine form of Randolph, meaning "shield-wolf." The name possibly refers to a war shield that made its owner invincible.

Rane (RAH-neh) Norwegian name which means "queen" or "pure." In Iceland Rane is a boy's name.

Rani (RAH-nee) Hindustani for "queen."

Ranita (rah-NEE-tah) Modern Israeli name meaning "song" or "joy." Popular variants are Ranice and Ranit.

Raquel (rah-KEHL) Spanish development of the Biblical Rachel, meaning "a ewe."

Rasia (RAH-see-uh) Flower name meaning "rose."

Ratri (rah-TREE) "Night." One of the many names for the revered Hindu goddess Sakti. See Sakti for more information.

Rawnie (RAW-nee) English Gypsy name which means "lady."

Razilee (rah-zi-LEE) Hebrew for "my secret." Also spelled Razili.

Rea (REH-uh) Flower name from the Greek for "poppy,"

the source of opium. Rea can also be translated as "a stream," making it a good astrological name for girls born under the water signs Pisces, Cancer, and Scorpio. Astrologers often advise such aquatic names if a horoscope contains too many wood or metal influences, the idea being that water controls wood and destroys metal. It is believed that a good star chart should contain a balance of the basic elements—earth, fire, air, water, metal, and wood—to permit the universal order to work smoothly during the person's life.

Rei (ray) Japanese for "gratitude." A favorite variation in Japan is Reiko.

Reina (reh-EE-nah) From the Latin word *regina,* this modern Spanish name means "queen."

Ren (ren) Delicate Japanese name meaning "water lily" or "lotus." The lotus is Buddhist symbol, first of purity, because the flower grows from muddy water and remains unstained, and second of perfection, because its fruit is ripe when the flower blooms and this embodies the oneness of Buddhist teaching and knowledge. The Buddhist paradise contains a pond filled with ambrosia and multi-colored lotus blossoms, and the flower is said to have sprung from the graves of devout Buddhists.

Rena (RAY-nah) Modern Greek name which means "peace." Other forms used today in Greece are Eirene, Ereni, Eirni, and Nitsa.

Renia (REN-yah) Polish name from either the Latin for "queen" or the Teutonic for "pure." Other Polish forms are Rega and Ina.

Reseda Flower name from Latin, referring to the fragrant mignonette.

Resi (REH-see) German nickname which means "reaper." See Tresa.

Reva (RAY-vah) An alternate name for the Narmada, one of the seven sacred Hindu rivers in India.

Rez Hungarian name which literally means "copper," for a girl with copper-colored hair.

Rhea Occult name from the Egyptian *Book of the Dead*, which because of its many incantations and spells has often been called the original book of magic. Rhea is another name for the goddess Nut, a deity with a serpent's head and human body who personifies the primeval waters in which the Creator lived in the beginning.

Ria (REE-ah) Spanish nature name referring to the mouth of a river.

Rida (REH-dah) Arabic for "favor," possibly implying the child is in God's favor. Also a boy's name.

Riesa (ree-AY-suh) Astrological name for a girl born under Aries, the Ram. Aries people are said to be the leaders of the zodiac, innovative, gregarious, energetic, and impulsive.

Rihana (ree-HAH-nuh) Muslim name meaning "sweet basil," which in Western myth is an emblem of poverty and hate.

Rimona (ri-MOH-nuh) Popular in Israel, Rimona comes from the Hebrew for "pomegranate."

Rin (reen) Japanese for "park," a place name occasionally used as a girl's name.

Risa Gaining popularity in the United States, Risa means "laughter."

Risha (REE-shah) Hindu astrological name for a child born during the solar month Vrishabha, corresponding to the sign Taurus, the Bull.

Rita A favorite Polish nickname. See Mara. Rita is also a pet form of the Spanish Margarite, from the Latin for "a pearl." Still another meaning comes from the Hindu religion, in which Rita refers to the concept of the underlying natural and moral order present in the universe.

Ritsa (REET-sah) In Greece this is a common pet form of Alexandra, from the Greek for "helper and defender of mankind." Another pet name is Aleka.

Rohana (roh-HAH-nah) Hindu name which means "sandalwood."

Ronli (rohn-LEE) Hebrew for "joy is mine." Variants are Rona, Roni, Ronia, Ronice, and Ronit, all of which simply mean "joy."

Rosaleen Irish diminutive of Rose, meaning "love." Dark Rosaleen is a symbolic name for Ireland.

Rosalinda (roh-sah-LEEN-dah) From the Spanish Rosa Linda, "beautiful rose." This can be used as either a single name or two names, divided into first and middle names. The English equivalent is Rosalind. The shortened form Rosa is popular in Italy, Denmark, and Holland.

Roselani (roh-se-LAH-nee) A compound English and Hawaiian name referring to a small red rose which grows in Hawaii. Roselani literally means "heavenly rose."

Rosita (roh-SEE-tah) Spanish flower name meaning "little rose." A favorite pet form also used as a given name is Zita.

Rozele (ROH-zhe-le) Lithuanian name for the rose. Other variations used in Lithuania are Roze and Rozyte.

Rozene (roh-ZAY-nuh) North Amercian Indian name for the rose. In Western astrology the rose is the flower of Gemini.

Ruana (roo:-AH-nah) Hindu object name. The ruana is a musical instrument used in India which resembles a viol. See Almira for an explanation of inanimate-object names.

Ruchi (ROO:-chee) Hindustani name meaning "a love

growing into a wish to please and shine before the beloved."

Rudra (ROO:-drah) Sacred Hindu name derived from the rudraksha plant, the berries of which are used for making rosaries. The god Siva, as he contemplates the destruction of the world, is said to shed rudraksha-seed tears. The seeds nearly always have several "faces," and it is believed that anyone finding a one-faced seed will have his every wish and a life of wealth, luxury and power.

Ruri (roo:-REE) Japanese for "emerald." A common variation is Ruriko. Naming children after precious stones dates back to an ancient belief that gems protect one from evil spirits. In astrology the emerald is the birthstone of Taurus, the Bull.

Rusalka (ROO-sahl-kah) A favorite in Czechoslovakia, this name means "wood nymph."

Ruzena (ROO:-zhe-nah) Czech flower name meaning "rose."

Ryba (REE-bah) Czech name meaning "fish," often used as a surname. In astrology the Fishes are the symbol of Pisces.

Sabina "Woman from the Sabine country. This name is used today in Bulgaria, Czechoslovakia, Finland, Italy, Poland, Russia, the Ukraine, Spanish-speaking countries, and the United States.

Sabra (SAH-bruh) The name for a native-born Israeli. Sabra comes from the Hebrew for "thorny cactus," which refers to a prickly but edible fruit native to the coastal plains of Israel. Occasionally used as a boy's name. A diminutive form is Sabrina.

Sacha (SAH-shah) A favorite Russian nickname. Also spelled Sasha. See Alexandra.

Sachi (SAH-chee) Japanese for "bliss." A popular variation is Sachiko, "bliss child."

Sada (SAH-dah) Japanese name meaning "the chaste."

Sadira Flower name from the Persian for "the lotus tree." See Kumuda and Ren for the significance of the lotus in Hindu and Buddhist beliefs.

Sadzi (sahd-ZEE) Carrier Indian name meaning "clock," literally "sun heart."

Sagara (sah-GAH-rah) Hindustani for "ocean." Often used as a name element.

Sagitta (sa-JEE-tuh) "Born under Sagittarius." Astrological name for a girl born under that sign of the zodiac. Variants include Sagita and the shortened Sagi.

Sakari (sah-KAH-ree) Common today among the Todas of India, this name means "sweet."

Saki (SAH-kee) Japanese for "cape."

Sakti (SAHK-tee) The name literally means "energy." One of the major goddesses in Hindu belief, Sakti embodies both virginal innocence and bloodthirsty destruction. As the eternal virgin, she is sometimes represented as a young girl of about fifteen. The Sakti of illicit love, in contrast, is associated with incest and adultery. As a goddess of terror, she is worshipped by death cults, and it is said that the blood of the sacrifices before her image is never allowed to dry.

Sakuna (sah-KOO:-nah) Used today in India, this name means "bird."

Sakura (sah-KOO:-rah) Japanese for "cherry blossom." In Japan the cherry blossom is the national flower and the flower of March, and a symbol of wealth and prosperity. In China it is the flower of April and a symbol of a good education.

Sala (SAH-lah) Sometimes shortened to Sal. The sala is a sacred Hindu tree, one beam of which brings a home blessings and peace. The tree is said to contain a spirit who if worshipped, brings rainfall; and it is believed that Buddha died under the sala's branches.

Salama (sah-LAH-mah) Arabic name which means "peace" or "safety," with a connotation of being protected.

Salome (sah-LOH-me) Hebrew for "peaceful."

Samara (sah-MAH-rah) Hebrew for "a guardian."

Sameh (SAM-e[h]) Common among Muslim Arabs, this name means "forgiver," referring to one of the ninety-nine qualities of God listed in the Koran.. Strictly orthodox Muslims believe a name should come from the Koran or Muhammad's immediate family.

Sanura (sah-NOO:-rah) Swahili name for a child who reminds her parents of a kitten.

Sanuye (sah-NOO:-ye) Pretty Miwok Indian name which means "red cloud coming with sundown."

Sanya (SAHN-yah) East Indian name for a child born on Saturday, from the word for Saturday, *Sanivaram*.

Sapata (sah-PAH-tah) Miwok Indian name from the word *sapatu*, "to hug." The connotation is "bear dancing with forefeet around a tree." The same name has also implied "bear hugging tree."
Other Miwok bear names include Hausu ("bear yawning as it awakes," from *hausus*, "to yawn"); Kutcuyak ("bear with good hair," from *kutci*, "good"); Lipetu ("bear going over a man hiding between rocks," from *lile*, "up," in this case meaning "up over" or "on top of"); and Notaku ("growling of a bear as someone passes by," from *notcaku*, "to growl").

Sari (SHAW-ri) Hungarian form of the Biblical Sarah, which means "princess." Other variations used in Hungary are Sara, Sarolta, Sarika, and Sasa.

Saril (shuh-RIL) Turkish name referring to the sound of running water.

Sarolta (SHAW-rohl-tah) Hungarian form of the French Charlotte, "petite" or "feminine." Also used in Hungary as a form of Sarah.

144

Satinka (sah-TEEN-kah) North American Indian name meaning "magic dancer."

Saura (SOW-rah) A Hindu sect devoted to the exclusive worship of the sun. Hence, a name for a child born under the zodiacal sign Leo, which is ruled by the sun.

Sawa (SAH-wah) Japanese for "marsh." Also a Miwok Indian name meaning "rock" and implying "rock on the edge of a river." The Indians believed that many spirits dwelt within rocks, an idea perhaps suggested by the many tools made from rock or the fire sparked from flint.

Seda Armenian name meaning "echo through the woods."

Sedna (SED-nah) The Eskimo goddess of food, who lives in the sea. According to legend, if her taboos are violated, she causes a storm which keeps seals, polar bears, and whales from leaving their homes. These animals were created from sections of her fingers which her father cut off.

Seki (SE-kee) Japanese for "great." The name is unusual because of an old superstition that if a child is given too ambitious a name, she will never live up to it. Seki can also mean "barrier," in the sense of a city or toll gate, or "stone."

Selima (se-LEE-mah) Arabic for "peace."

Selina (seh-LEE-nuh) Greek for "sprig of parsley" or "the moon." In astrology the moon is the ruler of the sign Cancer, the Crab. The many variations of this name include Selene, Selena, Selinda, Celina, Celinda, Sela, Sena, Selia, Cela, Cena, and Celia.

Sema (SEE-muh) This astrological name originally comes from Greek and means "a sign from the heavens."

Sen (sen) Japanese for "wood fairy," referring to an ancient hermit believed to live in the mountains and possess magical powers. The hermit lives for thousands of years, and hence the name expresses a hope for longevity. The sen, or sennin, is usually pictured as a wrinkled old man with a flowing white beard, which is why the name is more common for boys than for girls.

Sesha (SEH-shah) The great Hindu serpent who symbolizes time, and on whose coils the Creator Vishnu rested before creation.

Setsu (SET-soo) Japanese for "fidelity," referring to wifely virtue. Another form is Setsuko, "faithful child."

Shada (SHAH-dah) North American Indian name with the unusual meaning "pelican."

Shahar (shah-HAHR) Contemporary Muslim name meaning "the moon." In astrology the moon governs the sign Cancer.

Shaina (SHAY-nah) Yiddish for "beautiful." The many variations include Shaine, Shayne, Shayna, Shane, and Shanie.

Shakeh Common Armenian name sometimes shortened to Kay by Armenians in the United States. Many Armenians, however, have retained their heritage names and have resisted such changes.

Shammara (SHAH-mah-rah) "He girded his loins." Feminine form of an Arabic name used by Muslims.

Shani (SHAH-nee) Pretty Swahili name which means "marvelous."

Shappa (SHAH-pah) North American Indian name meaning "red thunder." Given to a child born during a violent storm.

Sharai (shah-RIGH) "A princess." The original Hebrew name from which the English Sharon is derived. In Hebrew the word *sharon* is a place name meaning "a plain."

Sharma Gaining popularity in the United States, Sharma appears to be an American creation from Sharon plus Mary. A variation is Sharmin, Sharon plus the feminine suffix *mine*.

Shika (shee-KAH) Japanese for "deer," implying docility and gentleness rather than grace and beauty. Shikako, "deer child," is also occasionally used.

Shina (SHEE-nah) Japanese for "goods," in the sense of possessions. It can also mean "virtue."

Shino (SHEE-noh) Japanese for "slender bamboo," a symbol of fidelity.

Shiri (SHEE-ree) Hebrew for "my song." Other variations are Shira and Shirah, which simply mean "song."

Shizu (SHEE-zoo:) A favorite in Japan, this name means "quiet" or "clear." Modern variants are Shizuyo, Shizue, Shizuko, and Shizuka.

Shoushan (shoo:-SHAHN) Armenian development of Susan, a flower name which means "lily."

Shumana (SHOO:-mah-nah) Hopi Indian name meaning "rattlesnake girl." From the Rattlesnake Cult. Also spelled Chumana.

Shura (SHOO:-rah) Contemporary Russian name from the Greek for "helper and defender of mankind." See Alexandra.

Shuri (SHOO:-ree) English Gypsy name. The exact meaning could not be found.

Sibeta (see-BAY-tah) Miwok Indian name from the word *sipe*, "to pull out." The connotation is "pulling white sucker fish from under a flat rock." In astrology the Fishes are the symbol of Pisces.

Sidra An occult name for any sign of the zodiac, Sidra simply means "related to a constellation" or "related to the stars."

Sigrid Scandinavian for "beautiful victory."

Sihu (SEE-hoo:) This North American Indian name means "a flower" or "a bush."

Siko (SEE-koh) The Mashona of Southern Rhodesia give this name to a baby girl who cries a lot the first day.

Silivia (see-lee-VEE-uh) Hawaiian development of the Latin Silva, meaning "from the forest."

Simba (SEEM-bah) "Lion" in Swahili. The Hindustani version is Simha. Both can be used as astrological names for those born under Leo, the Lion.

Sisika (si-SEE-kah) North American Indian name for a swallow or thrush.

Sita (SEE-tah) Hindu name which means "furrow" and refers to a mother earth goddess and the wife of the god Rama. The name is also used by the Zuni Indians, who adapted it from the Spanish Zita, "rose."

Sitala (see-TAH-lah) Miwok Indian name. The connotation is "valley quail running uphill."
Other Miwok quail names include Kukse, "valley quail starting to fly from the ground," from *kukse,* "to be frightened"; Moitoiye, "valley quail's topknot bobbing as the bird walks"; and Petno, "valley quail crouching in the brush as a hawk passes."

Siti (SEE-tee) Swahili for "lady."

Situla (si-TOO-luh) From the Latin for "well bucket." This is another name for the constellation and zodiacal sign Aquarius, the Water Bearer.

Sofi Contemporary Greek name meaning "wisdom." Other popular forms are Sofia, and to a lesser extent, Sophron and Sophia. The Spanish development of the name is Sofia, and the Turkish, Sofya.

Solana (soh-LAH-nah) Spanish for "sunshine."

Soma (SOH-mah) From the Hindustani for "moon," this name is given to a child born on Somavara, "Monday," in the solar month Karka, under the sign Cancer, which is ruled by the moon.

Sonel (soh-NAYL) Hebrew flower name which means "lily." The English equivalent is Susan.

Sonya (SOHN-yah) Popular in Scandinavia and Russia, Sonya comes from the Greek for "wisdom." A Scandinavian variation is Sonja, while Russian forms include Sofia, Sofiya, Sonechka, Sonyura, and Sonyusha.

Sora (SOH-rah) Used by North American Indians, this name means "a warbling song bird."

Soso (SOH-soh) Miwok Indian name implying "tree squirrel biting a tiny hole in a pine nut."

Spica (SPIGH-kah) Astrological name taken from the brightest star in the constellation Virgo, the Virgin. Spica is 190 light years from earth, and 5 times larger and 1,000 times brighter than the sun.

Stacy Modern American name created from either Anastassia, "of the Resurrection," or Eustacia, "peaceful" or "fruitful." A variant spelling is Stacey.

Stellara (stel-LAH-ruh) This astrological name, meaning "starry" or "child of the stars," can be used for a girl born under any sign of the zodiac.

Stesha (STEH-shah) Russian diminutive of Stephania, "crowned one."

Stina German nickname for Christel, "Christian."

Suela (soo:-EH-lah) Pet form of Consuela, "consolation," used in Spanish-speaking countries. Other variations include Suelita and Chela.

Sugi (SOO:-gee) Japanese nature name which means "cedar." A giant sugi or group of such trees is often associated with a Shinto shrine, and hence the tree has become almost symbolic of the shaded mystery of such sanctuaries. In Japan the cedar is also an emblem of moral rectitude.

Suke (SOO:-ke) Hawaiian development of Susan, "lily." Also spelled Suse.

Suki (SOO:-kee) Japanese for "beloved." Also a Miwok Indian name which means "chicken hawk with a long tail." See Liluye for other Miwok chicken hawk names.

Sula (SOO:-luh) Icelandic name for the gannet, a large sea bird. Also occasionally used in other countries as a nickname for Ursula or Ursola, "little she-bear." See Ursola.

Suletu (soo:-LEH-too) Miwok Indian name from the word *sulete*, "to fly around." The connotation is "California jay flying out of a tree." The jay occasionally appears in Indian creation legends as a mischief-maker who was doomed to eventually become a lesser creature on earth. In most myths the poor jay's tragic flaw is false pride.

Sumi (SOO:-mee) Japanese for "the clear" or "the refined."

Suni (SOO:-nee) The Zuni Indian word for "Zuni."

Sunki (SHOO:N-kee) Hopi Indian name which means "overtake," possibly referring to a proud feat in the father's life: the chasing and overtaking of wild game or an enemy. Used by the Horn Cult.

Surata (soo:-RAH-tah) Hindustani for "blessed joy," referring to a mystical experience achieved through sex.

Suri (SOO:-ree) "Knife." A nickname from the Todas of India for a girl or boy with a sharp nose. Once a name or nickname is used among the Todas, it cannot be bestowed again for four generations, and if by chance two people have the same name, one of them picks another.

Surya (SOO:R-yah) Hindu astrological name for a child born under Leo, which is ruled by the sun. In Hindu mythology Surya, the sun god, is pictured with a dwarfish, burnished-copper body and red eyes.

Susana (soo:-SAH-nah) Spanish for "lily" or "graceful lily." The English equivalent is Susan. Other variants are the Hungarian nickname Zsa Zsa and the Italian Suzetta.

Sutki (SHOO:T-kee) Hopi Indian name from the Cloud

Cult, meaning "a broken coil of potter's clay." This is probably either an event name or an object name, the object being the first thing the father saw after the child was born.

Suzamni (soo-ZAHM-nee) Carrier Indian name of French origin. Suzamni is a combination of Susan, "lily," plus Annie, "graceful."

Suzu (SOO:-zoo) A favorite in Japan. The name means "little bell" and refers to the suzu, a tiny metal bell often placed in a silk charm bag and attached to a child's girdle so that whenever she moves, a pretty tinkling is heard. Originally it was thought the sound would frighten demons; more recently it was believed the amulet would keep the child from falling. Other variants used today are Suzue, "branch of little bells," Suzuki, "bell tree," and Suzuko, "bell child."

Svetla (SVYET-lah) Common Czech name which means "light."

Syeira (SYIGH-ruh) A favorite among English Gypsies. The gypsy custom of borrowing names from other cultures and then significantly changing them creates problems in determining meaning. Syeira, however, may be a development of Sarah, "princess."

Tabia (tah-BEE-ah) Swahili for "talents."

Taci (TAH-shee) Zuni Indian name with the odd meaning "washtub," perhaps bestowed because it was the first object the father saw after the child was born.

Tadita (tah-DEE-tah) Omaha Indian name from the word *tothito,* referring to the running of pipe bearers in a Hedewachi ceremony. Tadita has been translated as "to the wind!" and more loosely as "a runner." A variant spelling is Tadeta.

Taima (tah-EE-mah) Used by some North American Indian tribes, this name means "crash of thunder." Given to a girl or boy born during a thunderstorm.

Taipa (tah-EE-pah) Miwok Indian name which literally

means "to spread wings." The more elaborate connotation is "valley quail spreading its wings as it
alights."

Taka (TAH-kah) Japanese name which has three widely
varying meanings: "tall," "honorable," or "a falcon."
Takako is also used. See Kazu.

Takala (TAH-kah-lah) Hopi Indian name meaning "corn
tassel." From the Cloud Cult.

Takara (tah-KAH-rah) Japanese for "treasure" or "precious object."

Takeko (TAH-keh-koh) Japanese for "bamboo," a symbol of fidelity.

Takenya (tah-KEHN-yah) Miwok Indian name. The connotation is "falcon swooping and knocking down its
prey with its wings."
Other Miwok falcon names include Hokoiya
("falcon hiding extra food"); Selibu ("falcon flying
along the edge of a bluff"); Selipu ("falcon darting
on an angle in the air"); and Wininu ("falcon circling
as it flies through the air").

Taki (TAH-kee) Japanese name referring to a plunging
waterfall.

Takuhi (tak-koo:-HEE) Armenian for "queen." Also
spelled Takoohi.

Tala (TAH-lah) Used by North American Indians, this
name means "wolf" and implies intelligence and good
luck.

Talasi (TAH-lah-shee) Hopi Indian name meaning "corn
tassel flower." From the Cloud Cult.

Talia (tah-LEE-uh) Hebrew for "heaven's dew." Another
spelling is Talya. The shortened Tal simply means
"dew," while Talor and Talora mean "dew of the
morning."

Talula (tah-LOO-lah) Choctaw Indian name which means
"leaping water." The *u* is pronounced like the *oo*

in *foot* rather than *moon*. The name has been Anglicized to Tallulah.

Tama (TAH-mah) North American Indian name meaning "thunderbolt." Also used in Japan, where it means "jewel."

Tamaki (TAH-mah-kee) Japanese for "armlet" or "bracelet." A popular variant is Tamako.

Tamar (tah-MAHR) Israeli name from the Hebrew for "a palm tree," implying grace and uprightness. Variants are Tamara and Tamarah, which may also be derived from an East Indian word for "spice." Tamara is used in several other countries, including Russia, the Ukraine, Czechoslovakia, Latvia, the United States, and Spanish-speaking countries.

Tami (TAH-mee) Japanese for "people." A popular variant is Tamiko.

Tammi Finnish nature name meaning "oak."

Tanaka (tah-NAH-kah) Japanese for dweller in (or near) a rice swamp." Usually used in Japan as a surname, though occasionally as a girl's name.

Tani (TAH-nee) Japanese for "valley."

Tansy Flower name used by the Hopi Indians of the Tansy-mustard Clan.

Tanya (TAHN-yah) "A fairy queen." A favorite Russian diminutive. Other forms are Tania and Tanechka.

Tao (taw) Chinese name which means "peach," one of the three sacred Buddhist fruits and a symbol of longevity and immortality. A similar name is Tao Hua, "peach blossom." The peach is called the tree of the fairy fruit because of the peach tree of the gods which grew in the mythical gardens of the Royal Lady of the West. The tree bloomed only once in three thousand years, and exactly three thousand years later yielded the Fruits of Immortality. It is said these peaches were eaten by the Eight Taoist Immortals.

153

Tara (TAH-rah) A Buddhist savior goddess.

Tarana (tah-RAH-nah) African Hausa name for a girl born during the day. Derived from the word *rana,* "day."

Tasarla (tah-SAHR-luh) English Gypsy name which, strangely enough, may mean either "morning" or "evening."

Tasida (tah-SEE-dah) Sarcee Indian name meaning "a rider." Its literal translation is "on-top-(of a horse)-he-sits." Also often used as a boy's name.

Tassos (TAH-sohs) Modern Greek name which means "reaper." The English equivalent is Theresa.

Tasya (TAHS-yah) A diminutive used primarily in Russia, occasionally in Spain. See Anastassia.

Taura (TAW-ruh) Astrological name for a girl born under Taurus, the Bull.

Tawia (tah-WEE-ah) African Fanti or Ashanti name for a child of either sex born after twins. Also a Polish nickname for Oktawia, "eighth," which in English becomes Octavia.

Tawnie (TAW-nee) English name meaning "little one." The masculine form is Tawno.

Tazu (TAH-zoo) Japanese for "rice-field stork," a symbol of longevity. Children in Japan are occasionally named after an animal, fish, or bird in the hope that the child will develop a particularly admirable quality possessed by the animal.
Other such totemic names include Chidori, "sanderling"; Kuma, "bear"; Taka, "hawk"; Tatsu, "dragon"; and Washi, "eagle."

Temima (teh-MEE-muh) Hebrew for "whole" or "honest."

Temira (teh-MEE-ruh) Hebrew name meaning "tall," expressing the hope that the child will grow tall. Also spelled Timora.

Tereza (teh-REH-zhuh) A great favorite in Brazil, Tereza is derived from Greek and means "reaper." The Spanish form is Teresa.

Teri (TE-ree) Contemporary Hungarian name from the Greek for "reaper." Pet forms in Hungary include Treszka, Terez, Terike, Teca, Rezi, and Riza.

Tesia (TE-shuh) Polish name from the Greek for "loved by God." Other Polish forms are Teofila and Fila. Tesia is also used in Poland as a pet form of Hortenspa, from the Latin for "gardener."

Tetsu (TET-suh) Japanese for "iron." This odd name for a baby stems from an ancient Oriental belief that demons and evil spirits were born during the Stone Age and therefore dread the influence of metals. Iron has always been considered especially potent and magical. Among the Kachins of Upper Burma, iron knives are brandished over a mother and her newborn baby, and old rags are burned in the hopes that the stench will drive demons away. In another part of Burma, on the Irrawaddy River, iron pyrites are believed to frighten alligators.

Thema (TAY-mah) Used in Ghana, this Akan name means "queen."

Thordis (THOHR-des) A favorite in Norway, Thordis means "dedicated to Thor," the Norse god of thunder. The popular Icelandic form is Thora. Another Scandinavian variant is Tora.

Tilda Estonian name from the Old German for "battle maiden." Other variations are Tilli, Tille, and Hilda. The English equivalent is Matilda.

Tima (TEE-muh) Found in several recent American birth columns, this name is possibly a creation from Tina or a feminine form of Timothy.

Timmi Originally a nickname for Timothea, "honoring God," Timmi is gaining use in the United States as an independent name.. Also spelled Timi.

Tina A nickname for many names throughout the world,

including the Russian Valentina, the Polish Khristina, the Greek Kostantina, and the American Christina.

Tiponya (ti-POHN-yah) Miwok Indian name which means "great horned owl sticking her head under her body and poking an egg that is hatching," from the word *tipe,* "to poke." The owl appears frequently in Indian lore. According to a Kiowa legend, when the medicine man dies he becomes an owl, and when the owl dies he turns into a cricket. The Eastern Cherokees believe the cry of the screech owl means illness or death, and the Penobscot Indians say if a man mocks a screech owl, the bird will burn him up. The Pawnees, on the other hand, believe the owl protects man from night evils.

Tirtha (TEER-tuh) Hindustani for "ford." Also used as a name element.

Tirza (TEER-zah) Hebrew name meaning "cypress tree" or "desirable."

Tisa (TEE-sah) Swahili for "ninth-born."

Tivona (tee-VOH-nuh) "Lover of nature." Used today in Israel.

Tiwa (TEE-wuh) Zuni Indian name which means "onions" and was probably bestowed because the first object the father saw after the child was born was an onion.

Tobit (toh-BEET) Used today in Israel for both girls and boys, Tobit means "good." Variants are Tova and Tovah.

Tokiwa (toh-KEE-wah) Japanese for "eternally constant," implying constancy as everlasting as the rocks.

Tolikna (toh-LEEK-nah) Miwok Indian name. The connotation is "coyote's long ears flapping." In many Indian legends the coyote created the world (see Kaliska). Another story says the adventurous beast once went to the edge of the world and sat on the hole where the sun comes up; then he rode the sun across the sky.

Other Miwok coyote names include Notcitcto ("coyote snarling over a piece of meat lying under his feet"); Wootci ("coyote barking"); Woto ("coyote sitting on a rock, barking, and moving his tail"); and Yutu ("coyote pretending not to notice a bird so he can seize it").

Tomo (TOH-moh) Japanese for "knowledge" or "intelligence."

Tonya (TOHN-yah) Russian pet form of Antonina, "inestimable" or "priceless." Another popular form in Russia is Tosya.

Tora (TOH-rah) Japanese for "tiger." See Tazu for other Japanese animal names.

Tori (TOH-ree) Japanese for "bird." The name is given in the hopes that the child will develop some admirable quality possessed by the bird, perhaps gentleness or physical grace.

Toshi (TOH-shee) Japanese for "year." A common variant is Toshiko, "year child."

Tosia (TOH-shuh) Polish nickname for Antonina, meaning "inestimable" or "priceless." Other forms used in Poland are Anta, Nina, and Tola.

Toski (TOHSH-kee) Hopi Indian name meaning "a squashbug." Used by the Cloud Cult.

Tosya (TOHS-yah) Russian nickname. See Tonya.

Totsi (TOHT-shee) Hopi Indian name meaning "moccasins." Used by the Horn Cult.

Trava (TRAH-vah) Czech name which means "grass," implying the freshness of spring.

Trella (TREH-yuh) Spanish for "little star." Trella is actually a shortened form of Estrella, "star," and both names are used today in Spain and Latin and South America.

157

Tresa German name from the Greek for "reaper." Other German forms are Therese, Theresia, Trescha, Resel, and Resi. See Tereza and Teri for variations used in other countries.

Trina (TREE-nah) Hindustani name which means "piercing," referring to the sacred kusa grass, with its needle-sharp points. See Kusa for further information.

Trinette French for "pure." See Katina.

Trisha (TREE-shah) "Thirst," one of the 350 Hindu classifications of love. In the United States the same name is a diminutive of Patricia.

Truda Polish name from the Old German for "battle maiden" or "spear strength." Variations used in Poland are Trudka, Giertruda, Gerta, and Gertrukda.

Tula (TOO:-lah) Hindu astrological name for a child born under Libra, which is symbolized by the Balance.

Tulann (too:-LAHN) Miwok Indian name. The connotation is "several bears fighting over food."

Tulsi (TOO:L-see) A favorite among the Hindus of Madras, used for both girls and boys. The name comes from the sacred tulasi plant, or Indian basil, which is believed to resemble the hair of the goddess Vrinda. Her spirit enters the plant each night, and thus it is forbidden at that time to pick the tulasi leaves. See Vrinda.

Tusa (TOO:-suh) Zuni Indian name which means "prairie dog."

Tuwa (TOO:-wah) Hopi Indian name which means "earth."

Tyna (TEE-nah) A nickname for many Czech names, including Kristyna, "Christian," and Celestyna, "heavenly."

Ulani (oo:-LAH-nee) Hawaiian for "cheerful."

Ulina From the ulina flower.

Uma (OO:-mah) Hindustani for "mother." One of the more than one thousand names for the goddess Sakti. See Sakti for more information.

Umeko (oo-ME-koh) Japanese for "plum blossom child." Another form is Ume, "plum blossom." In Japan the plum blossom is a symbol of patience and perseverance, and the emblem of the samurai, or military, class.

Una (OO:-nah) Hopi Indian name meaning "remember." The coyote is implied in the name because he is said to remember food he has buried.

Upala (oo:-PAH-lah) Used in India, this name refers to the opal, believed by the ancients to be a magical stone because it seemed to contain "all the colors of the heavens."

Urania (yoo:-RAY-nee-uh) The Greek Muse of Astronomy. The name means "heavenly" and is used today for a girl born under the zodiacal sign Aquarius, which is ruled by Uranus.

Urit (oo:-REET) Hebrew for "light." A common variation is Urice.

Ursola (OO:R-soh-luh) or oo:r-SOH-luh) "Little she-bear." The name is used in Bulgaria, Slovakia, Slovenia, Russia, Germany, Estonia, and Spanish-speaking countries. A variant spelling is Ursula. Popular pet forms include Ulla and Ursel, German; Sula, Urmi, and Ulli, Estonian; and Ursulina, Spanish.

Ushi (oo:-SHEE) In ancient Chinese astrology not only the months but also the hours, days, and years are named after signs of the zodiac. The name Ushi, "the ox," may be given to a child born in the hour of the ox, on the day of the ox, in the month of the ox, and in the year of the ox, which is 1973.

Utina (oo:-TEE-nah) Used by North American Indians, this name means "(woman of) my country."

Valda Scandinavian name from the Old Norse for "ruler" or "governor."

Valeska Feminine Polish form of Vladislav, from the Russian for "glorious ruler."

Valli (VAH-lee) Hindu name which comes from a plant native to India. In Estonia the same name is a pet form of Valentina, "strong and healthy."

Valma Modern Finnish name meaning "unwavering protector." See Vilma.

Vamana (van-MAH-nah) Hindu name also used for boys. Vamana was a dwarf who overcame the demon king Bali. He is believed to be an incarnation of the Hindu god Vishnu.

Vanda (VAHN-dah) Used in many Slavic countries, including Czechoslovakia, the Ukraine, and Poland, Vanda comes from the Old German for "wanderer." The name is also common in Lithuania, where two other forms are Vandute and Vandele. The English equivalent is Wanda.

Vanya (VAHN-yah) Russian name from the Hebrew for "gracious gift of God." A common variant is Vania. The English equivalent is Jane.

Varaza (vah-RAH-zah) Used in India, this name means "boar."

Vardis (vahr-DEES) Hebrew flower name which means "rose." Other common variants in Israel include Varda, Vardice, Vardit, Vardia, and Vardina.

Varuna (vah-ROO:-nuh) A Hindu god of the sea and the guardian of the western quarter of the compass.

Varvara (VAHR-vah-rah) Russian name from the Latin for "stranger." Favorite pet forms are Varya, Varenka, and Varyusha. A Slovak form is Varina, and the English equivalent is Barbara.

Vatusia (vah-TOO:see-ah) African Ovimbundu proverb name from the saying *Va tu sia,* "They leave us be-

160

hind." In other words, the dead are gone and we are left to mourn. This is a name a woman gives herself because of the anguish she has suffered.

Veda "Sacred understanding." Veda refers to the sacred Hindu writings which are believed to be uncreated and eternal. As a child's name, it may be loosely translated as "learned one."

Vedis Scandinavian name meaning "forest nymph," referring to the mythical Scandinavian sylvan spirit.

Vegenia (ve-ge-NEE-uh) Hawaiian name from the Latin for "maidenly." The English equivalent is Virginia.

Vera A favorite in Russia, Vera means "faithful." Pet forms are Verinka and Verochka. The name is also used today in the United States, Czechoslovakia, Latvia, Serbia, and Spanish-speaking countries.

Veronika (VAI-roh-nee-kah) Czech name from the Greek for "forerunner of victory." The English equivalent is Veronica.

Vida (VEE-dah) "Beloved." A feminine form of the Hebrew Dawid or David.

Vidonia (vee-DOH-nee-uh) Popular Portuguese nature name meaning "vine branch."

Viki (VEE-kee) Serbo-Croatian name meaning "victory." Other variations are Vika and Viktorija. In English the name is Victoria.

Vilma (VIL-mah) Used today in Russia, Czechoslovakia, and Sweden, Vilma is derived from the German Wilhelmina, "unwavering protector." The Finnish form is Valma, and the English, Wilma.

Vina (VEE-nah) A stringed musical instrument carried by the Hindu goddess of wisdom, science, and speech.

Virida (be-REE-dah) Spanish name meaning "green," connoting the freshness of spring. Color names have been used throughout the world as charms against evil spirits (see Akako). Virida, however, probably has no magical meaning.

Visolela (vee-soh-LAY-lah) African Ovimbundu name from the proverb "Longings are of waterfalls, but these you pick over are of the drying trays." Loosely translated, the saying means it is easy to use your judgment about the ordinary things of life, such as maize to be sorted in drying trays, but there are also desires of the heart which are as uncontrollable as waterfalls.

Viviana (vee-vee-AH-nuh) Hawaiian development of Vivian, from the Latin for "alive."

Vondila (vohn-DEE-lah) African Ovimbundu name a woman gives herself after she has lost a child. Vondila comes from the proverb *Va undila ohumba longalo; ocipala kundila,* "They borrow a basket and sieve; a face you do not borrow." More loosely translated, the name means there may be other children, but never with that same face.

Vrinda (VRIN-dah) A woman in Hindu mythology whose great virtue gave her husband divine power so he could not be controlled by the god Siva. She was seduced by the god Vishnu in the form of her husband, who then could be easily killed by Siva. Vrinda in turn, threw herself into the flames of her husband's funeral pyre, and Vishnu changed her body into the Gandaki River and her hair into the tulasi plant. See Tulsi.

Wakana (wah-kah-nah) Japanese name referring to the rape plant.

Wakanda (wah-KAHN-dah) Sioux Indian name meaning "inner magical power." See Orenda for a fuller explanation.

Wakenda (wah-KAYN-dah) Used by North American Indians, this name means "worshipped."

Waneta (wah-NAY-tah) North American Indian name meaning "the charger." The Anglo-Saxon Wannetta, "little pale one," has often been shortened to this form.

Warri (WAH-ree) Used by the first Afro-Americans taken from the Jekri tribe of Southern Nigeria. In America the name was often changed to Warrah and seems to have almost completely disappeared in a few generations.

Wauna (wah-OO:-nah) Miwok Indian name from the word *woani*, "to bark," and *wou*, "to crow" or "to whine." The implied meaning is "snow geese calling as they fly."

Wenona (weh-NOH-nah) North American Indian name which means "first-born daughter."

Wichasta (wi-CHAH-stah) Generally used for boys, this North American Indian name means "strong" or "manly."

Wilima (wee-LEE-muh) Hawaiian development of Wilma or Wilhelmina, from the Old German for "unwavering protector."

Willow Nature name meaning "freedom." In Rumania, among the Gypsies of Transylvania, the willow was believed to have the power to grant mothers easy delivery and to give the sick and old renewed vitality.

Winda (WEEN-dah) Swahili for "hunt."

Winema (we-NEH-mah) Miwok Indian name meaning "woman chief."

Wisia (VEE-shuh) Polish name meaning "victory." Other Polish variants are Wicia, Wikitoria, Wiktorja, and Wikta. The English equivalent is Victoria.

Wyanet (wee-AH-net) North American Indian name meaning "beautiful."

Xena (ZAY-nah) Contemporary Greek name meaning "hospitable." Another form is Polyxena. The English and Slovakian equivalent is Xenia.

Yachi (YAH-chee) Japanese for "eight thousand." Round numbers were once considered a good luck charm, and although the superstition has virtually vanished, many number names remain. A common variation is Yachiyo.

Yachne (YAHK[H]-ne) A favorite among Lithuanian and Polish Jews, this name comes from the Hebrew for "gracious."

Yaluta (yah-LOO:-tah) Miwok Indian name. The implied meaning is "women out on the flat telling each other there is a lot of farewell-to-spring seed." See Muliya for other Miwok farewell-to-spring names.

Yamka (YAHM-kah) Hopi Indian name which means "flower budding." Another Hopi name is Siyamka, "rabbit-brush flower budding."

Yamuna (yah-MOO:-nah) Another name for the Jumna, one of the seven sacred Hindu rivers of India. See Kalinda and Kalindi.

Yanaba (yah-NAH-bah) Navaho Indian name meaning "she meets the enemy." Like most Navaho girls' names, Yanaba refers to an event of war.

Yarkona (yahr-KOH-nuh) Hebrew name which literally means "green." The name may also come from the yarkona bird, with its greenish-gold feathers, found in the southern part of Israel.

Yarmilla (YAHR-mel-luh) Slovak for "trader in the marketplace," from the word *yarmarka,* "marketplace."

Yasmeen (YAS-meen) Popular Arabic nature name which comes from the jasmine flower. Common forms in India are Jasmine, Yasmine, and Yasiman.

Yasu (YAH-soo:) Japanese for "the peaceful" or "the tranquil." Also used in Yasuko.

Yelena (ye-LAY-nah) Russian form of either the Greek Helene "light," or the Latin for "lily flower." Pet forms are Lenusya and Liolya.

Yemina (ye-MEE-nuh) Hebrew for "right hand," connoting strength.

164

Yendelela (Yayn-de-LAY-lah) African name from the Ovimbundu proverb *Ya endelela ka lelalela pekonjo,* "It keeps going, does not stay fat on the hoof." The saying means that while a man may be respected among friends, he can still be an outcast among strangers.

Other Ovimbundu proverb names include Capopia, "I do not dispute God"; Citalala, "greenness is always in the forest, and goodness always somewhere in people"; and Cinosole, "the thing you like you do not eat with a stick but with your fingers," in other words, formality can get in the way of the true joys of life.

Yenene (yeh-NAY-neh) Miwok Indian name. The elaborate connotation is "wizard pressing his fingers on a sleeping person to " 'poison' him."

Yepa (YAY-pah) Used by North American Indians, this name means "the snow maiden."

Yeva (YEH-vah) Russian development of the Hebrew *chavva,* "life-giving." A common variant is Eva.

Yevetha (yuh-VAY-tuh) "Outcast." Used by the Sema Nagas of India for a lower-caste girl or boy. Such names are bestowed because an old superstition says that if a child of poor parents receives an ambitious name, such as "challenger" or "victor," she will die.

Yoki (YOH-kee) North American Indian name meaning "bluebird on the mesa."

Yoko (YOH-koh) Japanese name which means "positive child" or "female." The latter implies the dualism of the Oriental concept of the universe. The female principle Yo, allegedly existed in the beginning with the male principle, In. Yo and In lay dormant in the chaotic egg until it eventually split into heaven and earth.

Yolanda "Violet," the flower of the zodiacal sign Aquarius. Interestingly, in numerology the name Violet was a destiny number of eleven, while Aquarius is the eleventh sign of the zodiac. Aquarius, in turn, is ruled by the planet Uranus, which also corresponds to the master number eleven. A diminutive of Violet is Vietta.

Yoluta (yoh-LOO:-tah) North American Indian name for the farewell-to-spring flower." See Muliya for other Indian farewell-to-spring names.

Yonina (yoh-NEE-nuh) Hebrew for "dove." Variants include Yona, Yonit, Yonita, Jona, Jonina, and Jonati. Yona is often used as a boy's name.

Yori (YOH-ree) Japanese for "the trustworthy."

Yoshi (YOH-shee) Japanese for "the good" or "the respectful." A favorite variation is Yoshiko, "good child" or "respectful child." Also a boy's name.

Yoshino (yoh-shee-noh) Japanese for "good field" or "fertile field." The suffix -no, meaning "field," is attached to a number of Japanese names. Other examples include Kikuno, "chrysanthemum field"; Kurano, "storehouse field"; Orino, "weaving field"; Umeno, "plum-tree field"; and Urano, "shore field."

Yow (yoh) Chinese for the feminine right, as opposed to the masculine left. In Oriental and Hindu philosophies elaborate masculine-feminine systems have been worked out. For example, in the Hindu world the the soul and the consonants are masculine, the body and the vowels are feminine.

Yuki (YOO:-kee) Japanese for "snow." Variations are Yukie and Yukiko. The name can also mean "lucky."

Yuri (YOO:-ree) "Lily." Japanese flower name.

Yovela (yoh-VAY-luh) Hebrew for "rejoicing."

Yvette Modern American development of the Old French Yvonne, meaning "yew bow." The Scandinavian form of Yvette is Yvonne.

Zada (ZA-dah) Syrian name meaning "lucky one."

Zahara (ZAH-rah) Swahili for "flower."

Zaleya From the zaleya flower.

Zaltana (zahl-TAH-nuh) Used by North American Indians, this name means "high mountain."

Zanete (ZAH-ne-te) Contemporary Latvian form of Janina or Zanna, from the Hebrew for "gracious gift of God." The English equivalent is Jeanette.

Zarifa (zah-REE-fah) Pretty Arabic name meaning "graceful."

Zayit (zigh-EET) Hebrew for "olive." Also used in Israel as a boy's name. Variations include Zeta and Zetana.

Zea (ZAY-uh) Derived from Latin, Zea refers to a kind of grain. This harvest name is appropriate for girls born under the earth signs of the zodiac: Capricorn, Taurus, and Virgo.

Zel Persian for "a cymbal" or Turkish for "a bell."

Zelenka (ZE-layn-kah) Czechoslovakian name meaning "little green one," implying the child is innocent and fresh.

Zera (ZAY-rah) From the Hebrew *zera'im*, meaning "seeds."

Zerdali (zair-dah-LI) Turkish name with the unusual meaning "wild apricot."

Zigana (ZEE-gaw-nah) Hungarian for "gypsy girl."

Zihna (ZHEE-nah) An abbreviation of Ziyanta, "spinning," this Hopi Indian name is given to a child fond of whipping tops.

Zil (zil) A variant of the Turkish Zel, "a bell."

Zina (ZEE-nah) From the African Nsenga word for "name," Zina refers to a child's secret spirit name, known only to her family.

Zita (SEE-tah) Modern Spanish name meaning "little rose." A favorite pet form is Rosita.

Zizi (ZEE-zee) Hungarian development of the Hebrew

for "dedicated to God." Other variations used in Hungary are Erzsbet, Erzsi, Erssike, Erzsok, Boske, Boski, Bozsi, Beti, Liza, Liszka, and Zsoka. The English equivalent is Elizabeth.

Zizia From the zizia flower.

Zofia (SAW-fyuh) Slovak variant of the Greek Sofi. Other forms used in Slovakia are Zofie, Sofia, Zofka, and Zofinka. See Sofi.

Zoheret (zoh-HAIR-et) Hebrew for "she shines."

Zohra Muslim name meaning "the blooming." Also a name for the planet Venus, which governs the zodiacal sign Taurus, the Bull.

Zora (SAW-ruh) Slovak for "aurora" or "dawn."

Zorina (SAW-re-nuh) Slovak for "golden." Another variation used today is Zorana.

Zuri (ZOO:-ree) Swahili for "beautiful."

Zuza (ZOO:zah) Czech name meaning "lily" or "graceful lily." The English equivalent is Susan.

Zytka (ZET-kuh) This Polish nickname is used for many girls' names ending in -*ita,* including Rosita, Brigita, and Margarita. A shortened form is Zyta.

Part III

Boys' Names

Abasi (ah-BAH-see) Swahili name meaning "stern." In India the equivalent is Abbas, "stern of countenance," referring to one of the ninety-nine attributes of God listed in the Koran. Both forms are popular among Muslims.

Abdel (AHB-duhl or ahb-DOOL) Common Arabic name meaning "servant of." A favorite among Muslims, Abdel is used as an element in many names. Examples are Abdullah, "servant of God," Abdul Karim, "servant of the generous One," and Abdel Nasser, "servant of the victorious One."

Abi Turkish for "elder brother." Occasionally given to a first child when the parents plan to have other children.

Abran (ah-BRAHN) Popular Spanish development of the Hebrew Abraham, "father of a mighty nation" or "father of the multitude." Another Hebrew form is Abram, "exalted father."

171

Abrasax A magic name used in incantations to invoke spirits and their powers. The use of names in magic spells comes from a belief that knowing someone's name gives you power over him.

Acar (uh-KUHR) Turkish name meaning "bright."

Acayib (uh-jah-YIB) Turkish for "wonderful and strange."

Adal German name meaning "noble."

Adan (ah-DAHN) Spanish development of Adam, "earth" or "man of the red earth." Among the Yorubans, the name Adan (a-DAN) refers to a large bat and comes from the proverb "If you do not have a large bat, you sacrifice a small one." In other words, you simply do your best.

Adar (ah-DAHR) Syrian name meaning "ruler" or "prince," derived from the twelfth month of the Babylonian calendar. In Hebrew the name means "fire" and comes from the sixth month of the Jewish calendar.

Adeben (ah-deh-BEHN) Used by the Akan of Ghana, this name means "twelfth-born son."

Adel German name meaning "noble." Adel is used as an element in many names, including Adelar, "noble eagle," Adelard, "nobly resolute," Adelbern, "noble bear," and Adelhart, "nobly firm."

Adem (ah-DEM) Turkish development of Adam, "earth" or "man of the red earth."

Adigun (ah-dee-GOO:N) This name is used by the Yoruba-speaking people of Nigeria and means "righteous."

Adir (ah-DEER) Hebrew for "majestic" or "noble."

Adiv (ah-DEEV) Hebrew for "pleasant" or "gentle."

Adli (uhd-LEE) Turkish for "just."

Admon (ahd-MOHN) Israeli flower name for a red peony which grows in the upper Galilee.

172

Adni (AHD-nee) Occult name for the Pentagrams of Earth, which are used to invoke or banish spirits.

Adom (ah-DOHM) "Help from God." Akan name used in Ghana.

Adon (ah-DOHN) "Lord." Hebrew name which is also word for God.

Adri Modern Hindu name meaning "rock." Adri was a minor god in Hindu mythology who protected mankind and once rescued the sun from evil spirits who were trying to extinguish it.

Adrian "Dark one." Used today in the United States and in Spanish-speaking countries, where the name is pronounced ah-dree-AHN. A Spanish variation is Adriano.

Agler (AHG-lair) Modern Greek name which means "gleaming."

Agni (AHG-nee) The ancient Hindu god of fire. Agni is depicted with three heads, either four or seven arms, and seven tongues, each named, for lapping up the butter offered during sacrifices. He often has a ram at his side and rides in a glorious chariot driven by a red-limbed, golden-haired charioteer. The chariot's wheels are the seven winds.

Agu (ah-GOO:) Nigerian Ibo nature name meaning "leopard."

Agustin (ah-goo:-STEEN) Spanish for "belonging to Augustus, the exalted one." The modern American equivalent is Austin.

Ahanu (ah-HAH-noo:) North American Indian name meaning "he laughs."

Aharon (ah-hah-ROHN) Hebrew form of Aaron, "exalted" or "lofty."

Ahdik (AH-dik) Used by North American Indians, this name means "caribou" or "reindeer."

Ahil (AH-heel) Bulgarian name from the Greek for "he has no lips." Given to a thin-lipped child.

Ahir (uh-HEER) Turkish name meaning "end" or "last." For the last child a mother intends to have.

Ahmad (AH-mahd) A favorite Arabic name meaning "the most praised." Ahmad was occasionally used by Muhammad and is one of the more than five hundred names for the Prophet. An old saying holds that angels pray in every house where an Ahmad or Muhammad live. A variant is Ahmed.

Ahmed (AH-met- or AH-med) Muslim name. See Ahmad.

Ahmik (AH-mik) North American Indian name meaning "the beaver," a symbol of skill.

Ahren From the Old German for "eagle." In astrology the eagle is one of the symbols of Scorpio. Other eagle names for boys born under that sign are Adler and Aleron.

Ajani (a-ja-NEE) Yoruban nickname for "one who takes possession after a struggle."

Akando (ah-KAHN-doh) "Ambush." North American Indian name which possibly comes from the tradition of naming a child after a great feat performed by his father.

Akar (uh-KUHR) Turkish for "flowing" or "running," referring to water.

Akil (ah-KEEL) This common Arabic name means "intelligent" or "thoughtful."

Akim (ah-KEEM)Russian diminutive of the Hebrew Jehoiakim, "God will establish."

Akin (a-KEEN) A common Yoruban word suggesting talent or strength and used as a name meaning "hero" or "strong man." A favorite variation is Akins, "brave boy."

Akio (AH-kee-oh) Japanese for "bright boy." A variation is Akira.

Akon (ah-KOHN) "Ninth-born son." Used by the Ochi- and Ga-speaking people of Africa. Also spelled Akron.

Akoni (ah-KOH-nee) Hawaiian development of the Latin for "inestimable" or "priceless." The English equivalent is Anthony.

Akule (ah-KOO:-le) "He looks up." North American Indian name which possibly indicates one of the first things the child did after birth.

Ala (ah-LAH) Arabic for "glorious."

Alabi (a-la-BEE) Yoruban name given to a boy born after many girls.

Alain (ah-LAN) "Handsome" or "cheerful." One of the most popular boys' names in France today.

Aland (AL-uhnd) "Bright as the sun." Astrological name for a boy born under the sun sign Leo.

Alani (ah-LAH-nee) "Orange." This Hawaiian nature name refers to any kind of orange or orange tree, particularly the oahu tree, with its oblong, fragrant leaves used for scenting cloth. Like most Hawaiian names, this one is used for either sex. Other nature names include Aloalo, "hibiscus," Awapuhi, "flowering ginger," and Waioli, "singing water."

Alano (ah-LAH-noh) Spanish name meaning "handsome" or "cheerful." The English equivalent is Alan.

Alar (AY-luhr) "Having wings."

Albie Contemporary American creation from Albert, "noble and brilliant."

Albin (ahl-BEEN) Russian development of the Old German Alh-win, meaning "everyone's friend." The English equivalent is Alvin.

Alder Modern German nature name taken from the alder tree.

Alein (ah-LIGHN) Yiddish for "alone."

Alek Russian form of Alexander, "helper and defender of mankind." Among the many variations used in Russia are Alexandr, Alik, Lyaksandr, Sanya, Sasha, Shura, Shurik, Les, and Oles. The name originally comes from Greece, where a modern form is Alekos. In Portugal the name is Alexio, and in Scotland, Alister.

Aleser (AL-e-ser) A medieval corruption of the Arabic Asad, "lion," used to designate the constellation and zodiacal sign Leo, the Lion. Variants are Alasid, Asid, and Assid.

Alf (ahlf) A favorite in Norway, this name means "elfin." Also spelled Alv.

Alhim (AHL-heem) Occult name for the Pentagrams of Fire, used to invoke and banish spirits. Alhim also refers to the planet Venus, which governs the zodiacal sign Taurus.

Ali (ah-LEE) A favorite Arabic name, Ali means "Jehovah" or "the greatest" or "the highest." Popular among Muslims in Turkey, Egypt, Persia, Jordan, India, and Arabia. Ali was a son-in-law of the Prophet's, married to his daughter Fatimah.

Alim (a-LEEM) Arabic for "wise" or "learned." A variant is Alem.

Alister Common in Scotland. See Alek.

Almiron (AHL-mee-ruhn) Hindustani name which means clothes basket." The feminine equivalent is Almira. Naming children after common household objects is traditional in India because Hindus believe God is manifested in everything. Hence, each time you say the name, you are pronouncing the name of God, which is considered a step toward salvation.

Almon (ahl-MOHN) Hebrew for "forsaken" or "a widower."

Alnath (ahl-NATH) Arabic name for the first star in the horns of Aries, the Ram. Aries is known as "the first mansion of the moon" and is the first sign of the zodiac.

Alon (ah-LOHN) Hebrew nature name which means "oak tree."

Alrik Common in Sweden, Alrik comes from the Old German for "ruler of all."

Alroy (ahl-ROY) This Spanish name means "the king."

Altair Modern Greek name for a star of the first magnitude in the constellation Lyra. Also an Arabic name which means "the flying eagle."

Alter (AHL-ter) From the Latin for "other," or "another," or the Yiddish for "old one." Jewish people still occasionally give this name to the critically ill to confuse the demons.

Aluino (ah-loo:-EE-noh) Spanish for either "fair-complexioned" or "everyone's friend." A variation with the first meaning is Alva; another name with the latter meaning is Alvie. English equivalents are Alben and Alvin.

Alvar Nature name for a dwarf shrub native to Sweden.

Alvars (AHL-vahrs) Hindu name for a group of medieval mystical poets in South India.

Alvis (AHL-vees) Scandinavian name which means "all-knowing."

Amado (ah-MAH-doh) Used in Spanish-speaking countries, Amado comes from the Latin for "loving diety" or "lover of the divine." Variants include Amadeo and Amando.

Ameer (ah-MEER) This Arabic name means "a prince."

Amiel (ah-mee-AYL) Current Israeli name meaning "Lord of my people." A shorter form is Ami, "my people."

Amin (AH-min) Used in India, Amin means "faithful." Hebrew equivalents are Amitan and Amnon, the latter popular today in Israel.

Amon (AY-muhn) Originally derived from Hebrew, Amon means "related to the sun." The name is used today for the Leos of the zodiac, whose sign is ruled by the sun.

Anane (ah-NAH-neh) Ghanaian name for a fourth boy born in succession.

Andrey (ahn-DRAY) Russian name derived from the Greek Andreas, meaning "strong and manly."
Variations used throughout the world include Ondro (Czech); Anders (Danish, Norwegian, and Swedish); Andrew (English); Andreas and Evagelos (Greek); Andor, Andras, Endre, Andi, Andris, and Bandi (Hungarian); Andris (Latvian); Andrius Lithuanian); Aniol, Jedrus, and Jedrek (Polish); and Andre and Andres (Portuguese and Spanish).

Anka (uhn-KAH) Turkish name for either the legendary phoenix or the will-o'-the-wisp.

Annan (ah-NAHN) "Fourth-born son." Used by the Ochi- and Ga-speaking people of Africa.

Anoki (ah-NOH-kee) "Actor." North American Indian name.

Ansis (AHN-siss) Latvian name meaning "gracious gift of God." The English equivalent is John.

Antoan (an-twan) Vietnamese for "to be safe" or "secure."

Anton (AHN-tohn) From the Latin for "inestimable" or "priceless." The name is used today in Bulgaria, Slovakia, Russia, the Ukraine, Germany, Rumania, Serbia, Sweden, and Norway.
Popular variations include Antonin, Antek, Tonda, and Tonik (Czech); Anthony and Tony (English); Antoine (French); Andonios, Andonis, and Tonis (Greek); Antal, Anti, and Toni (Hungarian); Antonio (Italian and Spanish); Antons (Latvian); Antavas (Lithuanian); Antoni, Antek, Antos, Antonin, Tolek, and Tonek (Polish); Tosya, Tusya, and Antinko (Russian); and Antin (Ukrainian).

Anum (AH-noo:m) Used by the Akan-speaking people of Ghana for a "fifth-born son."

Apang (AH-pang) North American Indian name meaning "first-place winner."

Apenimon (ah-PEH-ni-muhn) North American Indian name meaning "trusty."

Archer Astrological name of Teutonic origin for a boy born under Sagittarius, the Archer.

Ardon (ahr-DOHN) Hebrew for "bronze."

Arel (ah-RAYL) Hebrew name meaning "lion of God." A common variant is Areli. In astrology the Lion is the symbol of Leo.

Aren (AH-ren) Norwegian and Danish name meaning "eagle" or "rule."

Ares (AY-reez) Occult name derived from Antares, the brightest star in the constellation Scorpio. Ares literally means "Mars," which is one of the planet rulers of the sign Scorpio.

Ari (ah-REE) Also spelled Arie, this Hebrew name means "lion," the symbol of the zodiacal sign Leo.

Arian (AIR-ee-uhn) Occult name for a boy born in the Age of Aquarius, an astrological era of two thousand years in which peace and brotherhood will reign. The Aquarian Age theoretically began in March, 1948, when the sun left the constellation Pisces, ruler of turmoil and conflict, and entered Aquarius. A variation of the name is Arius.

Aries Astrological name for a child born under Aries, the first sign of the zodiac. The name literally means "ram," the symbol of the sign.

Arif (ah-RIF) Turkish for "wise and intelligent."

Arkin Norwegian for "the eternal king's son." Often used as a surname.

Arley "The bowman" or "the hunter." Occult name for a boy born under Sagittarius, the Archer.

Arman (ahr-MAHN) This Russian name comes from the Old German for "army man." Other Russian variants are Armand and Armen. The Hungarian equivalent is Armin. English forms include Armand, Armin, and Armund.

Armon (ahr-MOHN) From the Hebrew for "castle" or "place." A variation is Armoni.

Arne (AHR-ne) "Eagle." One of the most popular names in Norway. Used to a lesser extent in Sweden and Denmark. A favorite form in Iceland is Arni. The English equivalent is Arney or Arnie.

Arnon (ahr-NOHN) Hebrew name which means "rushing stream," implying the child is energetic.

Aron (AH-rohn) "Lofty" or "exalted." Popular European name used today in Czechoslovakia, Hungary, Poland, Rumania, Scandinavia, and Russia. The English equivalent is Aaron.

Arpad (AWR-pahd) This Hungarian name was popularized by a Magyar national hero who founded a dynasty in 890 A.D.

Arpiar (ahr-pee-AHR) A favorite Armenian name meaning "sunny" or "of sunshine."

Arri This modern Greek name means "seeking the positive, or best) results." Also used today are Aristotelis and Telis.

Arrio Spanish name meaning "warlike."

Arslan (uhr-SLUHN) Turkish for "lion." In astrology the Lion is the symbol of Leo.

Arte (AHR-tee) American modern development of Arthur, "noble" or "bear man."

Artur (ahr-TOO:R) "Noble" or "bear man." Used in Russia, Bulgaria, Hungary, Estonia, Poland, Rumania, Scandinavia, and the Ukraine.

Arve (AHR-ve) One of the most popular names in Norway, Arve means "inheritor of property" or "heir."

Arvid Swedish and Norwegian name meaning "man of the people." Also used as a form of Arve, "heir."

Asadel (A-sa-del) Arabic for "most prosperous."

Asar This occult name comes from the Egyptian *Book of the Dead*, considered by many to be the original book of magic. Asar is another name for the god Osiris, the personification of the Nile Flood and hence the god of destruction. He was also thought to represent the sun after it sets and as such was a symbol of the motionless dead. It was through Osiris that the ancient Egyptians hoped to gain immortality.

Ash This is an occult name, since the ash is thought to bring good luck. A sprig of ash worn on the breast is said to give one prophetic dreams, and ash sap given to a newborn baby is supposed to frighten away evil spirits. Another superstition is if the first parings of a child's nails are buried beneath an ash tree, he will become a fine singer.

Asher Hebrew for "lucky," "blessed," or "happy."

Ashlin "Son of the pool surrounded by ash trees." Astrological name for boys born under the water signs Pisces, Scorpio, and Cancer. A similar name is Ashton, "son of the farm of ash trees," for those born under the earth signs Capricorn, Taurus, and Virgo.

Ashon (ah-SHON) "Seventh-born son." Used by the Ochi- and Ga-speaking people of Africa.

Ashur (ah-SHOO:R) Swahili name used in Tanzania for a child born during the Muslim month of Ashur.

Asiel (ah-see-AYL) Hebrew name which means "God has created him."

Asker (uhs-KAIR) Turkish for "soldier."

Aswad (ahss-WAHD) Arabic for "black."

Atar Astrological name for a child born on the ninth day of the month. This originally comes from an early

Persian custom of naming the ninth month and the ninth day of each month after Atar, the spirit of fire.

Atman (AHT-muhn) Hindu name meaning "the self."

Atuanya (ah-TOO:-ahn-yah) Used by the Ibo of Nigeria, Atuanya literally means "we throw the eyes." Loosely translated, the name means "unexpected" and is given to a son born when a daughter was expected.

Audric French name meaning "old and wise ruler." The English equivalent is Aldrich.

Audun (OW-doo:n) Currently popular in Norway, this name means "deserted" or "desolate." The feminine is Aud.

Aurek (AW-rek) Polish for "golden-haired." Other forms used today in Poland are Aureli and Elek.

Avedig (ah-veh-DEEG) Armenian name indicating the child's birth is "good news."

Avel Contemporary Greek name meaning "breath" and connoting the mortality of man.

Averil Ancient Anglo-Saxon name for April, now given to boys born in that month, under the zodiacal signs Aries and Taurus. Variants are Averell, Avril, and Averill.

Avi (ah-VEE) This Hebrew name means "Father," referring to God, and is an element in many modern Israeli names. Examples include Avidan, "God is just" or "Father of justice"; Avidor, "Father of a generation"; Aviel, "God is my Father"; Avital, "Father of dew"; Avner, "Father of light"; and Avniel, "My Father is my rock" or "My Father is my strength."

Aviv (ah-VEEV) Israeli name meaning "spring," "freshness" or "youth."

Awan (AH-wahn) This North American Indian name means "somebody."

182

Awun The god of destruction in the Formosan creation legend.

Axel (AHK-sel) Used in Sweden and Norway, Axel means "divine reward." The name is also a Scandinavian variation of the Hebrew Absalom, "father of peace." Another Swedish form is Axell, which is a surname as well.

Ayaz Turkish name meaning "frost on a clear winter night" or "dry cold on a winter day."

Azad (uh-ZUHD) Turkish for "free" or "born free."

Azi (ah-ZEE) Nigerian name which means "the youth," implying energy. Azi is often used as a name element, as in the surname Azikiwe, which literally means "the youth are filled with indignation."

Azim (A-zeem) Arabic for "defender," referring to one of the ninety-nine qualities of God in the Koran.

Azizi (ah-ZEE-zee) Used primarily in East Africa, this Swahili name means "precious."

Azriel (ahz-ree-AYL) Hebrew name meaning "God is my help."

Badem (bah-DEM) Turkish name meaning "almond," for a child with almond-colored skin or almond-shaped eyes.

Bal English Gypsy name for a child born with a lot of hair. Derived from the Tibetan word *bal*, "wool," and the Sanskrit *bala*, "hair."

Balder Scandinavian name for the "god of light" or "white god" in Old Norse mythology. Balder was the son of the god Odin and was killed when touched by a sprig of mistletoe. His zodiacal sign corresponds to Gemini, the Twins. A variant spelling is Baldur.

Baldwin "Bold friend" or "bold protector." The name is gaining use in the United States, possibly because of writer James Baldwin.

Balin (BAH-leen) Hindu name meaning "mighty soldier."

Other forms are Bali and Valin. In Hindu mythology Balin was a monkey king. A notorious tyrant, he had the power to extract half the strength from anyone who challenged him.

Balint Hungarian name from the Latin for "strong and healthy." Another form used in Hungary is Baline. The English equivalent is Valentine.

Bane (BAH-nuh) Hawaiian development of the Greek Barnabas, given to a child born after much praying and waiting by the parents. The English equivalent is Barney.

Baram Contemporary Israeli name meaning "son of a nation." Originally derived from Abraham, "father of a nation."

Baran (BAIR-uhn) Astrological name taken from Aldebaran, the brightest star in the constellation Taurus, the Bull. Aldebaran is 55 light years from earth, and 36 times larger and 100 times brighter than the sun.

Bardo Danish name meaning "son of the earth" or "farmer." Spanish forms are Barto, Bartoli, Toli, and Bartolome. The modern American equivalent is Barth.

Barse (bahrs) "Fresh-water perch." This name is popular for boys born under the zodiacal sign Pisces, symbolized by the Fishes.

Baruch Modern Greek name meaning "doer of good."

Basham (BAH-shuhm) "Rich soil." Earth name for boys born under the earth signs of the zodiac: Capricorn, Taurus, and Virgo.

Basilio (bah-SEE-lee-oh) Spanish name which means "kingly" or "magnificent." The English equivalent is Basil.

Basir (buh-SEER) Turkish for "intelligent and discerning."

Baul (bal) English Gypsy name which means "snail."

Bavol (BAH-vohl) English Gypsy name which means "wind" or "air."

Bay Vietnamese name given to a "seventh-born" child, or to a child born in July, the seventh lunar month, or on Saturday.

Beck Swiss nature name meaning "brook." Also one of the commonest surnames in Switzerland.

Bedir Turkish for "full moon." In astrology the moon governs the sign Cancer.

Bedrich (BED-rik[h]) Czech name from the Old German for "peaceful leader." Other Czech forms are Beda and Bedo. The English equivalent is Frederick.

Beldon Originally derived from Old English, Beldon is an ecological name meaning "child of the unspoiled, beautiful glen." A variant is Belden.

Belen Derived from Greek, this occult name means "an arrow" and is given to a child born under Sagittarius, the Archer.

Bello African Fultani name which is a contraction of Ballawo Bini, meaning "the helper (or promoter) of the Islamic religion."

Bem (behm) Used by the Tiv-speaking people of Nigeria, Bem means "peace."

Bemossed (beh-MOH-sehd) This North American Indian name means "the walker" and possibly refers to a long journey the father made by foot before the child was born.

Ben In Arabic and Hebrew this means "son" or "son of" and is frequently used as an element in Arabic names. The longer Hebrew name Benjamin means "son of my right hand."

Benci (BEN-tsi) Hungarian name meaning "blessed." Variants are Benedik and Benedek. Polish forms are Bendek, Benek, and Benedykt. The English equivalent is Benedict.

185

Benzi Currently popular in Israel as a shortened form of Ben Zion, "excellent son."

Berdy (BAIR-dee) Russian and Slovakian name from the Old German for "brilliant mind" or "brilliant spirit." The English equivalent is Hubert.

Berg Dutch, German, Swedish, and Yiddish for "mountain."

Berger Austrian name for "one who takes care of a flock" or "one who lives in the mountains." A given name, Berger is also one of the commonest surnames in Austria today.

Bergren Swedish for "mountain stream."

Berk (bairk) Turkish for "solid," "firm," or "rugged."

Bernhard This Swedish name means "brave as a bear." The shorter form Bern, "bear," is also used in Scandinavia. Both names connote strength and bravery. The English equivalent is Bernard.

Bersh (bairsh) English Gypsy name meaning "one year." A variation is Besh.

Bertin (bair-TEEN) Spanish name meaning "distinguished friend." Popularized by Saint Bertin.

Berto (BAIR-toh) Spanish nickname for Alberto, "bright and distinguished." Other pet forms are Beto and Veto.

Berty (BAIR-tee) Czech development of the Old English for "bright and distinguished." Other Czech forms are Bertik and Berta. The English equivalent is Albert.

Berwin "Friend of the harvest." Earth name for boys born under the earth signs of the zodiac: Capricorn, Taurus, and Virgo. The name also has ecological significance.

Beval (BAY-vahl) This English Gypsy name means "like the wind."

186

Bialy (BYAH-lee) Polish for "light-complexioned boy" or "white-haired boy." A variation is Bialas.

Bildad (beel-DAHD) Hebrew for "beloved," literally "Baal has loved."

Bily (BEE-lee) Czech form of Bialy. See Bialy.

Bimisi (bee-MEE-see) North American Indian name meaning "slippery." A slightly different name from the same root is Biminak, "slick roper."

Birk Contemporary American nature name derived from either Birch, "at the birch tree," or Birkey, "from the island of birch trees." Once a nickname, Birk is commonly used today as an independent name.

Bjorn (b.yern) Pronounced to rhyme with *turn,* Bjorn means "bear" and is one of the most popular names in Norway and Iceland. A reason for its popularity is its distinctive Norse flavor.

Blair "Child of the fields." Earth name for boys born under the earth signs of the zodiac: Capricorn, the Goat, Taurus, the Bull, and Virgo, the Virgin. An astrologer may advise such an earth name if a child's horoscope contains too many metal or water influences, since earth controls metal and destroys water. The name, then, is thought to restore the balance of the basic elements in the child's horoscope so the universal order will work smoothly throughout his life. For other earth names see Basham, Berwin, Boyce, Clay, Dagan, Gorman, Loudon, Nowles, Terrill, Wald, and Winfield.

Blas (blahs) Spanish development of the Latin Blasius, meaning "stammerer." No explanation could be found for this strange meaning, but Blas may have originated as a nickname for an older child who stuttered. The English equivalent is Blaze or Blaise.

Blaz (blahz) Serbo-Croatian form of the Old German Willihelm, "unwavering protector." The English equivalent is William.

Boaz (BOH-ahz) Hebrew for "swift and strong."

Bodaway (boh-DAH-way) North American Indian name meaning "fire maker."

Bodi (BOH-dee) This Hungarian name has the rather archaic meaning "may God protect the king."

Bodil (BOH-del) Norwegian and Danish for "commanding."

Bodua (boh-DOO:-ah) Used by the Akan-speaking people of Ghana, this name means "an animal's tail." Bodua is the ruling spirit of the Akan day corresponding to Sunday, and the name is given to a child born on that day.

Bogar (boh-GAHR) Derived from the name of a semilegendary Hindu sittar and alchemist of South India who visited China and brought back various sexmagic teachings.

Bohdan (BOH-dahn) A favorite in the Ukraine, this name means "given by God" and was popularized by the seventeenth-century Cossack leader Bohdan Chmelnyckyj. A variant spelling is Bogdan. Pet forms include Bogdashka and Danya. The name is also popular in Czechoslovakia, where the element *Boh,* meaning *"God,"* appears in a number of other names, the most common being Bohumil, "beloved of God," and Bohumir, "peace of God."

Bond Icelandic and English name meaning "tiller of the soil." Also spelled Bonde. Variants are Bonds and Bondon.

Bor (bohr) Originally an English Gypsy place name meaning "hedge."

Borg Scandinavian name meaning "one who lives in a castle."

Boris A favorite in Russia, Boris means "battler" or "stranger." Also common in Hungary and other Slavic countries.

Botan (boh-TAHN) Japanese for "peony," in Japan the flower of June.

Bour (BOH-oo:r) Ghanaian nature name from the word *obo,* meaning "rock." Also from the same source are Obo and Obour.

Bowle (BOHM-lay) This English Gypsy name means "snail." Another name with the same meaning is Baul.

Bowman "An archer." Occult name for a boy born under Sagittarius, the Archer.

Boyce "Son of the forest." Astrological name for a boy born under one of the earth signs of the zodiac. See Blair.

Bradburn "Broad brook." Astrological name for boys born under Pisces, the Fishes. Also appropriate for those born under the other two water signs of the zodiac: Cancer, the Crab, and Scorpio, the Scorpion.

Braden Nature name meaning "from the wide valley."

Bradshaw Ecological name meaning "large virginal forest."

Brahma (brah-MAH) The Creator in the Hindu trinity of gods. In Hindu mythology Brahma bursts from the lotus which grows from the navel of the god Vishnu, the protector.

Bram (brahm) Dutch name meaning "the lofty one is father." The English equivalent is Abram.

Brandeis (BRAHN-dighs) Used today in Czechoslovakia and Germany, Brandeis means "dweller on a burned clearing" or "one who comes from Brandeis," the name of three different places in Bohemia, a province of Czechoslovakia.

Brede (BREH-deh) Current Norwegian and Danish nature name meaning "glacier."

Brencis (BREN-tsiss) Latvian development of the Latin for "crowned with laurel." a victory symbol. English equivalents are Lawrence and the more contemporary Lorin.

Brendan (BREN-duhn) German for "aflame."

Brishen (BREE-shen) English Gypsy name for a child born during a rain.

Brodny (BROHD-nee) Slavic nature name for "one who lives near a shallow stream crossing.'

Brody (BROH-dee) Used in Germany, Russia, Ireland, and Scotland, this name has a number of possible meanings: "man with an unusual beard"; man from the barony of Brodie" or "man from the muddy place"; or "man from Brody in Russia." A variant spelling is Brodie.

Bron (brohn) Afrikaans for "source."

Bruns (broo:ns) German name meaning "Dark" or "brown." Another variation is Bruna.

Burian "He lives near the weeds." Generally as a surname in the Ukraine.

Burne "Child from the brook." Used for boys born under the water signs of the zodiac: Pisces, Cancer, and Scorpio. Other spellings include Bourn, Bourne, Byrn, Byrne, and Burn.

Burr (boo:r) Scandinavian name meaning "youth."

Cadao (ka-yaw) South Vietnamese name meaning "folk song" or "ballad."

Cahil (kah-HIL) Turkish for "young," "inexperienced," or "naive."

Calder Ecological name meaning "cool, clear spring." Also an astrological name for boys born under the water signs Pisces, Cancer, and Scorpio. A variation is Caldwell.

Caleb This Hebrew name has several possible meanings: "messenger," "heart," or "dog." A contemporary American variation is Cale.

Calut (kah-LOO:T) Turkish development of Goliath.

Cam (kahm) English Gypsy name meaning "beloved" and also referring to the sun. In astrology the sun governs the sign Leo.

Camlo (KAHM-loh) English Gypsy name meaning "lovely" or "amiable," derived from the name Kama or Cama, for the handsome black Hindu god of love. One dark-skinned Gypsy band uses Camlo as part of their tribal name, Kaulo Camloes, which is translated as "the beautiful blacks." A variant is Caumlo. Oddly enough, the same name is also used in Vietnam, where it means "sweet dew."

Cappi (KAHP-pee) English Gypsy name meaning "good fortune" or "profit."

Carlos (KAHR-lohs) Spanish for "strong and manly." A modern Greek form is Carolos. The English equivalent is Charles.

Carswell "Child of the watercress spring." Astrological name for boys born under the water signs of the zodiac: Pisces the Fishes, Cancer the Crab, and Scorpio, the Scorpion. If a child's horoscope contains too many wood or metal influences, an astrologer may advise a water name to restore the balance of the elements, the belief being that water controls wood and destroys metal. A horoscope which balances the basic elements—earth, fire, air, water, metal, and wood—allows the universal order to run smoothly throughout the person's life.

Carvel "A song." Manx name from the Isle of Man.

Casimir (kah-SEE-mer) This Polish name means "he announces peace."

Castel (kah STEHL) Spanish development of the Latin Castelar, "belonging to a castle."

Catalin The magic name of a wizard who often appears in Irish legends.

Caton (kah-TOHN) Modern Spanish name used in Spain

and Latin and South America. Caton comes from the Latin Cato, meaning "knowledgeable" or "wise."

Cemal (ke-MAHL in Arabic, ye-MAHL in Turkish) Common Arabic and Turkish name which means "beauty."

Cesar (SAY-sahr) "Long-haired" or "hairy." Modern Spanish name from the Latin Caesar.

Chad "Related to Mars." Occult name for those born under Aries, which is ruled by the war planet Mars. Mars also shares the rule of Scorpio with Pluto.

Chaim (k[h]ighm) Pronounced to rhyme with *time,* this Hebrew name means "life." French Jews translated the name as Vive.

Chal (chahl) English Gypsy name meaning "lad," "boy," or "son." Similar in meaning are the Scotch Chiel, the Old English Childe, and the Russian Chelovik.

Chale (CHAH-leh) Colloquial Spanish form of Carlos, "strong and manly."

Cham Vietnamese name meaning "hard worker."

Chane (CHAH-neh) This Swahili name refers to either a strip of tough leaf used for weaving mats or a bundle. Hence, Chane connotes the sturdy dependability of the weaving leaf.

Chaney (CHAH-ney) From the Old French for "oak wood." Also spelled Cheney.

Chanoch (k[h]ah-NOHK[K]) Hebrew equivalent of Clark, from the Old English for "clergyman" or "learned man."

Chase Originally derived from Old French, Chase means "hunter." The name is appropriate for a boy born when the sun is in Sagittarius, the Archer.

Che (cheh) Colloquial Spanish pet form of Jose, "he will increase." The English equivalent is Joe.

Chen (chen) Chinese for "vast" or "great." One story is told of a boy who was about to receive a fate name

192

when his father dreamed a god appeared and wrote the character Chen, proclaiming "Give him this name." The boy, Chang Chen (surname first), grew up to become a minister of state. Fate names, once kept secret, are now used freely in China, particularly by the better educated.

Cheslav (ches-LAHF) Russian name meaning "one who lives in a fortified camp." English equivalents are Chet and the older name Chester.

Chesmu (CHEHS-moo:) North American Indian name meaning "gritty."

Chi (chee) Used by the Ibo of Nigeria, this name refers to a kind of personal guardian angel. One's Chi comes into being when one is born, and follows one throughout life, a spiritual double believed to be the cause of all manner of misfortune and success.
Many Ibo names are derived from this one, including Cinese, "Chi is protecting"; Chileogu, "Chi is our protector" or "Chi is our defender"; Cis, which is another spelling or form of Chi; Chioke, "gift of Chi"; Chinelo, "thought of Chi"; and Chinua, "Chi's own blessing."

Chiah (KIGH-uh) A popular shortened form of Hezechiah popular among early Afro-Americans.

Chik (cheek) English Gypsy name meaning "earth."

Chim (kim) Vietnamese name meaning "bird."

Ciceron (see-seh-ROHN) Spanish development of the Latin Cicero, which means "chickpea."

Cilombo (chee-LOHM-boh) Used by the Ovimbundu of Angola, Cilombo literally means "roadside camp," a welcome sight to weary travelers in Africa. Hence, the implied meaning is "a sight for sore eyes." The name is a great favorite and is often given to girls as well.

Ciro (SEE-roh) Spanish name meaning "the sun." Derived from the Persian name Cyrus. In astrology the sun governs the sign Leo.

Clay "Of the earth," symbolizing mortality. Good occult name for boys born under the earth signs Capricorn, Taurus, and Virgo. See Blair for further information on earth names.

Clemens Common Danish name meaning "gentle" or "kind." The English equivalent is Clement.

Colman (KOHL-mahn) Icelandic for "head man" or "charcoal maker." The similar English name Coleman is believed to come from the Latin for "dove," a symbol of peace.

Colon (koh-LOHN) Spanish name from the Latin for "dove." English equivalents are Columbus and the more modern Columbo.

Coman (koh-MAHN) Arabic for "noble."

Conrado (kohn-RAH-doh) Modern Spanish name from the Old German for "bold counselor."

Corey This Irish and Scotch nature name means "he lives by a hollow (or misty) pool." Also spelled Cori and Cory, it is used today as a girl's name as well.

Cowan "Twin." Good astrological name for a boy born when the sun is in Gemini, the Twins. Another possible meaning is "hillside hollow."

Cris (krees) Spanish name shortened from Christopher, "Christ-bearer." Popularized by Saint Christopher, the patron saint of ferrymen and travelers.

Crispus The given name of Crispus Attucks, a black who was the first American to die for independence in the Boston Massacre. When the British soldiers appeared, Attucks cried, "Do not be afraid," and was shot minutes later.

Curcio (KOO:R-see-oh) Spanish name from the Old French for "courteous." The English equivalent is Curt.

Dabir (dah-BEER) Used in Algeria and Egypt, this name means "secretary" or "teacher."

Dag (dahg) "Day" or "brightness." A favorite today in Norway because of its distinctive Norse sound. The feminine form is Dagny.

Dagaim (dah-GIGHM) "Two fishes." Hebrew name for the constellation and zodiacal sign Pisces, the Fishes.

Dagan (dah-GAHN) From the Hebrew for "corn" or "grain" or the East Semitic for "earth." This name is given to boys born under the earth signs Capricorn, Taurus, and Virgo. The name can also refer to a Babylonian god of agriculture and fish, in which case it means "little fish" and is appropriate for boys born under Pisces, the Fishes.

Dalal (dah-LAHL) Like many names in India, this one indicates the bearer's profession or the father's trade, in this case "a broker."

Dalibor (DAH-lee-bohr) Popular Czech nature name meaning "he dwells in the valley."

Damek (DUH-mek) Czech name meaning "earth" or "man of the red earth," derived from the Hebrew Adham or Adam. Other Czech forms include Adamec, Adamek, Adamik, and Adamok.

Dandin (dahn-DEEN) A Hindu occult or holy man who carries a staff. When used for black magic, the staff is made of decayed bamboo, and in some sects it is thought to be alive and is even fed. Other sects believe the staff can dance.

Dane (DAH-ne) Scandinavian name meaning "a Dane" or "man from Denmark." Other variations used today are Dana and Dain. In Dutch Dane is a form of Daniel, "God is my judge."

Dani (DAH-nee) Modern Israeli development of Dan, "my judge." Dan originally comes from the Hebrew Dawnee.

Danior (DAH-nee-ohr) English Gypsy name for a child born with teeth.

Danladi (dahn-LAH-dee) Used by the Hausa in Nigeria for a child "born on Sunday."

Danya (DAHN-yah) "Given by God." Popular diminutive in the Ukraine. See Bohdan.

Dar (dahr) This Hebrew name means "pearl" or "mother-of-pearl."

Daren (DAH-rehn) Hausa name used in Nigeria for a boy "born at night." A favorite form is Dare.

Dario (dah-REE-oh) Spanish name from the Greek for "wealthy." The modern American equivalent is Darin.

Dasan (DAH-sahn) In the Pomo Indian creation legend Dasan and his father were leaders of a bird clan who came from the waters and brought civilization with them.

Daudi (dah-OO:-dee) Pretty Swahili name meaning "beloved one." Used primarily in East Africa.

Daulo (DOW-loh) "Jar." Syrian name for the constellation Aquarius, the Water Bearer. In the zodiac Aquarius is considered a masculine and therefore fortunate sign.

Davin (DAH-vin) Used in Scandinavian countries, this name means "brightness of the Finns," who were once thought to be the most intelligent people of the North.

Dawud (da-WOO:D) A favorite among Muslims Dawud is a form of the Hebrew David, "beloved." An alternate Arabic spelling is Dawood.

Decker This Belgian occupation name means "roofer" and is often used as a surname.

Dekel (DAY-kel) Modern Israeli name meaning "palm tree" or "date palm." Originally derived from Arabic.

Del Once an American nickname for Delbert, "bright day" or "sunny day," Del is used today as an independent name. It is also an English Gypsy name, pronounced like *dale* and meaning "he gives."

Delano (de-LAH-noh) From the Irish Gaelic for "a healthy black man."

Delmar (dehl-MAHR) Used in Spain and Latin and South America, this name combines the words *del mar,* meaning "of the sea." A French form is Delmer.

Delsin (DEHL-sin) North American Indian name which simply means "he is so."

Demothi (deh-MOH-tee) North American Indian name which means "talks walking" and probably originally referred to a personal trait.

Deniz (de-NIZ) Turkish name meaning "sea," implying huge waves or a storm. Also a common surname in Turkey.

Denys (de-NEES) Russian development of the Greek Dionysus, "god of wine." Variations include Denis and Denya. The English equivalent is Dennis.

Der (dair) German name meaning "ruler of the people." A shortened form of Derrick.

Deror (deh-ROHR) Hebrew for "freedom," "free-flowing," or "a swallow." Another form used in Israel is Derori.

Dichali (dee-CHAH-lee) North American Indian name meaning "he speaks often."

Didi (DEE-dee) Israeli diminutive of the older name Jedidiah, which means "loved by the Lord." Also spelled Deedee.

Diego (dee-EH-goh) Spanish name which means "the supplanter." Other favorite forms in Spanish-speaking countries are Jaime and Jayme. English equivalents are James and Jaymie.

Dima (DEE-mah) Russian nickname meaning "powerful warrior" or "army ruler." See Vladimir.

Dimitry (di-MEE-tree) Popular in Russia, Dimitry comes from the Greek for "belonging to Demeter," the goddess of fertility. Also spelled Dimitri and Dmitri. A pet form is Mitia. See Mimis for modern Greek variations.

Dinos (DEE-nohs) Greek nickname for Constantinos, from the Latin for "firm and constant." The latter name was popularized by Constantine, king of Greece in the late nineteenth and early twentieth centuries, and many forms are used today, including Konstantinos, Konstandinos, Kostas, Kotsos, Kostis, Costa, and Gus. Dinos and Kostas are among the most common boys' names in Greece today.

Dion Once an American nickname for Dennis, "god of wine," Dion is frequently used today as an independent name.

Diverous (dee-VAY-ruhs) Common English Gypsy name.

Doane This English name comes from the Celtic for "black."

Dobry (DOH-bree) Polish name meaning "good." Also a common surname in Poland.

Dodek (DOH-dek) Polish name meaning "noble wolf" or "noble hero." Other forms used in Poland are Adek and Adolf. Czech variations are Dolfa and Dolfi. The English equivalent is Adolph.

Dohosan (doh-HOH-suhn) North American Indian name which means "a small bluff."

Domingo (doh-MEEN-goh) Spanish name for a child "born on Sunday," from the Latin word for Sunday. English equivalents are Dom and Dominic.

Donalt (DOH-nahlt) Norwegian development of Donald, meaning "world ruler." Because of the current Norwegian trend toward distinctly Nordic names, this is not as popular as it once was.

Donat (doh-NAHT) Used in Russia, Donat comes from the Latin for "a gift." An Italian form is Donati, with variants Donato and Donatello. The English equivalent is Donato.

Donkor (dohn-KOHR) "Humble." Used by the Akan of Ghana.

Donnelly From the Celtic for "a brave black man."

Donohue From the Celtic for "dark."

Donovan This Celtic name means "dark warrior."

Dor (dohr) From the Hebrew for "a generation" or "a home." The feminine form is Doris.

Dorek (DOH-rek) Polish name meaning "gift of God." See Todor.

Dorian Originally derived from the Greek Dorios, Dorian means "child of the sea." The name is given to boys born under the water signs of the zodiac: Pisces, Cancer, and Scorpio.

Dorjan (DOHR-yawn) Hungarian name from the Latin for "dark man" or "black man." Another variant used in Hungary is Adorjan. The English form is Adrian.

Doron (doh-ROHN) Hebrew for "gift," implying the child is a gift of God.

Dotan (doh-TAHN) Modern Israeli name meaning "law." A common variation is Dothan.

Dovev (doh-VAYV) Hebrew name meaning "to whisper" or "to speak quietly."

Doyle "Black stranger" or "dark stranger." Derived from Celtic.

Dreng (drehng) Norwegian name meaning "hired farmhand" or "brave man."

Dude (DOO:-deh) English Gypsy name meaning "moon." In astrology the moon rules the sign of Cancer, the

Crab. In the tarot pack the card of the moon corresponds to Pisces.

Duff "Dark-faced" or "black-faced." Derived from Celtic.

Dukker (DOO:K-kuhr) English Gypsy name meaning "to bewitch" or "to tell fortunes." A variant is Duke, which has the connotation of bewitching with evil intentions.

Dumaka (doo:-MAH-kah) This is a short-sentence name from the Ibo of Nigeria, and the meaning "help me with hands" expresses the father's plan to put the boy to work.

Duman (doo-MUHN) Turkish for "smoke" or "mist." Generally used as a surname in Turkey.

Dunham From the Celtic for "dark man" or "black man."

Dur (doo:r) Hebrew for "to pile up" or "to encircle."

Durriken (DOO:-ree-ken) English Gypsy name which means "fortune-telling."

Durril (DOO:-reel) English Gypsy name which refers to a berry, particularly the gooseberry.

Dusan (DOO:-ssahn) Serbo-Croatian development of the Hebrew Daniel, meaning "God is my judge."

Dustin From the German for "a fighter," Dustin is gaining popularity in the United States, possibly because of actor Dustin Hoffman.

Dyami (dee-AH-mee) Used by some North American Indians, this name means "an eagle." The eagle is often mentioned in Indian names, and other examples include Bosaiya, "white down on the head of a young eagle"; Tokawa, "white head of the bald eagle"; and Wiluye, "eagle singing as it flies."

Dylan Welsh nature name meaning "the sea." In Welsh mythology Dylan the Dark was the son of the sea.

Dyre (DEE-re) Very popular Norwegian name meaning "dear" or "precious."

Edan (EE-dahn) Originally derived from Celtic, Edan means "fire." The name is used for boys born under the fire signs of the zodiac: Aries, Leo, and Sagittarius. Also a good name for a child whose horoscope contains too many wood influences, since fire destroys wood. A lucky horoscope balances the basic elements—earth, fire, air, water, metal, and wood—to permit the universal order to work smoothly throughout the person's life.

Eddy Scandinavian name which means "unresting."

Ede (EH-deh) Occult name which means "devour thou me" and is used to invoke the powers of spirits. In magic ritual Ede is followed by the name Edu, "thou dost devour me."

Edik (AY-deek) Used in Russia, this name means "wealthy guardian." See Eduard.

Edmon (ed-MOHN) Russian development of the Old English Eadmund, which means "prosperous protector." A more common form is Edmond, but neither is widely used today in Russia.

Eduard (e-DWAHRD) From the Old English for "wealthy guardian," this name appears today in Czechoslovakia, Germany, Estonia, Poland, Rumania, Russia, Holland, and the Ukraine. Another Russian variation is Edik. The Italian and Latvian form is Eduards. The English equivalent is Edward.

Einar (IGH-nahr) One of the most common names in Norway and Iceland, Einar means "individualist" or "nonconformist." A popular Danish version is Ejnar.

Elan (EH-lahn) Abbreviated form of the North American Indian name Elangonel, meaning "friendly."

Eldridge German for "mature counselor" or Anglo-Saxon for "fearful and terrible."

Elek (E-lek) This name is used in Hungary as a shortened form of Alexander, "helper and defender of mankind," and in Poland as a variation of Aurek, "golden-haired." Other Hungarian forms are Eli and Lekszi. The Spanish equivalent is Alejo.

Eli (EH-lee) Hawaiian development of the English Eli, from the Hebrew for "Jehovah" or "the highest."

Elia (eh-LEE-uh) Zuni Indian name derived from the Spanish Elias, meaning "Jehovah is my God." A Hebrew variation is Ellis. The English equivalent is Elijah.

Elkan (el-KAHN) Hebrew for "he belongs to God."

Elki (EL-kee) Miwok Indian name from the word *elkini*, "to hang over" or "to hang on top of." The connotation is "bear hanging intestines of people on top of bushes or rocks."

The bear often appears in Miwok names. Other examples include Liwanu ("bear growling," from *liwani*, "to talk"); Notaku ("growling of a bear as someone passes by"); Sewati ("curving of the bear's claws"); Tuketu ("bear making dust as it runs"); and Yelutci ("bear traveling through brush and over rocks without making a sound"). See Honon and Molimo for more bear names. See also Lusela and Sapata, listed in the girls' section.

Elmen German name meaning "like an elm tree."

Eloy (eh-LOHY) Spanish for "famous warrior."

Elrad (AYL-rahd) Hebrew for "God rules."

Elsu (EHL-soo:) This name is common among the Miwok Indians and means "falcon flying." The connotation is "falcon circling in the air." See Takenya, listed in the girls' section, for other falcon names.

Elton "From the old estate" or "from the old town." The name is gaining use in the United States, possibly because of pop singer Elton John.

Eman (EH-mahn) Czech name from the Hebrew for "God with us." A Slovak form is Manuel.

Emilio (eh-MEE-lee-oh) Spanish name meaning "flattering" or "winning one."

Eneas (eh-NEH-uhs) Spanish development of the Greek Aeneas, meaning "the praised one."

Enli (EHN-lee) Dene Indian name which literally means "here below dog" and implies "that dog over there." The name may originally have referred to a dog the father spotted shortly after the child was born.

Ennis From the Greek for "the ninth," this name is given to a boy born under Sagittarius, the ninth sign of the zodiac.

Enoch (ay-NOHK[K]) Hebrew for "educated" or "dedicated."

Enyeto (en-YEH-toh) Miwok Indian name referring to "the bear's manner of walking," from the word *ena,* "bent" or "crooked." See Lusela and Sapata, listed in the girls' section, for other bear names.

Erek (EHR-ek) Polish name meaning "lovable."

Erik This popular Scandinavian name means "ever powerful" or "eternal ruler." One of the most common names in Denmark and Sweden.

Erin Irish for "peace." Also a girl's name.

Ervin (AIR-vin) Used in Czechoslovakia and Hungary, this name means "friend of the sea." The English form is Erwin, which may also mean "white river."

Eshkol (aysh-KOHL) Hebrew name meaning "a grape cluster." Also a common surname in Israel.

Essien (ehs-see-EHN) Used on the Gold Coast by the Ochi- and Ga-speaking people for a "sixth-born son."

Etan (ay-TAHN) Hebrew for "firm and strong." Another form is Ethan.

Etu (AY-too:) North American Indian name meaning "the sun." In astrology the sun governs Leo, the fire sign.

Eugen (EW-gehn) Modern Greek name meaning "noble" or "born of good family." Another Greek variation is Eugenios. The English equivalent is Eugene.

Evan (E-vuhn) "Young warrior" or "young bowman." Astrological name for a boy born under Sagittarius, the Archer. A variation is Ewan. Both names originally come from Celtic.

Ezer (AY-zayr) Israeli name from the Hebrew for "help." Many Biblical names are derived from this source, including Azrikam, Azur, Ezri, Azariah, and Ezra, the latter used in Israel for girls as well. The Hawaiian form of Ezer is Ezera.

Ezhno (AYZH-noh) North American Indian name meaning "solitary" or "a loner."

Faber (FA-ber) German name meaning "bean grower." The Russian form is Fabiyan, with the pet name Fabi. The English equivalent is Fabian.

Fadey (fah-DAY) Ukrainian for "stouthearted" or "courageous." Variants include Faddei, Fadeyka, and Fadeyushka. English equivalents are Thad and Tad.

Fadil (FAH-deel) Arabic for "generous."

Fairleigh (FAIR-lay) "From the meadow of the bull" or "from the meadow of the ram." Other spellings include Farley, Farly, Fairlay, Fairlee, Farlay, Fairlie, and Farlee.

Fath (FAT.h) Arabic name meaning "victory."

Faxon This name, of Teutonic origin, means "long hair."

Fedor (fay-DOHR) Russian development of the Greek Theodoros, "gift of God," or possibly the Latin Franciscus, "free man." A favorite diminutive is Fedya.

Felike (fay-LEEKS) Russian name derived from the Latin for "fortunate" or "lucky."

Felipe (feh-LEE-peh) Spanish form of Philip, from the Greek for "lover of horses."

Fermin (fair-MEEN) Used in Spanish-speaking countries, this name means "firm and strong."

Fidel (fee-DEHL) Spanish for "faithful and sincere."

Filip (FEE-leep) From the Greek Philippos, "lover of horses." Filip is used today in Bulgaria, Czechoslovakia, Lithuania, Poland, Rumania, Russia, Serbia, Norway, and Sweden. A Polish nickname is Fil. A Spanish form is Filipo. The English equivalent is Philip.

Fineas (fee-NEH-ahs) Spanish name from the Greek for "mouth of brass."

Finley "Sun's ray" or "sunbeam." Astrological name for a child born under Leo, which is ruled by the sun.

Finn Currently used in Norway this name means "Laplander."

Fisk This name means "fishes," the symbol of the zodiacal sign Pisces. Also spelled Fiske.

Fletcher From the Middle English for "arrow featherer," referring to an archer's skill in putting feathers on his arrows. Good astrological name for a boy born under Sagittarius, the Archer.

Flint Although the word flint refers to a kind of hard stone, the name originally comes from the Old English for "a stream." Hence, astrologers use the name for a child born under one of the water signs of the zodiac: Pisces, Cancer, and Scorpio.

Fordel (FOHR-del) English Gypsy name meaning "forgives."

Forrester Ecological name meaning "protector of the forests." Variations include Forester, Forster, and Foster.

Francisco (frahn-SEES-koh) One of the most common Spanish names in the world, Francisco comes from the Latin for "free man" or "Frenchman." The many variations used in Spanish-speaking countries include Chico, Chicho, Chilo, Chito, Currito, Curro, Farruco, Frasco, Paco, Frascuelo, Pacorro, Pancho, Panchito, Paquito, and Quico. Swedish and Norwegian equivalents are Frans and Franzen. The Austrian form is Franz.

Fredek (FRE-dek) Used today in Bulgaria, Czechoslovakia, Hungary, Poland, Russia, and Scandinavia. Fredek is a form of either Frederick, "peaceful ruler," or Alfred, "elfin counselor."

Fredi This modern German name means "peaceful ruler." Variations are Friedel, Fritz, and Friedrich. A Swedish form is Fredrik. The English equivalent is Frederick.

Fynn (feen) Ghanaian nature name derived from the River Offin. Fynn is an Anglicized form of Offin used today. Many Ghanaian names come from rivers, rocks, mountains, trees, animals, and other elements of nature. Some examples are Odom, from the odum or oak tree; Fram, from the ofram tree; Prah, from the River Prah; Afram, from the River Afram; Sono, from the Akan word *esono,* "an elephant"; and Krobo, the name of several rivers and mountains in Ghana.

Gabi (GAH-bee) Modern Israeli name created from Gabriel, "God is my strength."

Gadi (GAH-dee) Hebrew name from the Arabic for "my fortune." A popular variation is Gadiel, "God is my fortune."

Galeno (gah-LEH-noh) Spanish name meaning "little bright one." The English equivalent is Galen.

Galt (gahlt) Used in Norway, this name means "high ground."

Gan Common Vietnamese name meaning "to be near." Often used as a surname.

Garai (GAH-rah-ee) Popular among the Mashona of Rhodesia, Garai means "to be settled."

Garald (gah-RAHLD) This Russian name means "spear brave" or "spear strong." Other forms include Garold, Gerald, and Garolds.

Garridan (GAH-ree-duhn) English Gypsy name meaning "you hid."

Garth Common in Scandinavia, Garth means "enclosure" or "protection."

Gaspar (gahs-PAHR) Spanish name meaning "master of treasure," from the Persian Kansbar.

Gavril (gahv-REEL) Used today in Russia, this name means "man of God." A favorite diminutive is Ganya.

Georgy (geh-OHR-gee) Russian development of George, "farmer." Pet forms include Gorya, Yurik, Yura, Yuri, Egor, and Zhorzh.

Gerhard Used in Scandinavian countries, this name means "spear brave" or "spear strong."

Gerik (GAI-rik) Polish for "prosperous spearman." A variant is Edek. The English form is Edgar.

Giamo (JAH-moh) Italian for "the supplanter." The English equivalent is James.

Gibor (gee-BOHR) This Israeli name means "strong."

Gil (geel) Spanish for "the shield bearer." The English equivalent is Giles.

Gilad (gee-LAHD) Popular in Israel, Gilad comes from the Arabic for "a camel hump." Variations include Gilead and Giladi.

Giles (gighlz) "Young goat." Astrological name for a boy born under Capricorn, which is symbolized by the Goat. Another possible meaning is "youthful, downy-bearded one."

Gillie (gee-lee-e) English Gypsy name meaning "a song."

Ginton (geen-TOHN) Modern Israeli equivalent of the original Hebrew name Ginson, "a garden."

Giovanni (joh-VAHN-nee) A favorite in Italy, from the Hebrew for "gracious gift of God." The English equivalent is John.

Givon (gee-VOHN) "Hill" or "heights." Modern Israeli name.

Goel (goh-AYL) "The redeemer." Modern Israeli name.

Goran (YOH-rahn) One of the most popular names in Sweden. The variant Jorgen is a favorite in Norway and Denmark. Both names come from the Latin or Greek for "farmer." The English equivalent is George.

Gorman "Man of clay." Astrological name for boys born under the earth signs Capricorn, Taurus, and Virgo. See Blair for further information on earth names.

Gosheven (goh-SHAY-ven) North American Indian name which means "the Great leaper."

Gowon (GOH-wohn) Used by the Tiv-speaking people of Nigeria, Gowon means "rainmaker." Given to a child born during a storm.

Gozal (goh-ZAHL) From the Hebrew for "a bird."

Gregor (GRE-gohr) Used today in Slovakia, Germany, Slovenia, and Norway, this name means "watchful one." The English equivalent is Gregory, and the Spanish, Gregorio.

Guido (GWEE-doh) Spanish for "life." The English form is Guy.

Gunnar (GOO:-nahr) Common today in Iceland and Norway, Gunnar comes from the Old Norse for "battle army." The English equivalent is Gunther.

Gur (goo:r) Hebrew for "lion cub." Many Israeli names come from this root, including Guri, "my lion cub," Guriel, "God is my lion" or "God is my strength and protection," and Gurion, "a lion," connotating strength. In astrology the Lion is the symbol of Leo.

Gus Greek nickname for Constantinos. See Dinos for more information.

Gustaf (goo:-STAHF) Swedish name meaning "stave of the Goths."

208

Guyapi (goo:-YAH-pee) North American Indian name meaning "candid."

Gyasi (JAH-see) "Wonderful child." Akan name used today in Ghana.

Habib (hah-BEEB) A favorite in Tunisia and Syria, and common in all Muslim countries, this name comes from the Arabic for "beloved."

Hadad (hah-DAHD) The Syrian god of virility, who was also known as Adad.

Hadar (hah-DAHR) A Syrian diety.

Hadden (HAD-duhn) This name means "child of the heather-filled valley" or "child from the heather hill." Also spelled Haddan and Haddon. A variation is Hadley, "child from the heather meadow."

Hadrian Common Swedish name meaning "dark one." Other forms used throughout the world include Adrian, English; Adorjan, Hungarian; Adok, Polish; Adrik and Andrian, Russian; and Andriyan, Ukrainian.

Hahnee (HAH-nee) North American Indian name meaning "a beggar," given to a child to fool evil spirits into thinking he is unloved and hence not worth their time.

Haidar (HIGH-dahr) Used today in India, Haidar means "lion," the symbol of the zodiacal sign Leo. The name is used mostly by Muslims, and other Muslim names with the same meaning include Hirsuma, Asad, and Lais.

Hakan (hah-KAHN) North American Indian name which means "fiery."

Hakeem (HA-keem) Popular Muslim name from the Arabic for "wise," one of the ninety-nine qualities of God listed in the Koran. Also common is the name Abdul Hakeem, "servant of the wise One."

Hakem (HA-kem) Arabic occupation name meaning

"ruler." Such names are often used by Muslim Arabs, and other examples include Haddad, "smith," Ferran, "baker," Kateb, "writer," Khoury, "priest," and Samman, "grocer."

Hakim Ethiopian name meaning "doctor."

Hakon (HAH-kohn) Scandinavian for "of the high (or exalted) race." Many kings of Norway have had this name.

Hale (HAH-le) Hawaiian development of the Old Norse for "army ruler." The English equivalent is Harold.

Halian (hah-lee-AHN) Zuni Indian form of the Spanish Julian. The Zuni received many Spanish names from the Franciscan fathers.

Halil (huh-LIL) This Turkish name means "intimate friend."

Halim (HAH-leem, in Turkish huh-LEEM) A common name in Muslim countries, which include Arabia, Persia, Jordan, Egypt, Turkey, and India. Halim comes from Arabic and means "mild," "gentle," or "patient."

Hamal (HA-mal) Arabic for "lamb." Hamal is also a bright star in the constellation Aries, the Ram. Hence, the name is appropriate for an Aries child.

Hamid A favorite in Iran and in most other Muslim countries. See Muhammad.

Hamlin "Lover of home." The name refers to the domesticity of those born under the zodiacal sign Cancer. Also a good name for a child born with Venus in his fourth house.

Hanan (hah-NAHN) "Grace" or "gracious." This is a modern Hebrew form of Johanan, which in English becomes John.

Hanif (HAH-neef) This Arabic name means "true believer (in the Moslem religion)."

Hans (hahns) Scandinavian form of John, "gracious gift of God." Popular today in Sweden.

Hanuman (hah-noo:-MAHN) A Hindu monkey chief and one of the favorite characters in Hindu literature. He was able to fly, and many stories are told about his fantastically long tail. Once Hanuman was sent by the god Rama to fetch some healing herbs from a mountain before the moon rose, and when the monkey god could not find the herbs, he carried the whole mountain back to his master. Uprooting the mountain took him so long, he could not finish the job before the moon came up, so Hanuman ate the moon and coughed it up again when he replaced the mountain.

Harald (HAH-rahld) Scandinavian war name meaning "army ruler." One of the most popular names in Sweden and Denmark.

Harb (hahrb) Arabic name meaning "war."

Harel (hah-RAYL) Currently used in Israel, Harel comes from the Hebrew for "God's mountain."

Hari (HAH-ree) Hindustani for "tawny." Hari is another name for the god Vishnu, the protector in the Hindu triad. A common variant is Haridas, the -*das* suffix indicating humility and complete subjection to Vishnu.

Harith (HA-rith) Arabic for "ploughman." A common variant is Harithah. Both names are also used for girls.

Harley From the German for "archer" or "deer hunter," this name is given to boys born under Sagittarius, the Archer.

Haroun (hah-ROO:N) Arabic form of the Biblical Aaron, meaning "lofty" or "exalted." A popular spelling is Harun.

Hasad (huh-SUHD) This Turkish name refers to the "harvest" or "reaping."

Hashim (HA-shim) Common Arabic name meaning

"broker." Hashim was a descendant of the Prophet Muhammad.

Hasin (hah-seen) Used in India, this name means "laughing."

Haskel (hah-SKAYL) Popular in Israel, Haskel comes from the Hebrew for "wisdom" or "understanding." It may also be a shortened form of Ezekiel, "strength." Another spelling used today is Haskell.

Hassan (HA-san) Arabic for "handsome." Also spelled Hasan. In Muslim-oriented cultures children of the same family often receive similar names. Hence, one family might have a Hassan, Muhassan, Husain, Khalid, Khallad, and Makhlad, all of which come from the word *salima,* "to be safe." The Hausa of Nigeria give this name to a first-born male twin, and the second twin, if a boy, is named Husseini.

Hassel German for "a man from Hassall (the witches' corner)" or "one who lives near a hazel tree." Also spelled Hassel.

Hastin (hah-steen) "Elephant." The name refers to a legendary hero in Hindu mythology who was born in an elephant lake.

Hayden (HAY-duhn) Nature name meaning "son of the rose-hedged valley."

Hedeon (heh-DAY-ohn) Ukrainian name meaning "destroyer" or "tree cutter." The English equivalent is Gideon.

Helaku (heh-LAH-koo:) Used by North American Indians, this name means "sunny day."

Helki (HEHL-kee) Miwok Indian name from the word *hele,* "to touch." The connotation is "jacksnipe digging into the ground with its bill." This bird is said to appear only in winter and is the source of several Miwok names. Other examples include Oya, "naming or speaking of the kuiatawila bird (jacksnipe)," and Tiktcu, "jacksnipe digging wild potatoes."

Heman (HAY-mahn) Hebrew for "faithful."

Hendrik (HEN-drik) "Ruler of a home" or "ruler of an estate" or "heir." Popular in Scandinavia, particularly in Denmark and Sweden, where a favorite variant is Henrik. Bulgarian forms are Henri and Henrim. The English equivalent is Henry.

Hersh (hairsh) Israeli name from the Yiddish for "a deer." Other forms include Hersch, Hirsch, and Herzl.

Hilel (hi-LEL) Arabic nature name which means "the new moon." Badr, another Arabic name, simply means "the moon." In astrology the moon governs the sign Cancer, while the moon card in the tarot pack corresponds to Pisces.

Hillel (hee-LAYL) Popular Israeli name from the Hebrew for "praised" or "famous." Hillel was a renowned Jewish scholar and spiritual leader who lived from about 70 B.C. to 10 A.D.

Hilmar Scandinavian name meaning "famous noble."

Hinun (hee-NOO:N) "God of clouds and rain." North American Indian name.

Hiroshi (hee-ROH-shee) Japanese for "generous."

Hisoka (hee-SOH-kah) Japanese for "secretive" or "reserved."

Ho Chinese for "the good."

Hod (hohd) Israeli name from the Hebrew for "vigorous" or "splendid."

Holic (HOH-lits) Czech occupation name meaning "barber."

Holleb Used in Poland and Germany, this name means "like a dove" or "one who lives at the sign of the dove," a symbol of peace. Also spelled Hollub and Holub, and often used as a surname.

Hollis (HOHL-lehs) Icelandic name meaning "of the great hall" or "island man."

213

Holt Ecological name meaning "son of the unspoiled forests."

Honon (HOH-nohn) This North American Indian name comes from the Miwok word for "bear."
Because of its great strength, the bear is prominent in Indian names. Other examples include Anawuye ("stretching a bear's hide to let it dry"); Esege ("bear showing its teeth when cross"); Molimo ("bear disappearing into the forest or going into the shade of trees"); and Uzumati ("grizzly bear," a nickname used for someone with an unpleasant disposition). See also Elki and Molimo.

Honovi (hoh-NOH-vee) "Strong." North American Indian name.

Hototo (hoh-TOH-toh) "The whistler." North Amercian Indian name.

Howi (HOH-wee) Miwok Indian name meaning "turtle-dove." The Miwoks used many dove names, some of which are Polneye, "dove feigning injury to fool someone, from *polangas,* "to fall"; Tcumetokti, "dove coming from the south"; and Wialu, "dove going away," from *wialum,* "to leave."

Howin (huh-ween) Chinese nature name meaning "a loyal swallow."

Hugo (HOO:-goh) "Intelligence" or "spirit." Used in Spanish-speaking countries, Sweden, and Germany. A Spanish variant is Hugon. The English equivalent is Hugh.

Hulin Among the Purim Kukis of China, this name is the exclusive property of the Marrim clan, and no one outside the clan is permitted to use it.

Hurley "Child of the sea and tides." Used for boys born under the water signs of the zodiac: Pisces, Cancer, and Scorpio. See Carswell for more information on water names.

Husain (hoh-SAYN) Muslim name meaning "little beauty."

A variant is Hussein, pronounced hoh-SIGH-een. Hussein was a descendant of the Prophet.

Hute (HOO:-te) North American Indian name for a star in the handle of the constellation Ursa Major, the Big Dipper.

Ian Scotch form of John, "gracious gift of God."

Ibrahim (i-brah-HEEM) Arabic form of the Hebrew Abraham, "father of a mighty nation." One of the most popular Muslim names in Turkey, Iran, India, Arabia, Egypt, and Jordan. The patriarch appears in both the Old Testament and the Koran.

Igasho (ee-GAH-shoh) North American Indian name meaning "a wanderer."

Ilias (ee-LEE-ahs) Also spelled Elias, this modern Greek name means "Jehovah is my God," from the Hebrew Elijah.

Ilom (ee-LOHM) Popular among the Ibo of Nigeria as an abbreviation of the name Ilomerika, "my enemies are many."

Ingmar "Famous son." Common in Scandinavia, particularly in Sweden. Also spelled Ingemar.

Iniko (ee-NEE-koh) Used by the Efek- or Ibibio-speaking people of Southern Nigeria for a child of either sex born during a time of civil war, invasion, or other disaster. Iniko literally means "time of trouble."

Inteus (een-TAY-oo:s) North American Indian name meaning "he shows his face." In other words, he is not ashamed.

Ioakim (ee-oh-AH-keem) Russian name from the Hebrew for "God will establish." Favorite pet forms in Russia include Akim, Jov, Iov, and Yov.

Ira Hebrew for "descendants."

Isaac From the Hebrew for "he will laugh." Isaac was the most common Jewish name during the twelfth century. Its popularity gradually dwindled until it was seldom used, but today the name is appearing more frequently, particularly in the United States.

Isak (ee-SAHK) A magic name meaning "identical point," used in incantations to invoke the powers of God.

Isas (i-SAHS) Japaese for "meritorious."

Istu (EES-too:) Miwok Indian name meaning "sugar-pine sugar." The sugar-pine was a principle source of food and often appears in Miwok names. Other examples include Sumtciwe, "fuzz on the sugar pine cone when it is young"; Uskuye, "cracking sugar pine nuts"; and Yoskolo, "breaking off sugar pine cones."

Ivan (ee-VAHN) Popular in Russia, Ivan is a development of the Hebrew Yehokhanan, "gracious gift of God." Favorite diminutives are Vania and Vanya. The English equivalent is John.

Ivar (EE-vahr) Popular in Sweden, this name means "yew-bow army."

Ives "Son of the yew bow" or "little archer." Astrologers use this name for boys born under Sagittarius, the Archer. A popular French variation is Yves.

Ivon (EE-vohn) From the Teutonic for "archer." Good astrological name for a boy born under Sagittarius, the Archer. Also spelled Yvon.

Iye (EE-yeh) North American Indian name meaning "smoke."

Jacinto (hah-SEEN-toh) Spanish name for the hyacinth. The feminine form is Jacinta.

Jacy North American Indian name. In Tupi-Guarani legend Jacy, the moon, is the creator of all plant life. The name may also refer to the planet Venus.

Jael (yah-AYL) Israeli name from the Hebrew for "mountain goat." Also a girl's name. In astrology the Goat is the symbol of Capricorn.

Jafar (jah-fahr) This contemporary Muslim name is popular in India and means "a little stream."

Jagger "To carry things in a cart." The name is gaining popularity in the United States, possibly because of pop singer Mick Jagger.

Jahi (JAH-hee) Swahili for "dignity."

Jaime (HIGH-meh) One of the most popular names in Spanish-speaking countries, Jaime means "the supplanter." Another common form is Diego. English equivalents are James and Jaymie.

Jakob (YAH-kohb) A favorite in Denmark, this name means "the supplanter." Also used in other Scandinavian countries and Germany. A similar Czech name is Jakub, with the nicknames Kuba and Kubes. The English equivalent is Jacob.

Jal (jahl) English Gypsy name which literally means "he goes," referring to a wanderer.

Jamil (jah-MEEL) Popular Muslim name from the Arabic for "handsome." Arabs have many euphemisms for common objects. Ibn Jamil, "father of Jamil," for instance, is a euphemism for "vegetables." Another example is Ibn Jami, a euphemism for "table" which comes from the personal name Jami, "collector."

Jan (yahn) Popular Czech form of Johanan, from the Hebrew Yohanan, "gracious gift of God" or "God is gracious." Other Czech forms are Janek, Jenda, Janos, Janko, Jano, and Honza. One of the most common Christian names in Slavic countries.

Jarek (YAH-rek) Polish name for a child born in January. Other forms are Janiusz, Janiuszck, Januarius, and Jarek.

Jaron (YAH-rohn) Hebrew for "to cry out" or "to sing."

Jaroslav (YAH-roh-slahf) "Glory of spring." One of the most popular names in Czechoslovakia today. The suffix -slav, or "glory," often appears in Czech names. Other examples include Budislav, "future glory," Ladislav, "glorious government," Miroslav, "glorious peace," and Vaclav, "glorious wreath."

Javas (JAH-vahs) Used in India, this name means "swift" or "quick."

Javier (hah-vee-AIR) Spanish Basque name meaning "owner of the new house."

Javin (yah-VEEN) Hebrew name. See Yarin.

Jay From the Old French for "blue jay."

Jayme (HIGH-meh) Current Spanish name. See Diego.

Jean French development of John, "gracious gift of God." By far the most popular boy's name in France today.

Jed Unusual Arabic name meaning "the hand."

Jedrek (YED-rik) Polish name meaning "strong and manly." A variation is Jedrus. See Andrey for other forms used in Poland and throughout the world.

Jeks (yehkss) Modern Latvian name from the Hebrew for "the supplanter." A more formal Latvian variation is Jeska. The English equivalent is Jacob.

Jens (yens) From the Hebrew for "God is gracious" or "gracious gift of God." Popular in Sweden, Norway, and Denmark. A Swedish variation is Jonam, and a Norwegian, Johan.

Jesper (YES-per) Swedish form of the Old French for "jasper stone." The English equivalent is Jasper.

Jibben (JEE-ben) English Gypsy name which means "life." Similar is the Gypsy Jivvel, "he lives."

Jin Chinese for "gold." The name is occasionally used if a child's horoscope is found to have too many wood influences. It is thought such names can overcome the evil in the stars because metal conquers wood.

Jiro (ji-ROH) Japanese for "the second male." *ro* meaning "male child."

Jivin (jee-veen) East Indian name which means "to give life." A variant is Jivanta, "long-lived," also used for girls.

218

Jo Japanese form of the Biblical Joseph, "God will increase."

Joel Hebrew for "God is willing."

Johan (YOH-hahn) One of the most popular names in Scandinavia. See Jens.

Joji (JOH-ji) Japanese form of George, "farmer."

Jolon (JOH-lohn) North American Indian name which means "valley of the dead oaks."

Jonah Hebrew peace name meaning "dove." The Spanish form is Jonas, pronounced hoh-NAHS. Jonas is also a favorite in Iceland, where it is pronounced YOH-nuhs.

Jone Welsh form of John, "gracious gift of God."

Jorge (HOHR-heh) Spanish name meaning "farmer" or "migrant worker." The English equivalent is George.

Jori (JOH-ree or YOH-ree) Hebrew for "descendent" or "flowing downward." Variations are Jory and the more formal Jordan.

Jose (hoh-SEH) Widely used in Spanish-speaking countries, Jose comes from the Hebrew for "God will increase." Favorite Spanish pet forms include Pepe, Pepillo, Pepito, Che, Chepe, Chepito, Josecito, and Joseito. The English equivalent is Joseph.

Josha (JOH-shuh) "Satisfaction." Used in India.

Jotham (YOH-tahm) This Hebrew name means "God is perfect."

Joy (johv) Russian pet form. See Ioakim.

Juan (hwahn) A favorite in Spanish-speaking countries. A form of John, "gracious gift of God."

Jude (joo:d) Contemporary Israeli form of Judah, "praise." Variants are Judd, Juda, and Judas.

Jules "Youthful" or "downy-bearded." An English nickname for Julius used today in the United States and France.

Julian (hoo:-lee-AHN) Spanish name meaning "belonging to Julius." The Zuni Indians borrowed the name and changed it to Halian. Another Spanish form is Julio.

Jumah (JOO:-mah) Muslim name for a child born on Friday, the holy day in the Muslim religion. Also spelled Jimoh.

Jun (joo:n) Chinese for "truth" and Japanese for "obedient." Also a girl's name.

Juri (YOO:-ree) Estonian for "farmer" or "migrant worker." Another popular form is Juss. Latvian equivalents are Juris, Jurka, and Juritis.

Kabil (kah-BEEL) Turkish development of the Biblical Cain, "possessed."

Kabir (k[h]ah-BEER) A medieval Hindu mystic who tried to combine some of the religious teachings of the Hindus and Muslims.

Kadar (KAH-dahr) Arabic for "powerful." An alternate spelling is Kedar.

Kadin (kah-DEEN) Arabic for "friend," "companion," or "confident."

Kadir (K[H]AH-deer) Unusual Arabic name meaning "green" or "green crop (of grain)," connoting freshness and innocence."

Kaga (KAH-gah) This North American Indian name is given to the tribe "writer" or "chronicler."

Kai (kigh) Hawaiian nature name meaning "sea" or "sea water." Also a girl's name.

Kakar (KUH-kuhr) "Grass." Used by the Todas of India.

Kala (KAH-lah) "Black" or "time." One of the many names for the Hindu god Siva.

Kalb (kahlb) Arabic for "dog." The name is rarely used today unless a family has lost many children and is trying to make the evil spirits believe the child is too worthless for them to bother with. A variation is Kilab, "dogs." The English equivalent is Caleb.

Kale (KAH-le) Hawaiian development of Charles, "strong and manly."

Kalil (k[h]ah-LEEL) Arabic for "good friend." An epithet of Abraham's. Other spellings include Kahlil, Khaleel, and Khalil. The same name is used in Israel, where it means "crown" or "wreath."

Kaliq (K[H]AH-liq) Arabic name meaning "creative" and referring to God.

Kalkin (kahl-KEEN) In Hindu literature Kalkin is the tenth incarnation of the god Vishnu and will come during the Age of Darkness. Some Hindu scholars say Kalkin is yet to come, others say he is already here. It is believed that Vishnu as Kalkin, or Kalki, will appear riding a white horse.

Kalle (KAH-le) A favorite in Scandinavia, particularly in Sweden and Finland, Kalle is a form of the German Karl, "strong and manly."

Kalman (KAWL-mahn) Hungarian form of the German Karl. Other Hungarian variations are Karoly, Karcsi, and Kari.

Kaloosh (kah-LOO:SH) Armenian name which means "blessed coming" or "blessed advent."

Kamali (kah-MAH-lee) Mashona name from Southern Rhodesia. Kamali is a spirit believed to help a newborn baby live while other children in the village are dying.

Kami (KAH-mee) "Loving." Another name for Kama, the handsome black Hindu god of love who rides a parrot and carries a bow of sugarcane strung with bees. His arrows are tipped with flowers.

Kamil (kah-MEEL) Popular Muslim name from the Arabic for "perfect," one of the ninety-nine qualities of God listed in the Koran.

Kane (KAH-ne) Currently used in Japan, where it means "golden," and in Hawaii, where it refers to "man" or "the eastern sky."

Kaniel (kah-nee-AYL) From the Hebrew for "stalk" or "reed."

Kantu (KAHN-too:) "Happy." Another name for Kama, the Hindu god of love. See Kami.

Kara (KAH-rah) Banti Eskimo nickname for a boy who has broken a finger.

Kardal (K[H]AHR-dal) Arabic for "mustard seed."

Karel (KAH-rel) Czech version of Charles. See Karl.

Karif (kah-REEF) Arabic name for a child born in "autumn." Also spelled Kareef.

Karim (ka-REEM) A favorite in Muslim countries, this Arabic name means "generous, friendly, precious, and distinguished," most often interpreted as simply "generous," which is one of the ninety-nine qualities of God listed in the Koran. Also spelled Kareem.

Karl Popular in Germany, Karl means "strong and manly." The name is also used in Bulgaria, Hungary, Serbia, and Scandinavian countries. A variation in Germany is Karal.
Other forms used throughout the world include Karel, Karol, and Karlik (Czech); Charles and Chuck (English); Charlot (French); Kalman, Karoly, and Karcsi (Hungarian); Kalle (Scandinavian); Carlo and Carlino (Italian); Karlens and Karlis (Latvian); Karol and Karolek (Polish); and Carlos (Portuguese and Spanish).

Karmel (kahr-MEHL) Modern Israeli name from the Hebrew for "vineyard," "garden," or "farm." Also a girl's name.

Kaseko (kah-SEH-koh) A Mashona woman of Southern Rhodesia who has been scorned because she has no children may proudly name her first-born Kaseko, "to mock" or "to ridicule."

Kasib (KAH-sib) Arabic for "fertile."

Kasim (kah-SEEM) Muslim name meaning "divided." Also spelled Kaseem.

222

Kasimir (KAH-se-mer) Slavic name meaning "commands peace."

Kasper German name derived from either the Greek for "precious stone" or the Persian for "a treasured secret."

Kass German name meaning "blackbirdlike." Pet forms include Kase, Kasch, and Kaese.

Kayin (kah-YEEN) "Celebrated." Yoruban name for a long-hoped-for child.

Keahi (ke-AH-hee) Hawaiian for "fire." Also a girl's name.

Keb A mystical name from the Egyptian *Book of the Dead*, considered by many to be the original book of magic. Keb was an ancient earth god upon whose back grew the trees and plants of the world. He is sometimes pictured with a goose on his head and is often called the great cackler because he supposedly laid the egg from which the world sprang. In Pyramid Texts he is the god of the dead, representing the earth in which the dead are laid.

Kedar (KEH-dahr) "Mountain lord." One of the 1,008 names for the Hindu god Siva. See Siva for further information.

Keddy Scotch variation of Adam, "man of the red earth." Other forms include Keddie and Keady.

Kedem (KE-dem) Hebrew for "ancient" or "old" or "from the east."

Keegan "Little fiery one." Astrological name for boys born under the fire signs Aries, Leo, and Sagittarius.

Keir (keer) "Dark-skinned." Derived from Celtic.

Kekoa (ke-KOH-uh) A shortened form of the Hawaiian name Kekoalauliionapalihauliuliokekoolau, which means "the fine-leafed koa tree on the beautiful green ridges of the Koolau (mountains)."

Kele (KEH-leh) "Sparrow hawk." Hopi Indian name from the Rattlesnake Cult. Also spelled Kelle.

Kelemen (KE-le-men) Hungarian name which means "gentle" or "kind." The English equivalent is Clement.

Kelii (ke-LEE) Hawaiian for "the chief."

Kell "From the spring." Astrologers use this name for boys born under the water signs Pisces, Cancer, and Scorpio.

Kem (kehm) English Gypsy name meaning "the sun," which in astrology rules the sign Leo.

Kenan The given name of the famed black pastor Kenan Kamwana of Malawi, who taught his followers not to pay heed to Britain's colonial government because the black people were the chosen children of God.

Kenn Ecological name meaning "clear, sweet water." Also an occult name for boys born under the water signs Pisces, Cancer, and Scorpio. See Carswell for the significance of water names in astrology.

Kerel Afrikaans for "young man."

Kerem (ke-REM) Turkish for "nobility and kindness."

Kerey (KEH-ree) English Gypsy name meaning "homeward bound." A variation is Keri. The Gypsy names Keir and Ker simply mean "house."

Kern From the Irish Gaelic *ceirin,* "little black one." Other Irish forms are Kearn, Kerne, and Kieran.

Kerry From the Irish Gaelic for "son of the black one" or simply "black one."

Kers The Todas of India take this name from the plant known to botanists as eugenia arnottiana, wight.

Kersen Indonesian name which means "cherry."

Kerwin "Little jet-black one." Used in Ireland.

Kesar (keh-SAHR) Russian name meaning "hairy" or "long-haired." Also used in the Ukraine.

Kesin (keh-SEEN) Hindu title for "long-haired beggars."

Kesse (KEH-se) Fanti or Ashanti name for a boy who is fat at birth. The feminine form is Kessie.

Kibbe (KEEB-beh) North American Indian name meaning "the night bird," from the Nayas Indians.

Kijika (kee-YEE-kah) North American Indian name for a child who "walks quietly."

Kil (keel) Used by the Todas of India, this name comes from a prayer. Another prayer name is Erai.

Kim Vietnamese for "gold" or "metal." The name is sometimes given to restore the balance of metal and wood influences in a child's horoscope. Kim is also used in the United States. For more information on its possible American origins, see the Kim listed in the girls' section.

Kin Japanese for "golden."

Kiral (ki-RUHL) Turkish for "king."

Kiril (KI-ril) Bulgarian name from the Greek Kyrillos, "lordly one." Other names from the same source include Cyrek and Cyra, Czech; Cyryl and Cyrek, Polish; Keereel, Ciro, Kirill, Kirila, Kiryl, and Korney, Russian; and Cirilo, Ciro, and Cirio, Spanish.

Kiritan (keer-ee-TAHN) "Wearing a crown." Another name for the Hindu gods Vishnu and Indra.

Kistna (KIST-nah) A favorite in Hindu India, this name refers to an Indian river which some texts classify as one of the seven sacred Hindu rivers. Kistna is also a shortened form of Krishna. See Krishna, listed in the girls' section.

Kistur (KEE-stoo:r) English Gypsy name meaning "a rider."

Kito (KEE-toh) Swahili for "jewel," implying the child is precious.

Kivi (KEE-vee) Israeli name which means "supplant," "protected," or "held by the heel." Variants are Kiva Akiva, and Akiba.

Kiyoshi (kee-YOH-shee) Japanese for "quiet," an admirable virtue.

Kizza (keez-SAH) Used in Uganda for a child "born after twins."

Kliment (KLEE-ment) Russian name from the Latin for "kind" or "gentle." Other modern Russian forms include Klemet, Klemeny, Klim, and Klyment. The Hungarian Klement, the German Klemens, and the Greek Klemenis come from the same source.

Knoton (K.NOH-tohn) North American Indian name meaning "the wind." A variant is Nodin.

Knud (k.noo:d) A favorite in Denmark, Knud means "kind."

Knut (k.noo:t) Common today in Norway and Sweden, this name comes from the Old Norse for "knot." The modern American equivalent is Canute.

Kokudza (koh-KOO:D-zah) Like many African names, this one reveals a preoccupation with death, which claims so many infants in Africa. Kokudza means "the child shall not live long," and the name may be given to trick the demons into believing no one cares if the child dies.

Kolya (KOHL-yah) Popular pet form in Russia. See Nikolos.

Konane (koh-NAH-ne) Hawaiian for "bright as moonlight." Also a girl's name.

Konni (KOH-nee) German name from the Old German for "bold adviser." Other German forms are Konrad, Kurt, and Conny.

Kono (KOH-noh) Miwok Indian name which suggests "a tree squirrel biting through the middle of a pine nut." The American Indian is perhaps the best source for nature names.
Other examples include Kalmanu ("lightning striking a tree"); Nikiti ("round and smooth like an abalone shell"); Otu ("collecting sea shells in a basket");

Siwili ("long tail of the fox which drags along the ground"); Wenutu ("sky clearing after being cloudy"); and Yotimo ("the yellow jacket carrying pieces of meat from a house to its nest").

Kontar (KOHN-tar) Used by the Akan of Ghana for "an only child."

Korb German for "basket."

Korudon (koh-ROO:-dohn) Greek for "helmeted one" or "crested one."

Kostas (KOH-stahs) Modern Greek name. See Dinos.

Kosti (KOH-stee) Finnish name meaning "staff of the Goths." The English equivalent is Gus.

Kovar (KOH-vahr) This Czech occupation name is the equivalent of the English Smith.

Krikor (kree-KOHR) Popular Armenian name from the Latin Gregorius, "watchful." St. Gregory is the patron saint of Armenia.

Krispin (KREES-pin) Slovakian for "curly-haired." In Poland the name is spelled Kryspin.

Kriss Latvian name meaning "Christian." Also used in Germany. Other Latvian forms are Kristafs and Krisus.

Krister (KREE-ster) "Anointed one." A Swedish form of Christ. The Norwegian form is Krist.

Kristian (KREE-stee-ahn) "Believer in Christ." A favorite in Sweden.

Kristo (KREE-stoh) Modern Greek nickname for Christoforos or Khristos, "Christ-bearer." English equivalents are Chris and Christopher.

Kruin (KROO:-in) Afrikaans name meaning "top of a tree" or "mountain peak."

Kulen (KOO:-lehn) Popular among the Todas of India, Kulen is a shortened form of Kulpakh. The meaning is unknown.

Kumar (koo:-MAHR) "Prince." One of the many names used in India to refer to royalty.

Kuper Yiddish name meaning "copper," given to a boy born with reddish or golden hair.

Kurt Hungarian and German name which means "bold counselor."

Kuzih (KOO:-zhi) Carrier Indian name which means "great talker."

Kwaku (KWAH-koo:) Akan name from Ghana for a boy born on Wednesday.

Kwam (kwahm) Zuni Indian form of the Spanish Juan, "gracious gift of God." Another Zuni variation is Kwan.

Kwame (KWAH-me) Common among the Akan of Ghana for a boy born on Memenda, or Saturday. The feminine equivalent is Ama.

Kwamin (KWA-men) Used by the Ga-speaking people of Africa for a boy born on Saturday.
Other Ga day-of-birth names are Kudjo, "Monday," Kwabina, "Tuesday," Kwaku, "Wednesday," Kwau, "Thursday," Koffi, "Friday," and Kwashi, "Sunday."

Kwasi (KWAH-see) Akan name for a boy born on *Kwasinda,* or Sunday. The feminine equivalent is Akosua.

Kwesi (KWEH-see) African Ochi name for a boy born on Sunday.
Other Ochi day-of-birth names are Kudju, "Monday," Akwau, "Thursday," Kwofi, "Friday," and Kwamina, "Saturday." Ochi names for children born on Tuesday and Wednesday are listed under Kwamin.

Kyle (kighl) Yiddish for "crowned with laurel," a victory symbol.

Laban (lah-BAHN) Hebrew for "white."

Lado (LAH-doh) Common among the Bari of Southern Sudan for a second-born boy. Lado is often used for a second-born twin, along with Ulan, the name for a first-born twin. Other Bari serial names include Wani or Wanike; "third-born boy," Pitia, "fourth-born boy," and Mogga, "boy born after twins," literally "he holds twins" or "he is held by twins."

Lais (lays) This Muslim name is common in India and means "lion." See Haidar.

Lal (lahl) Hindu for "beloved." Another name for Krishna. See Krishna, listed in the girls' section.

Lamar "Close to (or related to) the sea." Used for those born under the water signs of the zodiac: Pisces, Cancer, and Scorpio. The name has also been traced to the Old German for "land famous."

Lang Scandinavian name from the Old Norse for "tall man."

Langundo (lahn-GOO:N-doh) "Peaceful." North American Indian name.

Lani (LAH-nee) Hawaiian name meaning "sky." This is also a common element in many longer Hawaiian names. See Lani, listed in the girls' section.

Lanu (LAH-noo) Miwok Indian name which means "people passing one another at the pota ceremony when running around the pole." Miwok Indian names often reveal tribal customs.
Other examples include Noini, "putting a feather ornament on your head"; Pota, "a man running around the pota ceremony pole"; and Simutuye, "pinning together a squirrel's abdomen after is has been gutted."

Lars One of the most popular Norwegian names, Lars means "crowned with laurel." Also used in Denmark and Sweden. See Lorens.

Lashi (LAH-shee) English Gypsy form of Louis, "famous warrior." Also spelled Lasho. The Scotch equivalent is Lesley. Hungarian forms are Lajos and Lazlo.

Lavi (LAH-vee) Hebrew for "lion." Yiddish forms are

Leib and Leibel. In astrology the Lion is the symbol of Leo.

Leander "Like a lion." Occult name for a boy born under Leo, the Lion.

Leben (LAY-ben) Yiddish for "life."

Leif (leef) "Beloved." One of the most popular names in Norway. Also spelled Lief.

Lel (layl) English Gypsy name meaning "he takes."

Len (lehn) "Flute." Hopi Indian name from the Flute Cult. Often combined with other words to create names such as Lenmana, "flute maiden," and Len-hono-noma, "standing flute," referring to the flute ceremony.

Lenci (LEN-tsee) Hungarian development of the Latin for "crowned with laurel." Variants include Loreca and Lorinc.

Lenn A shortened form of Leonard, "lionlike." For the Leos of the zodiac.

Lenno (LEHN-noh) North American Indian name which means "man."

Lennor (LEH-nohr) English Gypsy name meaning "spring" or "summer."

Lensar (LEHN-sahr) English Gypsy name meaning "with his parents." A variation is Lendar, "from his parents."

Leon (leh-OHN) Spanish name from the Latin for "lion," the symbol of the zodiacal sign Leo.

Leonid (LAY-oh-nid) A favorite in Russia, this name comes from the Old Frankish for "brave as a lion." A common pet form is Lonya.

Leor (leh-OHR) Israeli name meaning "I have light." Also a girl's name.

Leron (leh-ROHN) Israeli name meaning "song is mine." Other forms include Lerone, Liron, and Lirone.

Lev (lef) Russian name from the Latin for "lion." Other variations are Levka and Levushka. Also used in the Ukraine. The English equivalent is Leo.

Levi (LAY-vee) Popular Israeli name from the Hebrew for "joined to," in the sense of joined with God. Other variants are Levy, Levey, and Lewi. A pet form is Lev.

Liam (LEE-uhm) One of the most popular names in Ireland, Liam is a shortened form of William, "unwavering protector."

Liang (lee-AHNG) Chinese for "good" or "excellent."

Liko (lee-koo:) This unusual Chinese name means "Buddhist nun" and is given to boys to suggest to the demon world the child is not of much value at the same time is protected by Buddha.

Linfred "Gentle peace." Used today in Germany.

Lio (LEE-oh) Hawaiian development of Leo, "lion."

Lise (LEE-se) Miwok Indian name which means "salmon's head just coming out of the water." According to one legend, the salmon were once locked up by two old hags so the Indians could not get to them. The coyote, who was talkative and polite in those days, tricked the hags into giving him the key to the salmon and unlocked the river for the Indians.

Liu (LEE-oo) Used by the Ngoni of Malawi, this name means "voice."

Liwanu (lee-WAH-noo) Miwok Indian name which means "bear growling."

Loe (LOH-e) Hawaiian development of Roy, "king."

Lokni (LOHK-nee) Miwok Indian name which means "rain coming through a small hole in the roof." A father might give this name to a boy born during a rainstorm.

Loman (LOH-mahn) Serbo-Croatian name meaning "delicate."

Lonato (loh NAH toh) North American Indian name meaning "flint."

Lono (LOH-noh) The Hawaiian god of peace and agriculture.

Lorant (LOH-rawnt) Hungarian name from the Latin for "crowned with laurel." Other Hungarian forms are Lorencz, Lorinc, and Lenci.

Lorens From the Latin for "crowned with laurel." Popular in Norway, where other forms are Laurans, Larse, and Lars. Also used in Sweden and Denmark.

Lory Malayan name for a particular species of parrot.

Lothar German name meaning "famous warrior." The Spanish development is Luis.

Loudon Teutonic name meaning "from the low valley." Also spelled Lowdon.

Luister Afrikaans for "a listener."

Lukyan (loo:-kee-AHN) Russian development of the Latin for "light" or "bringer of light" or "bringer of knowledge." A diminutive is Lukasha. Other variations include Luce, Lucius, and Licien, French; Loukas, Modern Greek; Lucas and Lucio, Spanish; Lukas, Swedish; and Lusio, Zuni Indian.

Lunt (loo:nt) Scandinavian name meaning "from the grove."

Lutherum (LOO:-theh-ruhm) "Slumber." English Gypsy name for a child who always sleeps.

Luyu (LOO:-yoo) Miwok Indian name from the word *luyani,* "to shake the head," implying "dove shaking its head sideways."

Luyunu (loo-YOO:-noo) Miwok Indian name. The violent connotation is "bear taking off a leg or arm of a person while eating him." Similar in meaning is the Miwok Neplu, "bear eating a man."

Luz (loo:s) Spanish for "light." Also a girl's name.

232

Lyron (lee-ROHN) Israeli name from the Hebrew for "lyric" or "lyrical." A variation is Liron, "song is mine."

Maggio Derived from Italian, this name is used for a boy born in May, under the zodiacal sign Taurus, the Bull, Gemini, the Twins.

Mahir (mah-HEER) Hebrew for "industrious" or "expert."

Maimun (MIGH-moo:n) Arabic name which means "lucky."

Makan Common name among the Purim Kukis of Manipur, a tiny tribe whose clans exercise monopolies over certain given names. Makan is also a girl's name.

Makis (MAH-kees) Modern Greek name meaning "who is like God?" Variants include Mihail, Mikhail, Michail, Mikhalis, and Mikhos. The English equivalent is Michael.

Maksim (mahk-SEEM) Russian development of the Latin for "greatest in excellence." A pet form is Maks.

Malik (MAH-lik) Muslim name meaning "master." According to some Muslims, the name God dislikes most is Malik Al-Amlak, which means "king of kings."

Mamo (MAH-moh) Hawaiian for "saffron flower" or "yellow bird." Also a girl's name.

Manchu (mahn-joo:) Chinese for "pure."

Manco (MAHN-koh) Used by the Incas of Peru, this name means "king."

Mandek (MAHN-dek) Polish for "army man." Other forms include Armand, Armandek, and Arek. The English equivalent is Armand.

Mander (MAHN-der) English Gypsy name meaning "from me."

Mando (MAHN-doh) Used in Spanish-speaking countries as a shortened form of Armando "army man."

233

Mandrill A large, ferocious, gregarious baboon of western Africa, the male of which has blue and scarlet patches on his face and rump.

Manipi (mah-NEE-pee) This North American Indian name means "a walking wonder."

Mansa (MAHN-sah) African word for an African king. In ancient Egyptian times these rulers basked in elegance. One mansa was always accompanied by at least three hundred servants and musicians, the latter with gold and silver guitars. Another mansa from Mali was so extravagant in his tastes that when he passed through Cairo on a pilgrimage to Mecca, he and his followers threw such a quantity of gold on the market that they undermined the price of the Egyptian dinar.

Mansur (man-SOO:R) "Divinely aided." Common Arabic name.

Manu (mah-NOO:) Akan name from Ghana for a "second-born son" if the male children are successive.

Manuel (mah-noo:-EHL) A favorite in Spanish-speaking countries, Manuel comes from the Hebrew for "God be with us." The Russian form is Manuil, with variants Manuel, Manuyil, and Emmanuil. The English equivalent is Emmanuel.

Marar (mah-RAHR) Used by the Wataware of Southern Rhodesia, this unusual name means "dirt." Also spelled Marara.

Marek (MAH-rek) Polish development of the Latin for "warlike one." Other Polish forms are Marcin and Marcinek. English equivalents are Martin and Mark.
Many names throughout the world come from the same Latin source, including Marko, Marcus, Marko, Martinka, Martin, and Tynek (Czech); Marc and Mertin (French); Markus and Martel (German); Marinos, Markos, and Martinos (Greek); Marton, Marci, Marcilka, Martino, and Marcilki

(Hungarian); Marco and Mario (Italian); Marts, Markus, and Martins (Latvian); Marcos, Marco, Martial, Mario, and Martins (Portuguese and Spanish); Marten (Swedish); Martyn (Ukrainian and Russian); and Marti (Swiss and Slovenian).

Marid (MAH-rid) Arabic for "rebellious."

Marnin (mahr-NEEN) Currently used in Israel, Marnin comes from the Hebrew for "one·who creates joy" or "one who sings."

Marrim (MAH-reem) Common name among the Purim Kukis, a tiny tribe of only a few hundred people who live in four villages near Waikhong, in Manipur State in China. Marrim is also a girl's name.

Mart (muhrt) Turkish name for a child born during the month of March.

Martel "Related to Mars." Astrological name for boys born under Aries and Scorpio, both of which are ruled by Mars. Martel is actually a form of Martin. See Marek for other ethnic forms.

Marut (MAH-ruht) Another name for the Hindu god Vayu, who controls the winds.

Marv Ecological name meaning "friend of the sea."

Maska (MAHS-kah) North American Indian name meaning "powerful."

Maslin (MAHS-lin or MAS-lin) Originally derived from Old French, Maslin means "little twin." Another spelling is Maslen. Astrologers use the name for boys born under Gemini, the Twins. Geminis are said to have dual personalities, with the abilities to adapt quickly to changing situations and to do two things at a time. They tend to be versatile, restless, and high-strung.

Masou (mah-SOH-oo) North American Indian name which refers to a fire diety.

Masud (mah-SOO:D) Swahili name derived from the Arabic for "fortunate."

Mato (MAH-toh) North American Indian name meaning "brave."

Matope (mah-TOH-peh) Used by the Mashona of Southern Rhodesia, Matope means "this shall be the last child."

Matt Estonian form of the Hebrew Matthew, "gift from Jehovah." The name is popular throughout the world, and other variations include Matei, Bulgarian; Matek and Matus, Czech; Matthieu, French; Mathe, German; Matvey, Motka, and Matyash, Russian; Mates and Mato, Slovakian; and Matro and Matias, Spanish.

Mauli (MOW-lee) Hawaiian name meaning "dark-skinned."

Mayer "Farmer." One of the commonest names in Austria and often used as a surname.

Mayon (MIGH-yon) In Hindu Tamil myth Mayon is an ancient equivalent of Krishna, the black god.

Mehmet (ME-met) A form of Muhammad particularly popular in Turkey. See Muhammad.

Mehtar (meh-tahr) East Indian name meaning "prince." Used to indicate noble ancestry, but also popular among poorer castes.

Malvern (MEHL-vehrn) "Great chief." Common North American Indian name.

Mendeley (men-de-LAY) Russian name from either the Yiddish for "comforter" or the Latin for "of the mind." Mendeley is also a modern Yiddish form of Menachem.

Mensah (men-sah) One of the most common names in Ghana and given to a "third-born male" in succession.

Mered (me-REHD) Hebrew for "revolt."

Merripen (MEH-ree-pen) English Gypsy name meaning

"life." Strangely enough, the name also means "death."

Mestipen (MEHS-tee-pen) English Gypsy name meaning "life," "fortune," or "luck."

Meyer Belgian name meaning "farmer."

Mikkel (MEE-kel) A favorite in Denmark, Mikel comes from the Hebrew for "who is like God?" The English equivalent is Michael.
In its many variations, the name is one of the most popular in the world. Other forms include Michal, Czech and Polish; Mikk, Estonian; Michel, French; Michah, Hebrew; Milkins, Mikus, Miks, and Mikelis, Latvian; Mihas, Rumanian; Mischa, Slovakian; Migil and Miguel, Spanish; and Mikael, Swedish.

Milap (MEE-lahp) North American Indian name meaning "he gives."

Mimis (MEE-mees) Popular in Greece as a pet form of Dhimitrios, which means "belonging to Demeter," the Greek fertility goddess. Other Greek forms include Dhimitris, Mitsos, and Mitros. Dhimitrios is also the source of the English Demetrius and the Russian Dimitry.

Mingan (MEEN-gahn) North American Indian name meaning "the gray wolf."

Misu (MEE-soo:) This Miwok Indian name means "rippling water."
Water names are common among the Miwoks, and other examples include Iskemu, "water running gently when the creek dries"; Miltaiye, "water in waves"; Uhubitu, "foul, stinking, stagnant water"; and Yottoko, "black mud at the edge of the water."

Mohan (MOH-hahn) Hindu for "delightful." Another name for Krishna, the most celebrated god in the Hindu pantheon.

Mojag (MOH-yahg) "Never quiet." North American Indian name for a baby who cries a lot.

237

Molimo (moh-LEE-moh) Miwok Indian name which means "bear going into the shade of trees."
The bear often appears in Miwok names, some of which are Hatawa ("bear breaking the bones of people or animals," from *hate*, "to press with the foot," and *atwa*, "to split"); Hoho ("bear growling"); Hulwema ("dead grizzly which has been shot and killed by a hunter"); Huslu ("bear with a lot of hair"); and Utatci ("bear scratching itself"). See also Elki and Honon.

Morgan "Born in the sea." Used for boys born under the water signs of the zodiac: Pisces, Cancer, and Scorpio. See Carswell for the significance of water names in astrology.

Morse "Son of the black one." American name derived from Latin. Variants include Morris, Maurice, and Morrison. The Dutch form is Maurits, and the Modern Greek, Moris.

Morven "Child of the sea." Astrological name for those born under the water signs of the zodiac: Pisces, Cancer, and Scorpio. The more common name Murray has a similar meaning.

Moshe (moh-SHAY) Hebrew form of Moses, meaning "saved (from the water)."

Mosi (MOH-see) Swahili for "first born." Used primarily in Tanzania.

Moswen (MOHSS-wehn) African name from Botswana for a child "light in color."

Motega (moh-TEH-gah) North American Indian name meaning "new arrow."

Muhammad The Prophet Muhammad universalized this name, which comes from the Arabic *hamida*, meaning "the praised one." There are more than five hundred variations, including Mahmud, Mehmet, Mohamet, Mehemet, Mahmoud, Amed, Ahmad, Hamid, Hammad, Humayd, Hamdrem, and Hamdun. A Muslim saying is "If you have a hundred sons, name them all Muhammad." With its many variations, Muhammad is the most popular boy's name among Muslims and is generally considered the most common boy's name in the world.

Munda (MOO:N-dah) Southern Rhodesian name meaning "garden." Anglicized to Mundan.

Muraco (MOO:rah-choh) North American Indian name meaning "white moon." In astrology the moon governs the sign Cancer, while the card of the moon in the tarot pack corresponds to Pisces.

Musenda (moo:-SEHN dah) African Baduma name meaning "nightmare." Given to a child if the mother has a vivid dream right before birth.

Nabil (nah-BEEL) Common Arabic name meaning "noble."

Nagid (nah-GEET) Hebrew for "prince" or "ruler."

Nahele (nah-HEH-le) Hawaiian for "forest" or "grove of trees."

Nahma (NAH-mah) North American Indian name meaning "the sturgeon."

Nalren (NAHL-rehn) Dene Indian name meaning "he is thawed out."

Namid (NAH-meed) "Star dancer." This North American Indian name probably refers to the coyote, who was so vain he wanted to dance with the stars. So one night he asked a star to sail by a mountain and take him by the paw, which she did. The next night the coyote got impatient for her to come by, so he jumped off the mountain himself, thinking if the star could fly, so could he. He was "ten whole snowfalls in falling, and when he landed, he was squashed as flat as a willow mat."

Namir (nah-MEER) Israeli name meaning "leopard," connoting swiftness.

Nandin (NAHN-deen) One of the 1,008 names for the

Hindu god Siva, the destroyer who eats flesh and hungers for blood sacrifices. See Siva.

Narain (nah-RIGHN) Common Hindu name shortened from Narayana, which is another name for the god Vishnu, protector and sustainer of the world.

Nard Persian for "the game of chess."

Nasser (NAS-ser) A favorite among Muslims, this name comes from the Arabic for "victorious," one of the ninety-nine qualities of God listed in the Koran. Also spelled Nassor by the Swahili-speaking people of Tanzania.

Natal (nah-TAHL) Spanish name for a boy born at Christmas. Originally derived from the French noel.

Nav (nahv) English Gypsy name from the Hungarian Nev, "name."

Nawat (NAH-waht) North American Indian name meaning "left hand."

Nayati (nah-YAH-tee) North American Indian meaning "the wrestler."

Nehru This East Indian name comes from the word *nahar,* "canal." The late Prime Minister Nehru was so named because a canal passed by the ancestral estates of his family.

Neith Occult name from the Egyptian *Book of the Dead,* often called the original book of magic. The goddess Neith personifies the place in the sky where the sun rises.

Nelek (NEL-ek) Polish pet form of Kornelek, "horn-colored" or "like a horn." Other forms used in Poland are Kornel and Kornek. The English equivalent is Cornel.

Nen Occult name from the Egyptian *Book of the Dead.* Nen personifies the inert, motionless primeval waters and is sometimes pictured with a human body and the head of a frog.

Neper (NEH-pair) Spanish name from the Greek for "of the new city." A Spanish variant is Napier.

Nepter Astrological name combining Neptune plus Jupiter, the two planets which jointly rule the· sign Pisces, the Fishes.

Neron (neh-ROHN) Spanish name from the Latin for "strong" or "stern." The English equivalent is Nero.

Neto (NEH-toh) Spanish for "earnest." A variation is Ernesto.

Newlin "Son of the new pool." Used as an astrological water name. A variant spelling is Newlyn. See Carswell for more information on water names.

Nibaw (NEE-baw) "I stand up." North American Indian name.

Nicabar (nee-kah-BAHR) Spanish Gypsy name meaning "to take away" or "to steal."

Nicanor (nee-kah-NOHR) Spanish name meaning "victorious army" or "victorious people." A variant is Nicolas. See Nikolos.

Nigan (NEE-gahn) North American Indian name meaning "ahead."

Nigel "Black" or "dark." Used in the United States.

Niki (NEE-kee) Polish nickname for Dominik and Donek, meaning 'born on Sunday" or "belonging to God." English equivalents. are Nick and Dominick. In Greece Niki is a girl's name meaning "victorious army."

Nikolos (nee-KOH-lohs) A favorite in Greece, Nikolos means "victorious army" or "victorious people." Greek variations are Nikolaos and Nikos. The English equivalent is Nicholas.
Other forms used throughout the world include Nikolas and Nikita (Bulgarian); Nikulas and Nikula (Czech); Mikulas and Miki (Slovakian); Nicole (French); Nikolaus, Klaus, and Claus (German);

Niklos, Miki, and Niki (Hungarian); Nicola (Italian); Nikolai, Nilek, and Kola (Polish); Nikolai and Kolya (Russian); Nils and Niklas (Swedish); Niles (Finnish); Nicolai (Norwegian); and Nicolas (Spanish).

Nissan (nees-SAHN) Hebrew for "flight."

Nissim (nees-SEEM) Hebrew for "sign" or "miracle."

Nitis (NEE-tes) North American Indian name meaning "friend" or "good friend." Also spelled Netis.

Nnamdi (nahm-DEE) Nigerian name meaning "my father is still alive." Given to a child thought to be the reincarnation of his father.

Nodin (NOH-din) North American Indian name meaning "the wind." A variant is Noton.

Noe (noh-EH) Spanish development of the Hebrew Noah, "quiet peace" or "rest."

Nowles (nohlz) "From the grassy slope in the forest." Earth name for boys born under the earth signs of the zodiac: Capricorn, Taurus, and Virgo. Other spellings include Knowles and Knolls. See Blair for further information on earth names.

Noy Israeli name meaning "beauty."

Numair (noo:-MIGHR) Arabic diminutive of Nimr, which means "panther."

Nuri (NOO:-ree) Used today in Israel, this name means "fire." Other popular forms are Nur, Nuria, and Nuriel, the last two meaning "fire of God."

Nuru (NOO:-roo) Swahili name meaning "light." Given to a child born during daylight. Also a girl's name.

Nusair (noo:-SIGHR) Arabic diminutive of Nasr, which means "vulture."

Obram Common name among the Purim Kukis of Manipur State in China. Also used for girls.

Odin The chief god in Norse mythology, source of all wisdom, patron of culture, and champion of heroes.

Odinum (oh-dee-NOO:M) Used by the Ochi- and Ga-speaking people of Africa, this name expresses the African's love for children. Odinum means "fifteenth-born son" or "fifteenth-born daughter."

Odion (OH-dee-ohn) The Benin of Nigeria give this name to the "first of twins."

Odissan (oh-DEES-sahn) African Ochi and Ga name for a "thirteenth-born son."

Odinan (oh-dee-NAHN) African Ochi and Ga name for a "fourteenth-born son."

Odon (OH-dohn) Contemporary Hungarian name meaning "wealthy protector." A pet form is Odi. The English equivalent is Edmund.

Offin (oh-FEEN) Ghanaian name. See Fynn.

Ogun (oh-GOO:N) In African Yoruban legend Ogun is the god of war and the son of the river and lake goddess.
Many Yoruban names come from this god, including Ogunkeye, "Ogun has earned honor," Ogunsanwo, "Ogun gives help," and Ogunsheye, "Ogun has performed honorably."

Ohanko (oh-HAHN-koh) North American Indian name meaning "reckless."

Ohin (oh-HEEN) Used by the Akan of Ghana, Ohin means "chief."
Titled positions are a common source of given names, and other such names include Bafour, a title held by junior chiefs; Barima, "real man" or "great leader," a title held by all Akan senior chiefs; and Bekoe, Bediako, and Arko, all of which means "born fighter" or warrior.

Oko (oh-KOH) Another name for the Yoruban god of war. See Ogun.

Okon (oh-KOHN) Efik name used in Africa for a boy "born at night."

Olaf A favorite in Norway, Olaf comes from the Old Norse for "ancestral relic." This was the name of five Norwegian kings. Also spelled Olav. A popular form in Iceland is Olafur.

Olery French name from the Old German for "ruler of all."

Oles (OH-les) Polish form of Alexander, "helper and defender of mankind." See Alek for Russian forms of the name.

Olorun (oh-loh-ROO:N) The supreme god of the Yoruban pantheon, Olorun was born from Olokun, the mighty ocean of the sky. The ancient diety is no longer worshipped.

Omar (OH-mahr) Arabic for "first son," "most high," or "follower of the Prophet." Also spelled Omer.

Onan (oh-NUHN) Turkish for "prosperous." Also a popular surname.

Onani (oh-NAH-nee) Used in Malawi, this Ngoni name means "look!"

Opie (OH-pee) From the Greek for "opium."

Orban (OHR-bawn) Hungarian name from the Latin for "city boy" or "born in the city."

Ordando (ohr-DAHN-doh) Spanish name. See Roldan.

Oren (oh-REHN) Hebrew name meaning "ash tree."

Orji (OHR-jee) Nigerian Ibo name meaning "mighty tree."

Orunjan (oh-ROO:N-jahn) The Yoruban god of the midday sun.

Otadan (oh-TAH-dahn) North American Indian name meaning "plenty."

Otman (OHT-mahn) Spanish name from the Old German for "prosperous man." A common variant is Oton.

Ottah (oht-TAH) Used by the Urhobo-speaking people of Nigeria for a child who is thin at birth.

244

Ouray (oh-RAY) North American Indian name meaning "the arrow." In astrology the Archer is the symbol of Sagittarius.

Pablo (PAH-bloh) Spanish form of Paul, from the Latin for "little." The Italian form is Paolo.

Paco (PAH-choh) North American Indian name meaning "bald eagle."

Paddy Contemporary American creation from Patrick, "noble one."

Paki (PAH-kee) Used in South Africa, this name means "witness."

Pal (pahl) English Gypsy name meaning "brother."

Palani (pah-LAH-nee) Hawaiian development of Francis, "free man" or "Frenchman." See Francisco for other forms.

Pall (pahl) One of the most popular names in Iceland, Pall comes from the Latin for "little."
Forms used in other countries include Pavel, Czech and Russian; Pal, Pali, and Palika, Hungarian; Pal, Swedish; Poul, Danish; Pawel, Paulin, Pawelek, and Inek, Polish; and Pablo and Paulo, Spanish.

Pallaton (PAHL-lah-tohn) North American Indian name meaning "fighter."

Pancho (PAHN-choh) Common Spanish name meaning "free one" or "Frenchman." See Francisco for other Spanish forms.

Parker Ecological name meaning "protector (or keeper) of the park."

Parlan "Farmer" or "son of the earth." Popular today in Scotland.

Pascal "Pass over." Hebrew name for a child born during the Passover season.

Pat (paht) North American Indian name meaning "fish." In astrology the Fishes are the symbol of Pisces.

Patamon (PAH-tah-mahn) North American Indian name which means "raging."

Patrin (PAH-trin) This English Gypsy name refers to a trail Gypsies make from handfuls of leaves or grass which are thrown along the way to guide those behind.

Pattin (PAHT-tin) English Gypsy name meaning "a leaf," connoting freshness. The Spanish Gypsy form is Patia.

Patwin (PAT-win) Popular North American Indian name meaning "man." According to a Liwaito legend, a great flood covered the Sacramento Valley and destroyed all men but one. After an earthquake opened the Golden Gate and drained off the water, this man mated with a crow and repopulated the earth with Patwin, modern man.

Pavel (PAH-vyel) Russian and Czech development of Paul, "little." See Pall for other variations.

Payat (PAY-yaht) "He is coming." North American Indian name.

Paz (pahs) Spanish for "peace." Also a girl's name.

Peder (PEH-dehr) One of the most popular names in Denmark, Peder means "rock" or "stone." The English equivalent is Peter. Many variations are used throughout the world, including Piotr and Petr, Bulgarian; Pierre, French; Petros and Panos, Modern Greek; Pieter, Dutch; Peet and Peeter, Estonian; Pietro, Piero, Pedro, and Pero, Italian; Petras, Lithuanian; Piotr and Pietrek, Polish; Petar, Rumanian; and Per and Peder, Swedish and Norwegian.

Pias (PEE-ahs) English Gypsy name meaning "fun."

Pilan (pee-LAHN) "Supreme essence." Also spelled Pillan. The thunder god and supreme being of the Araucanian Indians of North America.

Pilar (pee-LAHR) A favorite in Spanish-speaking countries, Pilar means "pillar" or "fountain base," referring to the Virgin Mary, pillar of the Christian religion. Also a girl's name.

Pili (PEE-lee) Swahili for "second-born son."

Pillan (peel-LAHN) A major diety among the Araucanian Indians, Pillan is the god of thunder, lightning, and other natural phenomena. See Pilan.

Pinon (pee-NOHN) A Tupi-Guarani Indian god who was born with a star-serpent wound about his waist and eventually became the constellation Orion.

Pirro (PEER-roh) Spanish name from the Greek for "with flaming hair."

Platon (plah-TOHN) Spanish for "broad-shouldered."

Pol Astrological nickname for a Gemini child. Pol is a shortened form of the Greek Pollux, the name of an orange star, the brighter of the two first-magnitude stars in the constellation Gemini, the Twins. The other star is Castor.

Pov (pohv) English Gypsy name meaning "earth."

Powa (POH-wah) North American Indian name meaning "rich."

Purdy (per-dee) Hindustani for "recluse" or "secluded one."

Quillan (KWIL-luhn) "Cub." Astrological name for a child born under Leo, the Lion. Leos are impulsive, confident, and dramatic, and are lovers of pomp and ceremony. They like to seem in charge of things, but in truth they would rather have fun.

Quintin (keen-TEEN) Spanish for "fifth-born child."

Quirin (KWER-in) A magic stone supposedly found in the lapwing's nest. The quirin is also known as the traitor's stone, and according to occultists, when placed on the head of a sleeping person, the stone causes him to reveal his innermost thoughts.

Rabi (ra-BEE) Common Arabic name meaning "breeze," connoting the fragrance, for example, of new-mown hay or the earth after a spring rain. Also used for girls.

Nature names are popular in Arabic countries, and others include Asfour, "bird"; Baghel, "ox"; Kharouf, "lamb"; Saqr, "falcon"; Sarsour, "bug"; Shunnar, "pheasant"; and Yasmeen, "jasmine."

Radman (RAHD-muhn) Slovak name meaning "joy."

Radomil (RAH-doh-mil) "Love of peace." Popular in Czechoslovakia.

Rafael (rah-fah-EHL) A favorite in Spanish-speaking countries, Rafael means "God has healed." Also used today in Rumania. The English equivalent is Raphael.

Rafi (re-FEE) Arabic for "exalting." The Prophet Muhammad objected to this name as being too proud.

Ragnar (RAHG-nahr) Norwegian and Swedish name meaning "mighty army." The English equivalent is Rayner or Rainer.

Rahman (rah-MAHN) Popular Muslim name from the Arabic for "compassionate" or "merciful," one of the ninety-nine qualities of God listed in the Koran. A favorite combination is Abdul Rahman or Abd-al-Rahman, "servant of the merciful One," which is considered one of the two names God loves best. The other is Abdul Allah or Abd-Allah, "servant of God."

Rahmet (ruh-MET) Turkish development of Rahman, "God's compassion" or "God's mercy."

Raiden (RIGH-den) Japanese thunder god, usually depicted as a red demon carrying a drum and having two claws on each foot.

Raini North American Indian name. In the legends of the Mundruku tribe of the Tupi-Guarani, the god Raini created the world by placing it in the shape of a flat stone on another god's head.

Ramadan (rah-mah-DAHN) The ninth month of the

Muslim year, during which pious Muslims fast from sunrise to sunset.

Ramman (RAHM-mahn) Akkadian name for the constellation Aquarius, the Water Bearer. Also the name of an old Akkadian storm god.

Ramon (rah-MOHN) Spanish for "wise protector."

Ramsden Derived from the Old English for "ram's valley," this name is used by astrologers for boys born under Aries, the Ram. The variation Ramsey, or Ramsay, means "ram's island."

Ranon (rah-NOHN) Modern Israeli name from the Hebrew for "to sing" or "to be joyous." Also spelled Ranen. The similar Hebrew name Ranan means "fresh."

Rapier The surname of James T. Rapier (1839-1884), a black congressman from Alabama who called for strong enforcement of the civil rights legislation passed in the years following the Civil War. Rapier urged blacks to unite and form labor unions and organized the first conclave of black working men. The name has had some popularity in the United States.

Ravi "Conferring." One of the titles of the Hindu sun god Surya, who is also considered one of the twelve guardian of the months of the year. In India the Ravi River is a tributary of the sacred Indus.

Ravid (rah-VEET) Hebrew for "jewelry" or "ornament."

Raviv (rah-VEEV) Hebrew for "rain" or "dew."

Razi (RAH-zee) Popular in Israel, Razi comes from the Aramaic for "secret" and literally means "my secret." Other forms are Raz, "secret," and Raziel, "secret of God."

Reddy Originally a surname, Reddy is now used as a given name for a child whose parent has red hair.

Rendor (REN-dohr) Hungarian for "policeman."

Rene (re-NAY) French for "reborn."

Renenet (RE-ne-net) Occult name from the Egyptian *Book of the Dead*, considered by many to be the original book of magic. Renenet is the personification of fortune and good luck and is usually associated with the god Shai, who embodies fate.

Rey (ray) Spanish development of the French *roi*, "king." The English equivalent is Roy.

Reyhan (REH-hahn) Arabic for "favored by God."

Rez Hungarian name meaning "copper," given to a boy born with copper or reddish hair.

Rico (REE-koh) Spanish name from the Old German for "noble ruler" or "ruler of all." The English equivalent is Alaric. Rico and Richi are also pet forms of the Spanish Ricardo, whose English equivalent is Richard.

Rida (REH-dah) Arabic for "favor," implying the child is in God's favor.

Riki (Ree-kee) Estonian nickname for Frederick, "peaceful ruler," and Heinrich, "ruler of an estate." Variations are Heino and Henno.

Rimon A favorite in Israel, Rimon comes from the Hebrew for "pomegranate."

Rimril This name is the special property of the Marrim clan of the Purim Kukis of Manipur, a small Tibeto-Burmese tribe in China. Other names belonging to the Marrim clan are Rimhen, Rimnir, Rimhel, Hulin, Rimlal, and Rimshu. The meaning of these names could not be found.

Ringo Japanese for "apple." Since the apple is an Oriental symbol of peace, the name has the connotation "peace be with you."

Roald (ROO:-ahld or ROO:ahl) One of the most common names in Norway, Roald comes from the Old German for "famous ruler." The name was popularized by Roald Amundsen, the Norwegian polar explorer.

Robi (ROH-bee) Hungarian nickname for Robert, "shining with fame." Other forms of Robert used throughout the world include Berdy and Bobek, Czech; Robin, Robinet, and Robers, French; and Roberto and Ruperto, Spanish and Italian.

Rodas (ROH-dahs) Spanish name from the Greek for "place of the roses."

Rohan (ROH-hahn) Hindustani for "sandalwood," connoting the fragrance of sweet incense.

Rohin (roh-HEEN) Used in India, this name means "on the upward path."

Roi Common today in India, Roi means "king." Also spelled Roy, Rae, Ray, and Rao.

Roldan (ROHL-dahn) Spanish development of Roland, from the Old German for "from the famous land." Another Spanish form is Ordando.

Rolf (rohlf) Currently used in Sweden and Norway, Rolf means "swift wolf" or "wolf counsel."

Rolon (roh-LOHN) This Spanish name originally comes from Old German and means "famous wolf."

Romney Old Welsh for "curving river." Appropriate for boys born under the water signs of the zodiac: Pisces, Cancer, and Scorpio. See Carswell for more information on water names.

Roni (ROH-nee) Hebrew for "my joy." Variations include Ron, "joy" or "song," Ronel, "joy of God" or "song of God" and Ronli, "joy is mine" or "song is mine."

Rosmer "Child of the sea" or "sea horse." Astrological water name. See Carswell.

Roth German for "red-haired" or "ruddy-complexioned." Often used as a family name.

Rouvin (ROO:-veen) This modern Greek name comes

from Hebrew and means "behold a son." The equivalent in Spanish-speaking countries is Ruben.

Royd Scandinavian name meaning "from the forest clearing."

Rudo (ROO:-doh) Used by the Shona-speaking people of Zimbabwe, this name means "love."

Rudolf Slavic and Scandinavian form of Rudolph, from the Old German for "famous wolf." The Spanish development is Rudolfo.

Rufo (ROO:-foh) Spanish for "red-haired."

Ruperto (roo:-PAIR-toh) Spanish name. See Robi.

Rurik Slavic form of Rory, "red king," or Roderick, "famous ruler." Also used in Scandinavia.

Sabriam Probably a corruption of Abraham and used in occult incantations to invoke the powers of the spirits. Mystics have paraphrased the name to mean "Ho for the Sangraal! Ho for the cup of Babalon! Ho for mine Angel pouring Himself forth into my soul!"

Saburo (sah-boo-roh) Japanese for "third-born male."

Sahale (sah-HAH-leh) North American Indian name meaning "above."

Sahen (shah-hehn) Used in India, this name means "falcon."

Sakima (sah-KEE-mah) North American Indian name meaning "king."

Salih (SAH-lee) Arabic for "good" or "right."

Salim (sah-LEEM) Swahili name from the Arabic for "peace." Salim is also popular in Arabic countries, where it is pronounced SA-lim and means "safe."

Salmalin (sahl-mah-leen) Hindustani for "taloned." Salmalin is another name for Garuda, the half-giant, half eagle vehicle of the Hindu god Vishnu. Garuda is pictured with the body, arms, and legs of a man, the talons, beak, and head of an eagle, and a white face, red beak, and golden body. He was hatched from a monstrous egg five hundred years after his mother laid it.

Salomon (sah-loh-MOHN) Spanish development of Solomon, "peaceful."

Salvador (sahl-vah-DOHR) Spanish name meaning "the Savior." Another variation is Xavier.

Samein (sa-MIGH-an) A favorite among Arabic Christians, this is a development of the Biblical Simeon, "to hear" or "to be heard." Also spelled Saman.

Sammon Arabic for "grocer." Usually used as a surname.

Samuru (sah-moo-roo) Japanese form of the Biblical Samuel, "His name is God" or "God has heard."

Sanat (SAH-naht) Hindustani for "ancient." Another name for the Hindu god Brahma.

Sander (SAHN-der) Bulgarian form of the Greek Alexandros, "helper and defender of mankind."

Sani (sah-NEE) The Hindu personification of the planet Saturn. Much evil occultism is associated with this god, and some scholars believe all left-hand sun cults are actually Saturn cults. Sani is usually depicted clothed in black and riding a vulture. His other names include Asita, "black," Kona, "angular," and Manda, "slow." In astrology the planet Saturn governs the sign Capricorn.

Sanson (sahn-SOHN) Spanish form of the Hebrew Shimshon, "the sun's man" or "splendid man." The English Sampson and Samson come from the same source. The Danish, Dutch, and Swedish variant is also Samson.

Sarad (SAH-rahd) Hindu name for child born in the "autumn."

Sarojin (sah-roh-jeen) Hindu name meaning "lotuslike." The lotus is revered by the Hindus because Brahma was born in the center of the sacred flower.

Sarngin (SAHRN-geen) Another name for the Hindu god Vishnu, the protector, who carries a bow called the *sarnga*.

Sartan (SAHR-tuhn) Hebrew designation for the constellation and zodiacal sign, Cancer, the Crab. Chaldean and Greek astrologers believed that the Gate of Men, through which souls passed to enter into human bodies, was found in Cancer. The sign is also known as the House of the Moon because the moon was supposedly located in Cancer during creation.

Sef An Egyptian lion god whose name means "yesterday" and is taken from the *Book of the Dead*. In astrology the Lion governs the sign Leo.

Segel Hebrew for 'treasure." Derived from the Biblical phrase *Am Segulah,* "a treasured people," often used to refer to Israel.

Seif (SIGH-eef) Arabic for "sword of religion."

Seker In the Egyptian *Book of the Dead* Seker personifies motionless and dead matter and sits enthroned in total darkness. He is called "the greatest god who was in the beginning and dwells in the blackness."

Selmar "Child of the rolling sea." Astrological name for boys born under the water signs Pisces, Cancer, and Scorpio. An alternate spelling is Selmer.
Other similar water names include Seabert, "glory of the sea"; Seabrook, Seabrock, and Sebrock, "from the brook by the sea"; Seger and Seager, "sea warrior" or "sea spear"; Seward, "guardian of the sea"; and Sewell, "child of the powerful sea."

Senon (SEH-nohn) Spanish name meaning "living" or "given life by Zeus." A corruption of the Spanish Zenon.

Senwe (SEHN-weh) African Baduma name meaning "a dry stalk of grain" and given to a frail child who resembles a thin stalk.

Sepp German name from the Hebrew Yoseph, "God will

increase." Other modern German forms are Josef, Jupp, Beppi, and Peppi.

Sergio (SAIR-jee-oh) Italian for "the attendant." The English equivalent is Serge.

Sevilen (se-vi-LEN) Turkish for "beloved." Often used as a surname.

Shalom (sha-LOHM) Hebrew for "peace." Also spelled Sholom.

Shamir (shuh-MEER) Hebrew name referring to a strong rocklike material which can cut through metal.

Shanon (shuh-NOHN) Hebrew for "peaceful" or "secure." A variant is Shanan.

Shane Modern Irish form of John, "gracious gift of God."

Sharif (shah-REEF) Arabic for "honest." A common name in Arabic countries.

Sheehan "Little peaceful one."

Shem (shem) Hebrew for "name," implying a good reputation.

Shen (shen) This occult name comes from the Egyptian *Book of the Dead,* often called the original book of magic because of the many incantations and spells it contains. The name refers to an Egyptian amulet which symbolized eternal life and was often placed by the feet of the dead.

Sheratan The second brightest star in the constellation Aries, the Ram. Hence, a name for a child born under that sign.

Sherborn Old English for "from the clear, pure brook." Used as an ecological and astrological water name. Variant spellings are Sherborne and Sherburn. See Carswell for more information on water names.

Shing (sheeng) Chinese for "victory."

Shiro (shee-roh) Japanese for "fourth-born son."

Sigfrid German name from the Old German for "peace-

255

full" or "victorious." The Norwegian form is Sigvard.

Sigurd (SEE-gerd) Popular today in Scandinavian countries, Sigurd means "victorious guardian." The name originally comes from Old Norse mythology.

Silvain "From the forest." Used in France, where other forms are Silvie and Silvestre.

Simen (SEE-men) This English Gypsy name means "alike" or "equal" or "it is we," implying a resemblance between the newborn baby and his parents.

Sipatu (see-PAH-too:) Miwok Indian name from the word *sipe,* "to pull out." The unusual connotation is "softening a fox's tail after skinning the animal by repeatedly shoving a stick into the tail."

Siva (SHI-vah) One of the most popular Hindu names in India, from the god Siva, the destroyer. According to Hindu mythology, Siva has 1,008 qualities or names, which include Nandin, "destroyer," Natesa, "dance lord," and Hara, "seizer." He is usually pictured with either one or five faces, four arms, and a third eye, which burst forth to save the world from darkness when his two eyes were playfully covered by his wife. The eye can allegedly reduce men to ashes. Siva is depicted as a ferocious flesh-eater who adores blood sacrifices, and he often has with him a black dog who gobbles flesh without chewing. He once created a demon to devour one of his enemies, but when the poor soul begged to be forgiven, Siva relented. The starving demon demanded to be fed, and Siva ordered him to eat his own feet, which he did. In fact, he ate all of himself but his head.

Sivan (SEE-vahn) This Hebrew name comes from the ninth month of the Jewish calendar, corresponding in astrology to Gemini, the Twins.

Slade "Child of the valley." Earth name originally derived from Old English. Used by astrologers for boys born under the earth signs Capricorn, Taurus, and Virgo. See Blair for the significance of earth names.

Slane (SLAH-nuh) Czech for "salty."

Slavik (SLAH-vik) Russian pet name. See Stanislav.

Slevin Irish Gaelic for "mountaineer." Earth name for boys born under the earth signs of the zodiac: Capricorn, Taurus, and Virgo. Also spelled Sleven, Slaven, and Slavin.

Sofian (SOH-fee-an) Arabic for "devoted."

Sol (sawl) "The sun" or "child of the sun." Astrological name for a boy born under Leo, the Lion, which is ruled by the sun.

Songan (SOHN-gahn) North American Indian name meaning "strong."

Stancio (STAHN-see-oh) Used in Spain and Latin and South America as a shortened form of Constancio, "the firm, constant one."

Stane (SSTAN-e) Serbian diminutive of Stanislav, "glorious position." A variant is Stanko.

Stanislav (stah-nee-SLAHF) One of the most popular names in Russia, Stanislav means "glorious position." Also common in Serbia, Czechoslovakia, and the Ukraine. Russian pet forms are Stas and Slavik. A common Serbian diminutive is Stane. The Polish equivalent is Stasio.

Starr "Star." Astrological name from Middle English.

Stephan (ste-PAHN) A favorite in Russia, this name means "crowned one." Pet forms are Stefan and Stepka.

Stiggur (STEEG-guhr) English Gypsy name with the unusual meaning "gate."

Sudi (SOO:-dee) A favorite Swahili name used in East Africa, Sudi means "luck."

Sultan (soo:l-TAHN) Swahili for "ruler."

Suti (SOO:-tee) Occult name from the Egyptian *Book of*

the Dead. Suti is "the great god who carrieth away the soul, eateth hearts, and feedeth upon filth, the guardian of the darkness."

Sven (sven) One of the most common names in Norway, Sven means "youth." A favorite Danish variation is Svend. The name is widely used because of the current trend in Scandinavia toward Norse-sounding names.

Tabib (tuh-BIB) Turkish for "doctor" or "physician."

Tabor (TAH-bohr) Used in both Hungary and Turkey, Tabor means "camp" or "fortified encampment."

Tadeo (TAH-deh-oh) Spanish name from the Latin for "praise." Common variations are the Czech Tades and Tadeas, and the Polish Tadzio and Tadek. Modern American equivalents are Thad and Tad.

Tadi (TAH-dee) Omaha Indian name meaning "wind." The feminine form is Tadewi.

Tadzi (TAHD-zee) Used by the Carrier Indians of Canada, this name means "the loon."

Tahir (TAH-hir) Arabic for "pure." Common as a Muslim name in Egypt, Persia, Turkey, Arabia, Jordan, and India.

Tait (tight) Scandinavian name which means "cheerful."

Takis (TAH-kees) Modern Greek diminutive of the name Panaghoitis. Other variants are Panos and Panayotis.

Tal (tahl) Israeli name meaning "dew" or "rain." Another form is Talor, "dew of the morning." Also used for girls.

Tales (TAH-lehs) Spanish development of the Greek Thales, "flourishing." The philosopher Thales was one of the seven wise men of ancient Greece and the first man to accurately record a solar eclipse. He also not so wisely believed the world was made entirely of water, the air being expanded water and the earth simply compressed water.

258

Talli (TAHL-lee) In Lenape Indian lore Talli led the tribe after the great flood to the Snake Land, where they rebuilt civilization.

Talman (TAHL-mahn) Hebrew name from the Aramaic for "to injure" or "to oppress." Also spelled Talmon.

Taman (TAH-mahn) "Dark" or "black." Serbo-Croatian name.

Tamas (Taw-MAHS) Hungarian development of the Greek for "twin." In astrology the Twins are the symbol of Gemini. See Tomas for other variations.

Tanek (TAH-nek) Polish name from the Greek for "immortal." Other forms used in Poland are Atek and Atanazy. In Lithuania the equivalent is Tanis.

Tani (TAH-nee) Japanese for "valley."

Tano (TAH-noh) Ghanaian name derived from the River Tano. Also spelled Tanno. Many names in Ghana are taken from nature. See Fynn for more examples.

Tarn A small lake or pool in the mountains.

Taro (TAH-roh) Japanese for "first-born male." Loosely translated, Taro means "big boy."

Tarrus Astrological name for a child born under Taurus, the Bull. Taurus is actually another form of the name and literally means "bull." The variant Tari can also be used for Sagittarians.

Tas (tahs) English Gypsy name referring to the nest of a bird.

Tate (TAH-teh or Anglicized to tayt) North American Indian name meaning "windy" or "a great talker."

Tauno (TOO:noh) Contemporary Finnish name which means "world mighty" or "world ruler." The English equivalent is Donald.

Taurin (TAW-rin) Astrological name for a boy born under Taurus, the Bull. An alternate spelling is Tawrin. Taureans are the builders and financiers of the zodiac.

They plod determinedly toward success and security, and are loyal, dependable, and patient.

Tavis (TA-vis) "Twin." Astrologers use this name for boys born under Gemini, the Twins. Tavis is actually a Scotch form of Thomas, and English variations are Tevis and Tavish.

Tawno (TAW-noh) English Gypsy name which means "small" or "tiny." The feminine form is Tawnie.

Tayib (tayb) Used in India, this name means "good" or "delicate."

Telek (TE-lek) Polish for "iron cutter."

Telem (TEH-lem) Hebrew nature name which means "ford near a cliff." Telem also refers to a furrow. The English equivalent is Clifford.

Tem (taym in Gypsy) English Gypsy name which means "country.' The same name is found in the Egyptian *Book of the Dead,* where Tem is the oldest of the gods, the Creator who lived when "not was sky, not was earth, not were men, not were born the gods, not was death." He dwelled in the celestial waters and thought of the creation of the world. When these ideas were spoken aloud, the world came into being.

Teman (TAY-muhn) Modern Israeli name from the Hebrew for "right side," referring to the south.

Terrill An artificial sphere representing the earth. Hence, a name for boys born under the earth signs of the zodiac: Capricorn, Taurus, and Virgo.

Teva (TAY-vah) Hebrew for "nature."

Thanos (THAN-nohs) Contemporary Greek name meaning "noble" or "bear man." Variants are Thanasis and Athanasios. The English equivalent is Arthur.

Theron (THAIR-uhn) From the Greek for "a hunter." Astrological name for a boy born under Sagittarius, the Archer.

Thor (thohr) One of the most popular names in Denmark, from the Old Norse thunder god. A favorite variation in Norway is Tor. Other widely used forms include Thorbjorn, "Thor's bear" or "thunder bear," Thorleif, "Thor's beloved," and Thorvald, "Thunder ruler." The feminine equivalent is Thordis.

Tidzio (tee-dsee-OH) Perhaps one of the most uncomplimentary names in the world, Tidzio is bestowed in China to make evil spirits believe the child is despised by everyone so they will seek someone more beloved to harm. The meaning is "swine urine." Such debasing names are usually reserved for frail, unhealthy children or only sons.

Tilden "From the valley of good liberals." Other similar names include Tilford, "from the ford belonging to the good liberals," and Tilton, "from the estate of good liberals."

Timin (tee-MEEN) From the Arabic *tinnin,* "sea serpent." Timin is a huge, fabulous fish in Hindu mythology. Even bigger is Timin-gila, "swallower of Timin," and bigger still is Timin-gila-gila, who swallows Timin-gila. The Sea Monster is the Hindu symbol for the lunar month corresponding to the zodiacal sign Capricorn.

Timur (tee-MOO:R) Hebrew for "tall" or "stately."

Tino (TEE-noh) Spanish nickname for Augustino, "son of the exalted one." Used in Spain, Latin and South America.

Tito (TEE-toh) Spanish and Italian form of Titus, from the Greek for "of the giants." The modern Greek form is Titos.

Tivon (tee-VOHN) Hebrew for "naturalist" or "lover of nature.

Tobal (toh-BAHL) Spanish pet form of Cristobal, which means "Christ-bearer." Other forms are Chris, Cris, and Tobalito. English equivalents are Christopher and Chris.

Tobbar (TOHB-bahr) English Gypsy name meaning "road." *Boro-tobbar-killipen* is the Gypsy name of high toby or highway robbery.

Toby Diminutive of the Hebrew Tobias, "God is my good." Popular today particularly in Ireland.

Todor (TOH-dohr) Used in Hungary and the Ukraine, Todor means "gift of God." Ukrainian variants are Todorko and Todos. Polish forms are Feodor, Fedor, Tolek, Teos, Teodor, and Dorek.

Tohon (toh-HOHN) North American Indian name meaning "cougar."

Tolek (TOH-lek) A favorite nickname in Poland. See Anton and Todor.

Tomas (toh-MAHS in Spanish, TOH-mahs in most Slavic countries) From the Greek and Aramaic for "twin," this name is used today in Czechoslovakia, Lithuania, Portugal, Russia, Sweden, Norway, and Spanish-speaking countries. English equivalents are Thomas and Tammen.
Other variations include Tomasek and Tomasko, Czech; Thumas, French; Thoma, German; Tamas and Tomi, Hungarian; Toomas, Estonian; Tomasso, Italian; Toms, Latvian; Tomek, Tomcio, Tomislaw, and Slawek, Polish; and Tomaz and Tome, Portuguese.

Tomi (TOH-mee) Used in widely separated cultures. To the Kalabari of the Niger delta, Tomi means "the people." In Japan the name means "rich," and in Hungary it is a nickname for Tamas.

Tomlin Old English for "little twin." Good astrological name for a child born under Gemini, the Twins. A variation is Tomkin.

Toni Slavic and Hungarian form of the Latin for "inestimable" or "priceless." See Anton.

Topwe (TOHP-way) This is an example of a Southern Rhodesian "second name," given when a child reaches maturity, usually at twelve or fourteen, and suggesting a personal quirk. Topwe refers to a vegetable the child loved to eat.

Tor (too:r) Used by the Tiv-speaking people of Nigeria, Tor means "king." In Scandinavia the same name, pronounced tohr, is a popular variation of Thor. See Thor.

Toshio (toh-SHEE-oh) Common Japanese name meaning "year boy."

Tovi (TOH-vee) Hebrew for "my good." The short form Tov means "good."

Tukuli (too-KOO:-lee) Miwok Indian name. The elaborate connotation is "caterpillar traveling headfirst down a tree during the summertime." The name is derived from *tukini*, "to throw oneself endwise."

Insect names are common among the Miwoks and often reveal the Indian's subtle observation of the natural world. Examples include Hesutu ("lifting a yellow jacket's nest out of the ground"); Momuso ("yellow jackets piled up in their nest during the winter"); Muata ("little yellow jackets in the nest"); Nokonyu ("katydid's nose being close to its mouth"); Patakasu ("small ant biting a person hard"); and Tiimu ("black and white caterpillar coming out of the ground").

Tunu (TOO:noo:) Miwok Indian name which means "deer thinking about going to eat wild onions."

Tupi (TOO:-pee) Miwok Indian name from the word *tupi*, "to pull out" or "to pull up." The implied meaning is "throwing a salmon into the river bank." Fish are frequently mentioned in Miwok names. Other examples include Kosumi ("fishing for salmon with a spear," from *kose*, "to throw at"); Leyati ("the shape of an abalone shell"); Lii ("a fat turtle poking its head out of the water"); Lupu ("silvery quality of an abalone shell"); Metikla ("reaching a hand under water to catch a white sucker fish"); and

263

Pelisu ("eating fish for lunch while fishing at the river").

Turi (TOO:-ree) Nickname for the Spanish Arturo, "noble" or "bear man."

Tyee (TIGH-ee) North American Indian name meaning "chief." Another form is Tyonek, "little chief."

Tymon (TEE-mohn) Polish name from the Greek for "honoring God." A variation is Tymek. The English equivalent is Timothy.

Uzoma (oo:-ZOH-mah) Used by the Ibo of Nigeria for any child born during a journey. Abiona is the Yoruban counterpart.

Vadin (VAH-deen) Hindustani for "speaker," implying scholarly or learned discourse.

Valin (VAH-leen) A Hindu monkey king. See Balin.

Van A feathered monster or dragon in Armenian myth.

Varden Earth name meaning "from the green hills." Variants include Verden, Vardon, and Verdon. See Blair for the significance of earth names in astrology.

Vartan (VAHR-tahn) Popular Armenian flower name meaning "rose."

Vasilis (vah-SEE-lees) Greek name meaning "kingly" or "magnificent." Modern variants include Vasos and Vasileios. The English equivalent is Basil.

Vasin (VAH-seen) Used in India, this name means "ruler" or "lord."

Vassily (vah-SEE-lee) Russian development of the German Wilhelm, "unwavering protector." Other common diminutives are Vas, Vasilek, Vasya, and Vasyuta. The English equivalent is William.

Velden "From the country of grass."

Vencel (VEN-tsel) Hungarian for "wreath" or "garland."

Vered (VAI-red) Hebrew for "a rose."

Verney (VER-nee) "Spring." This name is given to boys

born under the spring signs of the zodiac: Aries, Taurus, and Gemini.

Vidor (VEE-dohr) Hungarian development of the Latin for "cheerful." The English equivalent is Hilary or Hillery.

Viljo (VEEL-yoh) Very popular today in Finland, Viljo is a form of William, "unwavering protector." The Danish form is Vilhelm.

Virge (verj) Astrological name meaning "virgin." For the Virgos of the zodiac. The same name is sometimes used as a nickname for Virgil, "staff bearer."

Vishnu The humblest diety in the Hindu pantheon, Vishnu is considered the protector of all creation and often comes to earth in human form to battle evil.

Vito (VEE-toh) Spanish name originally derived from the Latin *Vitalis*, "relating to life." Variants include Vital and Vitaliano.

Vladimir (vlah-DEE-meer) A favorite in Russia, Vladimir means "powerful warrior" or "army ruler." Common diminutives are Dimka, Dima, Volidik, and Volodinka.

Vladlen (VLAHD-len) This name became popular in Russia after Lenin came into power and is a combination of Vladimir plus Lenin.

Waban (wah-BAHN) North American Indian name meaning "the east wind."

Wakiza (wah-KEE-zah) North American Indian name meaning "desperate fighter."

Wald Earth name meaning "grove" or "rolling field." See Blair for the significance of earth names.

Walden This earth name comes from the Old English for "child of the forest valley." Closely associated with Thoreau's Walden Pond.

Wapi (WAH-pee) This North American Indian name means "lucky."

Wasi (WAH-see) A derogatory nickname among the Carrier Indians of Canada, Wasi means "lynx" and refers to someone who has a head too rounded to be attractive to the Carriers. Such names are seldm used in the person's presence.

Welby Nature name derived from the Old English for "from the farm by the spring."

Wemilat (weh-MEE-laht) North American Indian name for a child born to wealthy parents. The meaning is "all given to him."

Wemilo (weh-MEE-loh) North American Indian name which means "all speak to him," implying all respect him.

Wen (wayn) English Gypsy name for a child born in "winter."

Wesh (waysh) English Gypsy name which means "forest" or "woods."

Wicent (VE-tsent) Polish development of the Latin for "conqueror." Popular Polish variants are Wicek, Wicus, Wicenty, Wincenty, and Vincenty.

Wichado (wee-CHAH-doh) North American Indian name which means "willing."

Wilanu (wee-LAH-noo) Miwok Indian name. The implied meaning is "pouring water on acorn flour in a leaching place."

Wildon (WIGHL-duhn) "Wild valley."

Wilhelm (VEL-helm) Common in Germany, Poland, and Sweden, this name means "unwavering protector." German variants are Willi and Willy, Polish are Wilek and Wilus. The Latvian form is Vilis. The English equivalent is William.

Wilny (WEEL-nee) "Eagle singing while flying." North American Indian name.

Wilu (WEE-loo:) Miwok Indian name which means "chicken hawk calling *wi*."

Wimund (WIGH-muhnd) "Sacred peace." Occult name for a boy born in Age of Aquarius. See Arian.

Winfield (WIN-feeld) From the Teutonic for "friend of the soil" or "friend of the earth."

Wingi (WEEN-gee) North American Indian name which means "willing."

Winward "My friend's (or brother's) forest" or "my brother's keeper."

Woody Modern American name which originated as a nickname for Woodrow or Woodward, "lives near the hedge by the forest."

Wuliton (WOO-li-tuhn) North American Indian name meaning "to do well."

Wunand (WOO:nahnd) North American Indian name meaning "God is good."

Wuyi (WOO:-yee) This Miwok Indian name means "turkey vulture soaring."

Wynono (wi-NOH-noh) North American Indian name for a "first-born son."

Xavier (zah-vee-AIR) Spanish name meaning "bright." Another spelling is Javier. The name has also been interpreted to mean "owner of the new house."

Yadid (yah-DEED) Hebrew for "friend" or "beloved."

Yadin (yah-DEEN) Hebrew for "He (God) will judge." Also spelled Yadon.

Yakecen (YAH-keh-shen) Dene Indian name meaning "sky on song."

Yakez (YAH-kehz) Carrier Indian name meaning "heaven," shortened from the words *ya kezudzepe,* literally translated as "sky on his ears in," or "within heaven's ears."

Yamut (ya-MOO:T) Uncommon Arabic name meaning "he shall die," given only when a family has lost many children. The name is bestowed in the hope that the demons will leave the child alone because he has an ugly name.

Yancy North American Indian name which means "Englishman."

Yannis (YOHN-nees) Modern Greek form of the Hebrew for "gracious gift of God." Variants are Ioannis and Yannakis. The English equivalent is John.

Yarb (yahrb) English Gypsy name meaning "herb," implying a fragrant scent.

Yarin (yah-REEN) Hebrew name meaning "to understand." Anglicized to Javin.

Yasah (ya-SAHR) Arabic for "wealth." The Prophet objected to this name as being too proud.

Yazid (YA-zid) Arabic name which dates to remote antiquity and is identical in meaning to the Hebrew Joseph, "He will increase." The only difference is the "he" in the Arabic name refers to the bearer of the name, while the Hebrew "He" refers to Jehovah.

Yemon (yeh-MOHN) Japanese name which means "guarding the gate."

Yerik (YAY-reek) Modern Russian diminutive of Yeremiy, originally from the Hebrew for "appointed by God." Other Russian forms are Yarema and Yaremka. The name originally comes from Hebrew. English equivalents are Jeremy and Jeremiah.

Yucel (yoo:-JEL) Turkish for "sublime." Often used as a surname.

Yukio (yoo:-KEE-oh) Japanese for "snow boy," implying "boy who goes his own way."

Yuma (YOO:-mah) "Son of a chief." North American Indian name.

Yunus (yoo-NOOS) Turkish development of the Hebrew Yonah, meaning "dove," a symbol of peace. The English equivalent is Jonah.

Yuri (YOO:-ree) Popular diminutive in Russia. See Georgy.

Yusef (YOO:-sef) Arabic development of the Hebrew Joseph, "he shall increase." Another form is Yazid. Also used today in Czechoslovakia, Germany, and Poland.

Yutu (YOO:-too:) Miwok Indian name from the word *yutme,* "to claw." The connotation is "coyote making a feint so he can seize a bird."

Yves (eev) French for "little archer" or "son of the yew bow." In astrology the Archer is the symbol of Sagittarius.

Zahid (za-HED) Arabic for "self-denying" or "ascetic."

Zahur (zah-HOO:R) Swahili for "flower."

Zaid (ZIGH-eed or ZIGH-ed) Shortened Arabic form of Yazid, a development of Joseph. See Yazid.

Zak (zahk) Czechoslovakian for "a schoolboy."

Zaki (ZA-kee) Arabic for "intelligent."

Zamir (zah-MEER) Currently popular in Israel, Zamir means "a bird" or "a song." Also spelled Zemer.

Zareb (za-REB) Used in the Sudan, Zareb means "protector against enemies."

Zarek (ZAH-rek) Polish name from the Greek for "may God protect the king." A Polish variation is Baltek.

Zeeman From the Dutch for "seaman." Used for boys born under the water signs of the zodiac: Pisces, Cancer, and Scorpio.

Zeheb (ze-HEB) Turkish for "gold."

Zeke (ZAY-keh) Shortened Israeli form of Zechariah, "the memory of the Lord." The name may also come from the Aramaic for "shooting star" or "spark."

Zeki (ze-KI) Turkish for "intelligent" or "quick-witted."

Zelimir (SAL-e-mer) Slavic name meaning "he wishes peace."

269

Zenon (seh-NOHN) Spanish name from the Greek for "living" or "given life by Zeus."

Zenos (ZEH-nohs) "Jupiter's gift." Astrological name for boys born under Sagittarius and Pisces, which are ruled by Jupiter.

Zesiro (zeh-SEE-roh) Common in Uganda, this name means "elder twin."

Ziven (ZI-ven) Czech, Polish, and Russian name meaning "vigorous and alive." Variations are Ziv and Zivon.

Zorya (ZOHR-yah) Ukrainian for "star."

For You and Your Family

Dr. Turtle's Babies
William John Turtle, M.D.

All new parents find themselves plagued by questions on a variety of everyday situations—situations that can, without the proper answers, become real problems. Let a doctor answer your questions about: how to prepare for baby's homecoming; when and how to feed an infant; how to know when baby is sick; when to call a doctor; what to do about pacifiers and thumb-sucking; how to discipline; when to start toilet training; how to create a safe, stimulating environment for baby; how to schedule free time away from baby; how to establish good and lasting emotional patterns.

A pocket-size paperback   (U31-065, $3.95, U.S.A.)
     (U31-066, $4.95, Canada)

Anyone Can Have a Happy Child
Jacob Azerrad, Ph.D.

The author, a clinical psychologist, bases his program for successful parenting on the premise that a happy child is one who has a positive outlook on life, self-esteem and the esteem of others, and the ability to express warmth and understanding.

A pocket-size paperback   (U32-284, $3.50, U.S.A.)
     (U32-285, $4.50, Canada)

More Essential Books for Every Parent's Library

Couples with Children
Randy Meyers Wolfson and Virginia DeLuca

The inevitable changes that occur in a husband-wife relationship when there's a new baby in the house deal a great shock to a marriage. This book is the first to address these dramatic, stressful changes and offer support and advice for the first few months of parenthood. The authors include a detailed bibliography of books of interest to new parents as well as an excellent, extensive list of places to contact for support (clinics, counselors, etc.).

A pocket-size paperback   (U30-269, $3.50)

The Encyclopedia of Baby and Child Care
Lendon H. Smith, M.D.

An updated and revised edition of the all-inclusive reference guide to the health, treatment, and behavior of children from birth through adolescence. The book is separated into distinct, specialized encyclopedias on specific topics, such as "Emergencies and First Aid" and "Diet, Feeding and Nutrition"; each offers fully cross-referenced definitions, explanations, treatments, and even specialized medical terminology. An invaluable handbook for all parents and future parents.

Available in large-size quality paperback   (U37-502, $9.95, U.S.A.)
                                             (U37-503, $11.50, Canada)

To order, use the coupon below. If you prefer to use your own stationery, please include complete title as well as book number and price. Allow 4 weeks for delivery.